JavaScript Web Applications

JavaScript Web Applications

Alex MacCaw

Beijing · Cambridge · Farnham · Köln · Sebastopol · Tokyo

JavaScript Web Applications
by Alex MacCaw

Copyright © 2011 Alex MacCaw. All rights reserved.
Printed in the United States of America.

Published by O'Reilly Media, Inc., 1005 Gravenstein Highway North, Sebastopol, CA 95472.

O'Reilly books may be purchased for educational, business, or sales promotional use. Online editions are also available for most titles (*http://my.safaribooksonline.com*). For more information, contact our corporate/institutional sales department: (800) 998-9938 or *corporate@oreilly.com*.

Editor: Mary Treseler
Production Editor: Holly Bauer
Copyeditor: Marlowe Shaeffer
Proofreader: Stacie Arellano

Indexer: Fred Brown
Cover Designer: Karen Montgomery
Interior Designer: David Futato
Illustrator: Robert Romano

Printing History:

August 2011: First Edition.

ISBN: 978-1-449-30351-8

[LSI]

1313086775

Table of Contents

Preface

JavaScript has come a long way from its humble beginnings in 1995 as part of the Netscape browser, to the high-performance JIT interpreters of today. Even just five years ago developers were blown away by Ajax and the yellow fade technique; now, complex JavaScript apps run into the hundreds of thousands of lines.

In the last year, a new breed of JavaScript applications has appeared, giving an experience people were used to on the desktop, but that was unheard of on the Web. Gone are the slow page requests every time a user interacts with an application; instead, JavaScript engines are now so powerful we can keep state client side, giving a much more responsive and improved experience.

It's not just JavaScript engines that have improved; CSS3 and HTML5 specs haven't finished the drafting stage, but they are already widely supported by modern browsers such as Safari, Chrome, Firefox, and—to some extent—IE9. Beautiful interfaces can be coded in a fraction of the time previously required, and without all that notorious image cutting and splicing. Support for HTML5 and CSS3 is getting better every day, but you'll need to decide—based on your client base—whether to use these technologies.

Moving state to the client side is no simple task. It requires a completely different development approach to server-side applications. You need to think about structure, templating, communicating with the server, frameworks, and much more. That's where this book comes in; I'll take you through all the steps necessary to create state-of-the-art JavaScript applications.

Who Is This Book For?

This book isn't for JavaScript newbies, so if you're unfamiliar with the basics of the language, I advise you to pick up one of the many good books on the subject, such as *JavaScript: The Good Parts* (*http://oreilly.com/catalog/9780596517748*) by Douglas Crockford (O'Reilly). This book is aimed at developers with some JavaScript experience, perhaps using a library like jQuery, who want to get into building more advanced

JavaScript applications. Additionally, many sections of the book—especially the appendixes—will also be a useful reference for experienced JavaScript developers.

How This Book Is Organized

Chapter 1

The chapter starts with a discussion of JavaScript's history and covers some of the underlying influences of its current implementation and community. We then give you an introduction to the MVC architectural pattern, in addition to exploring JavaScript's constructor functions, prototypal inheritance, and how to create your own class library.

Chapter 2

This chapter gives you a brief primer on browser events, including their history, API, and behavior. We'll cover how to bind to events with jQuery, use delegation, and create custom events. We'll also explore using non-DOM events with the PubSub pattern.

Chapter 3

This chapter explains how to use MVC models in your application, as well as for loading and manipulating remote data. We'll explain why MVC and namespacing are important and then build our own ORM library to manage model data. Next, we'll cover how to load in remote data using JSONP and cross-domain Ajax. Finally, you'll learn how to persist model data using HTML5 Local Storage and submitting it to a RESTful server.

Chapter 4

This chapter demonstrates how to use a controller pattern to persist state on the client side. We'll discuss how to use modules to encapsulate logic and prevent global namespace pollution, then we'll cover how to cleanly interface controllers with views, listening to events and manipulating the DOM. Finally, we'll discuss routing, first using the URL's hash fragment, and then using the newer HTML5 History API, making sure to explain the pros and cons of both approaches.

Chapter 5

This is where we cover views and JavaScript templating. We cover the different ways of dynamically rendering views, as well as various templating libraries and where to actually store the templates (inline in the page, in script tags, or with remote loading). Then, you'll learn about data binding—connecting your model controllers and views to dynamically synchronize model data and view data.

Chapter 6

In this chapter, we'll get into the details of JavaScript dependency management using CommonJS modules. You'll learn the history and thinking behind the CommonJS movement, how to create CommonJS modules in the browser, and various module loader libraries to help you with this, such as Yabble and RequireJS. Next, we'll discuss how to automatically wrap up modules server side, increasing performance and saving time. Finally, we'll cover various alternatives to CommonJS, such as Sprockets and LABjs.

Chapter 7

Here, we'll get into some of the benefits HTML5 gives us: the File API. We'll cover browser support, multiple uploads, receiving files that are dragged onto the browser, and files from clipboard events. Next, we'll explore reading files using blobs and slices, and displaying the result in the browser. We'll cover uploading files in the background using the new XMLHttpRequest Level 2 specification, and finally, we'll show you how to give your users live upload progress bars and how to integrate uploads with jQuery's Ajax API.

Chapter 8

We'll take a look at some of the exciting developments with real-time applications and WebSockets. First, the chapter covers real time's rather turbulent history and its current support in the browsers. Then, we'll get into the details of WebSockets and their high-level implementation, browser support, and JavaScript API. Next, we'll demonstrate a simple RPC server that uses WebSockets to connect up servers and clients. We'll then take a look at Socket.IO and learn how real time fits into applications' architecture and user experience.

Chapter 9

This chapter covers testing and debugging, a crucial part of JavaScript web application development. We'll look at the issues surrounding cross-browser testing, which browsers you should test in, and unit tests and testing libraries, such as QUnit and Jasmine. Next, we'll take a look at automated testing and continuous integration servers, such as Selenium. We'll then get into the debugging side of things, exploring Firefox and WebKit's Web Inspectors, the console, and using the JavaScript debugger.

Chapter 10

This chapter covers another important—but often neglected—part of JavaScript web applications: deployment. Chiefly, we'll consider performance and how to use caching, minification, gzip compression, and other techniques to decrease your application's initial load time. Finally, we'll briefly cover how to use CDNs to serve static content on your behalf, and how to use the browser's built-in auditor, which can be immensely helpful in improving your site's performance.

Chapter 11

The next three chapters give you an introduction to some popular JavaScript libraries for application development. Spine is a lightweight MVC-compliant library that uses many of the concepts covered in the book. We'll take you through the core parts of the library: classes, events, models, and controllers. Finally, we'll build an example contacts manager application that will demonstrate what we've learned from the chapter.

Chapter 12

Backbone is an extremely popular library for building JavaScript applications, and this chapter will give you a thorough introduction. We'll take you through the core concepts and classes of Backbone, such as models, collections, controllers, and views. Next, we'll explore syncing model data with the server using RESTful JSON queries and how to respond to Backbone appropriately server side. Finally, we'll build an example to-do list application that will demonstrate much of the library.

Chapter 13

This chapter explores the JavaScriptMVC library, a popular jQuery-based framework for building JavaScript web applications. You'll learn all the basics of JavaScriptMVC, such as classes, models, and controllers, as well as using client-side templates to render views. The chapter ends with a practical CRUD list example, demonstrating how easy it is to create abstract, reusable, memory-safe widgets with JavaScriptMVC.

Appendix A

This appendix provides a brief introduction to jQuery, which is useful if you feel you need to brush up on the library. Most of the book's examples use jQuery, so it's important to be familiar with it. We'll cover most of the core API, such as traversing the DOM, manipulating the DOM, and event binding, triggering, and delegating. Next, we'll approach jQuery's Ajax API, making GET and POST JSON requests. We'll then cover jQuery extensions and how to use encapsulation to ensure you're being a good web citizen. Finally, we'll take a look at a practical example: creating a Growl jQuery plug-in.

Appendix B

Appendix B covers Less, a superset of CSS that extends its syntax with variables, mixins, operations, and nested rules. Less can really reduce the amount of CSS you need to write—especially when it comes to CSS3 vendor–specific rules. This appendix covers Less's major syntax enhancements and how to use the command line's tools and JavaScript library to compile Less files down to CSS.

Appendix C

The last appendix is a CSS3 reference. It provides a bit of background on CSS3, explains vendor prefixes, and then takes you through the major additions to the specification. Among other CSS3 features, this appendix covers rounded corners, rgba colors, drop shadows, gradients, transitions, and transformations. It ends with a discussion about graceful degradation using Modernizr and a practical example of using the new box-sizing specification.

Conventions Used in This Book

The following typographical conventions are used in this book:

Italic

Indicates new terms, URLs, email addresses, filenames, file extensions, and events.

`Constant width`

Indicates computer code in a broad sense, including commands, arrays, elements, statements, options, switches, variables, attributes, keys, functions, types, classes, namespaces, methods, modules, properties, parameters, values, objects, event handlers, XML tags, HTML tags, macros, the contents of files, and the output from commands.

`Constant width bold`

Shows commands or other text that should be typed literally by the user.

`Constant width italic`

Shows text that should be replaced with user-supplied values or by values determined by context.

 This icon signifies a tip, suggestion, or general note.

 This icon indicates a warning or caution.

Accompanying Files

This book's accompanying files are hosted on GitHub (*https://github.com/maccman/book-assets*). You can view them online or download a zip locally (*https://github.com/maccman/book-assets/zipball/master*). All the assets are separated by chapter, and any required libraries are also included. Most examples in this book are also available as standalone files.

Whenever a particular asset is referenced inside a chapter, it will be in the form of *assets/chapter_number/name*.

Code Conventions

Throughout this book we'll use the `assert()` and `assertEqual()` functions to demonstrate the value of variables or the result of a function call. `assert()` is just shorthand for indicating that a particular variable resolves to true; it is a common pattern that's especially prevalent in automated testing. `assert()` takes two arguments: a value and an optional message. If the value doesn't equal true, the function will throw an error:

```
var assert = function(value, msg) {
  if ( !value )
    throw(msg || (value + " does not equal true"));
};
```

`assertEqual()` is shorthand for indicating that one variable equals another. It works similarly to `assert()`, but it accepts two values. If the two values aren't equal, the assertion fails:

```
var assertEqual = function(val1, val2, msg) {
  if (val1 !== val2)
    throw(msg || (val1 + " does not equal " + val2));
};
```

Using the two functions is very straightforward, as you can see in the example below. If the assertion fails, you'll see an error message in the browser's console:

```
assert( true );

// Equivalent to assertEqual()
assert( false === false );

assertEqual( 1, 1 );
```

I've slightly sugar-coated `assertEqual()` since, as it stands, object comparison will fail unless the objects share the same reference in memory. The solution is a deep comparison, and we've included an example of this in *assets/ch00/deep_equality.html*.

jQuery Examples

A lot of the examples in this book rely on jQuery (*http://jquery.com*), an extremely popular JavaScript library that simplifies events, DOM traversing, manipulation, and Ajax. I've decided this for various reasons, but it's mostly because jQuery greatly clarifies examples, and it is closer to the JavaScript most people write in the real world.

If you haven't used jQuery, I strongly advise you to check it out. It has an excellent API that provides a good abstraction over the DOM. A brief jQuery primer is included in Appendix A.

Holla

Built as a companion to this book, Holla (*http://github.com/maccman/holla*) is a JS group chat application. Holla is a good example application because it encompasses various best practices covered in this book. Among other things, Holla will show you how to:

- Use CSS3 and HTML5 to create beautiful interfaces
- Drag and drop to upload files
- Lay out your code using Sprockets and Less
- Use WebSockets to push data to clients
- Create a stateful JavaScript application

Clone the code from Holla's GitHub repository (*http://github.com/maccman/holla*) and take a look. Many of the examples in this book have been taken from Holla's source; see Figure P-1.

Figure P-1. Holla, an example chat application

Author's Note

I wrote this book as I traveled around the world for a year. I wrote some parts in African huts without electricity and Internet, others in Japanese washitsus overlooking temples and blossoming trees, and some even on remote Cambodian islands. In short, I had a great time writing this, and I hope reading it gives you just as much pleasure.

Some people deserve their share of the blame. Thanks go to Stuart Eccles, Tim Malbon, Ben Griffins, and Sean O'Halpin for giving me the chances and opportunity to find my passion; and to James Adam, Paul Battley, and Jonah Fox for mentoring and putting up with my asininities.

Thanks also to the technical reviewers, who really helped shape the book: Henrik Joreteg, Justin Meyer, Lea Verou, Addy Osmani, Alex Barbara, Max Williams, and Julio Cesar Ody.

Most importantly, thanks to my parents for their unwavering support.

Safari® Books Online

 Safari Books Online is an on-demand digital library that lets you easily search over 7,500 technology and creative reference books and videos to find the answers you need quickly.

With a subscription, you can read any page and watch any video from our library online. Read books on your cell phone and mobile devices. Access new titles before they are available for print, and get exclusive access to manuscripts in development and post feedback for the authors. Copy and paste code samples, organize your favorites, download chapters, bookmark key sections, create notes, print out pages, and benefit from tons of other time-saving features.

O'Reilly Media has uploaded this book to the Safari Books Online service. To have full digital access to this book and others on similar topics from O'Reilly and other publishers, sign up for free at *http://my.safaribooksonline.com*.

How to Contact Us

Please address comments and questions concerning this book to the publisher:

O'Reilly Media, Inc.
1005 Gravenstein Highway North
Sebastopol, CA 95472
(800) 998-9938 (in the United States or Canada)
(707) 829-0515 (international or local)
(707) 829-0104 (fax)

We have a web page for this book, where we list errata, examples, and any additional information. You can access this page at:

http://www.oreilly.com/catalog/9781449303518

To comment or ask technical questions about this book, send email to:

bookquestions@oreilly.com

For more information about our books, courses, conferences, and news, see our website at *http://www.oreilly.com.*

Find us on Facebook: *http://facebook.com/oreilly*

Follow us on Twitter: *http://twitter.com/oreillymedia*

Watch us on YouTube: *http://www.youtube.com/oreillymedia*

## CHAPTER 1

MVC and Classes

Early Days

JavaScript development has changed markedly from how it looked when it was first conceived. It's easy to forget how far the language has come from its initial implementation in Netscape's browser, to the powerful engines of today, such as Google's V8. It's been a rocky path involving renaming, merging, and the eventual standardization as ECMAScript. The capabilities we have today are beyond the wildest dreams of those early innovators.

Despite its success and popularity, JavaScript is still widely misunderstood. Few people know that it's a powerful and dynamic object-oriented language. They're surprised to learn about some of its more advanced features, such as prototypal inheritance, modules, and namespaces. So, why is JavaScript so misunderstood?

Part of the reason is due to previous buggy JavaScript implementations, and part of it is due to the name—the *Java* prefix suggests it's somehow related to Java; in reality, it's a totally different language. However, I think the real reason is the way most developers are introduced to the language. With other languages, such as Python and Ruby, developers usually make a concerted effort to learn the language with the help of books, screencasts, and tutorials. Until recently, though, JavaScript wasn't given that endorsement. Developers would get requests to add a bit of form validation—maybe a lightbox or a photo gallery—to existing code, often on a tight schedule. They'd use scripts they'd find on the Internet, calling it a day with little understanding of the language behind it. After that basic exposure, some of them might even add JavaScript to their resumes.

Recently, JavaScript engines and browsers have become so powerful that building full-blown applications in JavaScript is not only feasible, but increasingly popular. Applications like Gmail and Google Maps have paved the way to a completely different way of thinking about web applications, and users are clamoring for more. Companies are hiring full-time JavaScript developers. No longer is JavaScript a sublanguage relegated to simple scripts and a bit of form validation—it is now a standalone language in its own right, realizing its full potential.

This influx of popularity means that a lot of new JavaScript applications are being built. Unfortunately, and perhaps due to the language's history, many of them are constructed very poorly. For some reason, when it comes to JavaScript, acknowledged patterns and best practices fly out the window. Developers ignore architectural models like the Model View Controller (MVC) pattern, instead blending their applications into a messy soup of HTML and JavaScript.

This book won't teach you much about JavaScript as a language—other books are better suited for that, such as Douglas Crockford's *JavaScript: The Good Parts (http:// oreilly.com/catalog/9780596517748)* (O'Reilly). However, this book will show you how to structure and build complex JavaScript applications, allowing you to create incredible web experiences.

Adding Structure

The secret to making large JavaScript applications is to *not* make large JavaScript applications. Instead, you should decouple your application into a series of fairly independent components. The mistake developers often make is creating applications with a lot of interdependency, with huge linear JavaScript files generating a slew of HTML tags. These sorts of applications are difficult to maintain and extend, so they should be avoided at all costs.

Paying a bit of attention to an application's structure when you start building it can make a big difference to the end result. Ignore any preconceived notions you have about JavaScript and treat it like the object-oriented language that it is. Use classes, inheritance, objects, and patterns the same way you would if you were building an application in another language, such as Python or Ruby. Architecture is critical to server-side applications, so why shouldn't the same apply to client-side apps?

The approach this book advocates is the MVC pattern, a tried and tested way of architecting applications that ensures they can be effectively maintained and extended. It's also a pattern that applies particularly well to JavaScript applications.

What Is MVC?

MVC is a design pattern that breaks an application into three parts: the data (Model), the presentation layer (View), and the user interaction layer (Controller). In other words, the event flow goes like this:

1. The user interacts with the application.
2. The controller's event handlers trigger.
3. The controller requests data from the model, giving it to the view.

4. The view presents the data to the user.

Or, to give a real example, Figure 1-1 shows how sending a new chat message would work with Holla.

Figure 1-1. Sending a new chat message from Holla

1. The user submits a new chat message.
2. The controller's event handlers trigger.
3. The controller creates a new Chat Model record.
4. The controller then updates the view.
5. The user sees his new chat message in chat log.

The MVC architectural pattern can even be implemented without libraries or frameworks. The key is to divide up the responsibilities of the MVC components into clearly defined sections of code, keeping them decoupled. This allows for independent development, testing, and maintenance of each component.

Let's explore the components of MVC in detail.

The Model

The model is where all the application's data objects are stored. For example, we might have a User Model that contains a list of users, their attributes, and any logic associated specifically with that model.

A model doesn't know anything about views or controllers. The only thing a model should contain is data and the logic associated directly with that data. Any event handling code, view templates, or logic not specific to that model should be kept well clear of it. You know an application's MVC architecture is violated when you start seeing view code in the models. Models should be completely decoupled from the rest of your application.

When controllers fetch data from servers or create new records, they wrap them in model instances. This means that our data is object oriented, and any functions or logic defined on the model can be called directly on the data.

So, rather than this:

```
var user = users["foo"];
destroyUser(user);
```

We can do something like this:

```
var user = User.find("foo");
user.destroy();
```

The first example is not namespaced or object oriented. If we have another `destroy User()` function defined in our application, the two will conflict. Global variables and functions should always be kept to an absolute minimum. In the second example, the `destroy()` function is namespaced behind User instances, as are all the stored records. This is ideal, since we're keeping global variables to a minimum, exposing fewer areas to potential conflicts. The code is cleaner and can take advantage of inheritance so functions like `destroy()` don't have be defined separately on every model.

Models are explored in much more depth in Chapter 3, which covers topics such as loading in data from servers and creating object-relational mappers (ORMs).

The View

The view layer is what's presented to the user and is what she interacts with. In a JavaScript application, the view would be made up mostly of HTML, CSS, and Java-Script templates. Apart from simple conditional statements in templates, the views shouldn't contain any logic.

In fact, like models, views should also be decoupled from the rest of the application. Views shouldn't know anything about controllers and models—they should be independent. Mixing up views with logic is one of the surest paths to disaster.

That isn't to say MVC doesn't allow for presentational logic—as long as it's not defined inside views. Presentational logic resides in what are called *helpers*: scripts solely for small utility functions related to the view.

The example below, which includes logic inside views, is something you shouldn't do:

```
// template.html
<div>
  <script>
    function formatDate(date) {
      /* ... */
    };
  </script>
  ${ formatDate(this.date) }
</div>
```

In the code above, we're inserting the `formatDate()` function directly into the view, which violates MVC, resulting in an unmaintainable mess of tag soup. By separating out presentational logic into helpers, as with the example below, we're avoiding that problem and keeping our application's structure MVC-compliant.

```
// helper.js
var helper = {};
helper.formatDate = function(){ /* ... */ };

// template.html
<div>
  ${ helper.formatDate(this.date) }
</div>
```

In addition, all presentational logic is namespaced under the helper variable, preventing conflicts and keeping the code clean and extendable.

Don't worry too much about specifics regarding views and templates—we cover them extensively in Chapter 5. The aim of this section is to familiarize you with how views relate to the MVC architectural pattern.

The Controller

Controllers are the glue between models and views. Controllers receive events and input from views, process them (perhaps involving models), and update the views accordingly. The controller will add event listeners to views when the page loads, such as those detecting when forms are submitted or buttons are clicked. Then, when the user interacts with your application, the events trigger actions inside the controllers.

You don't need any special libraries or frameworks to implement controllers; here's an example using plain old jQuery:

```
var Controller = {};

// Use a anonymous function to enscapulate scope
(Controller.users = function($){

  var nameClick = function(){
    /* ... */
  };

  // Attach event listeners on page load
  $(function(){
    $("#view .name").click(nameClick);
  });

})(jQuery);
```

We're creating a users Controller that is namespaced under the Controller variable. Then, we're using an anonymous function to encapsulate scope, preventing variable pollution of the global scope. When the page loads, we're adding a *click* event listener to a view element.

As you can see, controllers don't require a library or framework. However, to comply with MVC's architectural requirements, they must be separated from Models and Views. Controllers and states are covered in more detail in Chapter 4.

Toward Modularity, Creating Classes

Before we get to the nitty-gritty of MVC, we're going to cover some preliminary concepts, such as JavaScript classes and events. This will give you a solid foundation before moving on to some of the more advanced concepts.

JavaScript object literals are fine for static classes, but it's often useful to create classical classes with inheritance and instances. It's important to emphasize that JavaScript is a prototype language, and as such doesn't include a native class implementation. However, support can be emulated fairly easily.

Classes in JavaScript often get a bad rap, criticized for not being part of the "JavaScript Way," a term that means essentially nothing. jQuery is effectively neutral when it comes to structural methodology or inheritance patterns. This can lead JavaScript developers to believe they shouldn't consider structure—i.e., that classes aren't available or shouldn't be used. In reality, classes are just another tool, and as a pragmatist, I believe they're as useful in JavaScript as in any other modern language.

Rather than class definitions, JavaScript has constructor functions and the new operator. A constructor function can specify an object's initial properties and values when it is instantiated. Any JavaScript function can be used as a constructor. Use the new operator with a constructor function to create a new instance.

The new operator changes a function's context, as well as the behavior of the return statement. In practice, using new and constructors is fairly similar to languages with native class implementations:

```
var Person = function(name) {
  this.name = name;
};

// Instantiate Person
var alice = new Person('alice');

// Check instance
assert( alice instanceof Person );
```

By convention, constructor functions are upper camel-cased to differentiate them from normal functions. This is important because you don't ever want to call a constructor function without the new prefix.

```
// Don't do this!
Person('bob'); //=> undefined
```

The function will just return undefined, and since the context is the window (global) object, you've unintentionally created a global variable, name. Always call constructor functions using the new keyword.

When a constructor function is called with the new keyword, the context switches from global (window) to a new and empty context specific to that instance. So, the this

---

keyword refers to the current instance. Although it might sound complicated, in practice, you can treat it like native class implementations in other languages.

By default, if you don't return anything from a constructor function, this—the current context—will be returned. Otherwise, you can return any nonprimitive type. For example, we could return a function that would set up a new class, the first step in building our own class emulation library:

```
var Class = function(){
  var klass = function(){
    this.init.apply(this, arguments);
  };
  klass.prototype.init  = function(){};
  return klass;
};

var Person = new Class;

Person.prototype.init = function(){
  // Called on Person instantiation
};

// Usage:
var person = new Person;
```

Confusingly, due to a JavaScript 2 (*http://www.mozilla.org/js/language/js20-1999-02 -18/classes.html*) specification that was never implemented, class is a reserved keyword. The common convention is instead to name class variables as _class or klass.

Adding Functions to Classes

Adding class functions to a constructor function is the same as adding a property onto any object in JavaScript:

```
Person.find = function(id){ /*...*/ };

var person = Person.find(1);
```

To add instance functions to a constructor function, you need to use the constructor's prototype:

```
Person.prototype.breath = function(){ /*...*/ };

var person = new Person;
person.breath();
```

A common pattern is to alias a class' prototype to fn, which is a bit less verbose:

```
Person.fn = Person.prototype;

Person.fn.run = function(){ /*...*/ };
```

In fact, you'll see this pattern throughout jQuery plug-ins, which essentially just add functions to jQuery's prototype, aliased to jQuery.fn.

Adding Methods to Our Class Library

Currently, our class library includes functionality for instantiating and initializing instances. Adding properties to classes is the same as adding properties to constructor functions.

Properties set directly on the class will be equivalent to static members:

```
var Person = new Class;

// Static functions are added directly on the class
Person.find = function(id){ /* ... */ };

// And now we can call them directly
var person = Person.find(1);
```

And properties set on the class' prototype are also available on instances:

```
var Person = new Class;

// Instance functions are on the prototype
Person.prototype.save = function(){ /* ... */ };

// And now we can call them on instances
var person = new Person;
person.save();
```

However, in my opinion, that syntax is a little convoluted, impractical, and repetitive. It's difficult to see, at a glance, a list of your class' static and instance properties. Instead, let's create a different way of adding properties to our classes using two functions, extend() and include():

```
var Class = function(){
  var klass = function(){
    this.init.apply(this, arguments);
  };

  klass.prototype.init  = function(){};

  // Shortcut to access prototype
  klass.fn = klass.prototype;

  // Shortcut to access class
  klass.fn.parent = klass;

  // Adding class properties
  klass.extend = function(obj){
    var extended = obj.extended;
    for(var i in obj){
      klass[i] = obj[i];
    }
    if (extended) extended(klass)
  };

  // Adding instance properties
```

```
klass.include = function(obj){
  var included = obj.included;
  for(var i in obj){
    klass.fn[i] = obj[i];
  }
  if (included) included(klass)
};

return klass;
};
```

In the improved class library above, we're adding an `extend()` function to generated classes, which accepts an object. The object's properties are iterated through and copied directly onto the class:

```
var Person = new Class;

Person.extend({
  find:   function(id) { /* ... */ },
  exists: functions(id) { /* ... */ }
});

var person = Person.find(1);
```

The `include()` function works in exactly the same way, except properties are copied onto the class' prototype, rather than directly onto the class. In other words, the properties are on the class' instance, rather than statically on the class.

```
var Person = new Class;

Person.include({
  save:    function(id) { /* ... */ },
  destroy: functions(id) { /* ... */ }
});

var person = new Person;
person.save();
```

We're also implementing support for `extended` and `included` callbacks. If these properties are present on the passed object, they'll be invoked:

```
Person.extend({
  extended: function(klass) {
    console.log(klass, " was extended!");
  }
});
```

If you've used classes in Ruby, this should all look very familiar. The beauty of this approach is that we've now got support for modules. Modules are reusable pieces of code, and they can be used as an alternative to inheritance for sharing common properties among classes.

```
var ORMModule = {
  save: function(){
    // Shared function
```

```
    }
};

var Person = new Class;
var Asset  = new Class;

Person.include(ORMModule);
Asset.include(ORMModule);
```

Class Inheritance Using Prototype

We've been using the prototype property a lot, but it hasn't really been explained yet. Let's take a closer look at what it is exactly and how to use it to implement a form of inheritance in our classes.

JavaScript is a prototype-based language and—rather than make distinctions between classes and instances—it has the notions of a *prototypical object*: an object used as a template from which to get the initial properties for a new object. Any object can be associated as a prototype of another object, sharing its properties. In practice, you can look at this as a form of inheritance.

When you fetch a property on an object, JavaScript will search the local object for the property. If it isn't found, JavaScript will start searching the object's prototype and continue up the prototype tree, eventually reaching Object.prototype. If the property is found, its value is returned; otherwise, undefined will be returned.

In other words, if you start adding properties to Array.prototype, they'll be reflected across every JavaScript array.

To subclass a class and inherit its properties, you need to first define a constructor function. Then, you need to assign a new instance of the parent class as the prototype for your constructor function. It looks like this:

```
var Animal = function(){};

Animal.prototype.breath = function(){
  console.log('breath');
};

var Dog = function(){};

// Dog inherits from Animal
Dog.prototype = new Animal;

Dog.prototype.wag = function(){
  console.log('wag tail');
};
```

Now, we can check to see whether the inheritance works:

```
var dog = new Dog;
dog.wag();
dog.breath(); // Inherited property
```

Adding Inheritance to Our Class Library

Let's add inheritance to our custom class library. We'll pass through an optional parent class when creating a new class:

```
var Class = function(parent){
  var klass = function(){
    this.init.apply(this, arguments);
  };

  // Change klass' prototype
  if (parent) {
    var subclass = function() { };
    subclass.prototype = parent.prototype;
    klass.prototype = new subclass;
  };

  klass.prototype.init = function(){};

  // Shortcuts
  klass.fn = klass.prototype;
  klass.fn.parent = klass;
  klass._super = klass.__proto__;

  /* include/extend code... */

  return klass;
};
```

If a parent is passed to the Class constructor, we make sure any subclasses share the same prototype. This little dance around creating a temporary anonymous function prevents instances from being created when a class is inherited. The caveat here is that only instance properties, not class properties, are inherited. There isn't yet a cross-browser way of setting an object's __proto__. Libraries like Super.js (*http://github.com/maccman/super.js*) get around this problem by copying the properties, rather than implementing proper dynamic inheritance.

Now, we can perform simple inheritance by passing parent classes to Class:

```
var Animal = new Class;

Animal.include({
  breath: function(){
    console.log('breath');
  }
});

var Cat = new Class(Animal)
```

```
// Usage
var tommy = new Cat;
tommy.breath();
```

Function Invocation

Like everything else in JavaScript, functions are just objects. However, unlike other objects, they can be invoked. The context inside the function—i.e., the value of `this`—depends on where and how it's invoked.

Apart from using brackets, there are two other ways to invoke a function: `apply()` and `call()`. The difference between them has to do with the arguments you want to pass to the function.

The `apply()` function takes two parameters: a context and an array of arguments. If the context is null, the global context is used. For example:

```
function.apply(this, [1, 2, 3])
```

The `call()` function has exactly the same behavior, yet it is used differently. The first argument is the context, while each subsequent argument is delegated to the invocation. In other words, you use multiple arguments—rather than an array like with `apply()`—to pass arguments to the function.

```
function.call(this, 1, 2, 3);
```

Why would you want to change the context? This is a valid question because other languages get on fine without allowing explicit context changes. JavaScript uses context changes to share state, especially during event callbacks. (Personally, I feel this was a mistake in the design of the language, as it can be confusing for beginners and introduce bugs. However, it's too late to change it now, so you need to learn how it works.)

jQuery takes advantage of `apply()` and `call()` throughout its API to change context—for example, when using event handlers or iterating using `each()`. This can be confusing at first, but it's useful when you understand what's happening:

```
$('.clicky').click(function(){
  // 'this' refers to the element
  $(this).hide();
});

$('p').each(function(){
  // 'this' refers to the current iteration
  $(this).remove();
});
```

To access the original context, a common pattern stores the value of `this` in a local variable. For example:

```
var clicky = {
  wasClicked: function(){
    /* ... */
```

```
    },

    addListeners: function(){
      var self = this;
      $('.clicky').click(function(){
        self.wasClicked()
      });
    }
  };

  clicky.addListeners();
```

However, we can use `apply` to make this much cleaner, wrapping the callback within another anonymous function, which preserves the original context:

```
  var proxy = function(func, thisObject){
    return(function(){
      return func.apply(thisObject, arguments);
    });
  };

  var clicky = {
    wasClicked: function(){
      /* ... */
    },

    addListeners: function(){
      var self = this;
      $('.clicky').click(proxy(this.wasClicked, this));
    }
  };
```

So, in the above example, we specify the context to be used inside the click callback; the context jQuery invokes the function in is ignored. In fact, jQuery's API includes something to do just this—you guessed it, `jQuery.proxy()`:

```
  $('.clicky').click($.proxy(function(){ /* ... */ }, this));
```

There are other useful reasons to use `apply()` and `call()`, such as delegating. We can delegate calls from one function to another, and even alter the passed arguments:

```
  var App {
    log: function(){
      if (typeof console == "undefined") return;

      // Turn arguments into a proper array
      var args = jQuery.makeArray(arguments);

      // Insert a new argument
      args.unshift("(App)");

      // Delegate to the console
      console.log.apply(console, args);
    }
  };
```

Above, we're making an array of arguments and then adding our own. Finally, the call is delegated to `console.log()`. If you're not familiar with the `arguments` variable, it's set by the interpreter and contains an array of arguments with which the current scope was called. It's not a true array though—for example, it's not mutable—so we have to convert it to something usable with `jquery.makeArray()`.

Controlling Scope in Our Class Library

The proxy function described in the previous section is such a useful pattern that we should add it to our class library. We'll add a proxy function on both classes and instances, allowing us to keep the class' scope when handing functions off to event handlers and the like:

```
var Class = function(parent){
  var klass = function(){
    this.init.apply(this, arguments);
  };
  klass.prototype.init = function(){};
  klass.fn = klass.prototype;

  // Adding a proxy function
  klass.proxy = function(func){
    var self = this;
    return(function(){
      return func.apply(self, arguments);
    });
  }

  // Add the function on instances too
  klass.fn.proxy = klass.proxy;

  return klass;
};
```

We can now use the `proxy()` function to wrap up functions, making sure they're invoked in the right scope:

```
var Button = new Class;

Button.include({
  init: function(element){
    this.element = jQuery(element);

    // Proxy the click function
    this.element.click(this.proxy(this.click));
  },

  click: function(){ /* ... */ }
});
```

If we didn't wrap the `click()` callback with a proxy, it would be called within the context of `this.element`, rather than `Button`, causing all sorts of problems. A new specification of JavaScript—ECMAScript, 5th Edition (*http://en.wikipedia.org/wiki/ECMA Script#ECMAScript.2C_5th_Edition*) (ES5)—has also added support for controlling invocation scope with the `bind()` function. `bind()` is called on a function, making sure the function is called in the context of the specified `this` value. For example:

```
Button.include({
  init: function(element){
    this.element = jQuery(element);

    // Bind the click function
    this.element.click(this.click.bind(this));
  },

  click: function(){ /* ... */ }
});
```

This example is equivalent to our `proxy()` function, and it makes sure the `click()` function is called with the correct context. Older browsers don't support `bind()` but, luckily, support can be shimmed easily and implemented manually if needed. A shim basically implements a compatibility layer on legacy browsers, directly extending the relevant object's prototypes, allowing you to use features of ES5 today without worrying about older browsers. For example, a shim that would support `bind()` would look like this:

```
if ( !Function.prototype.bind ) {
  Function.prototype.bind = function( obj ) {
    var slice = [].slice,
        args = slice.call(arguments, 1),
        self = this,
        nop = function () {},
        bound = function () {
          return self.apply( this instanceof nop ? this : ( obj || {} ),
                             args.concat( slice.call(arguments) ) );
        };

    nop.prototype = self.prototype;

    bound.prototype = new nop();

    return bound;
  };
}
```

`Function`'s prototype is only overwritten if the feature doesn't already exist: newer browsers will continue to use their native implementations. Shimming is especially useful for arrays, which have had a bunch of new features added in recent JavaScript versions. I personally use the es5-shim (*https://github.com/kriskowal/es5-shim*) project because it covers as many of the new features in ES5 as possible.

Adding Private Functions

So far, any property we've added to our classes has been open to the world and can be changed at any time. Let's now explore how to add private properties to our classes.

A lot of developers end up prefixing private properties with an underscore (_). Although these can still be changed, it makes it obvious that they're part of a private API. I try to steer clear of this approach because it looks rather ugly.

JavaScript does have support for immutable properties; however, this isn't implemented across the main browsers, so we'll have to wait before using this method. Instead, we'll use JavaScript anonymous functions to create a private scope, which can only be accessed internally:

```javascript
var Person = function(){};

(function(){

  var findById = function(){ /* ... */ };

  Person.find = function(id){
    if (typeof id == "integer")
      return findById(id);
  };

})();
```

We're wrapping all our class' properties in an anonymous function, then creating local variables (`findById`), which can only be accessed in the current scope. The `Person` variable is defined in the global scope, so it can be accessed from anywhere.

Never define a variable without using the `var` operator, since it always creates a global variable. If you need to define a global variable, do so in the global scope or as a property on `window`:

```javascript
(function(exports){
  var foo = "bar";

  // Expose variable
  exports.foo = foo;
})(window);

assertEqual(foo, "bar");
```

Class Libraries

As with a lot of concepts in this book, it's good to understand the theory behind classes, but often in practice, you'll use a library. jQuery doesn't include class support natively, but it can easily be added with a plug-in like HJS (*http://plugins.jquery.com/project/HJS*). HJS lets you define classes by passing a set of properties to `$.Class.create`:

```
var Person = $.Class.create({
  // constructor
  initialize: function(name) {
    this.name = name;
  }
});
```

To inherit classes, pass their parent as an argument when creating them:

```
var Student = $.Class.create(Person, {
  price: function() { /* ... */ }
});
```

```
var alex = new Student("Alex");
alex.pay();
```

To add class properties, set them directly on the class:

```
Person.find = function(id){ /* ... */ };
```

HJS' API also includes a few utility functions, such as `clone()` and `equal()`:

```
var alex = new Student("Alex");
var bill = alex.clone();
```

```
assert( alex.equal(bill) );
```

HJS isn't your only option; Spine (*http://maccman.github.com/spine*) also has a class implementation. To use it, just include spine.js (*http://maccman.github.com/spine/spine.js*) in the page:

```
<script src="http://maccman.github.com/spine/spine.js"> </script>
<script>
  var Person = Spine.Class.create();

  Person.extend({
    find: function() { /* ... */ }
  });

  Person.include({
    init: function(atts){
      this.attributes = atts || {};
    }
  });

  var person = Person.init();
</script>
```

Spine's class library has a similar API to the library we've been building throughout this chapter. Use `extend()` to add class properties and `include()` to add instance properties. To inherit from them, pass parent classes to the `Spine.Class` instantiator.

If you're widening your gaze beyond jQuery, Prototype (*http://prototypejs.org*) is definitely worth checking out. It has an excellent class API (*http://prototypejs.org/learn/class-inheritance*) that was the inspiration for a lot of other libraries.

jQuery's John Resig has an interesting post on implementing classical inheritance with the library (*http://ejohn.org/blog/simple-javascript-inheritance*). It's well worth reading, especially if you're interested in the nitty-gritty behind the JavaScript prototype system.

## CHAPTER 2

Events and Observing

Events are at the core of your JavaScript application, powering everything and providing the first point of contact when a user interacts with your application. However, this is where JavaScript's unstandardized birth rears its ugly head. At the height of the browser wars, Netscape and Microsoft purposely chose different, incompatible event models. Although they were later standardized by the W3C, Internet Explorer kept its different implementation until its latest release, IE9.

Luckily, we have great libraries like jQuery and Prototype that smooth over the mess, giving you one API that will work with all the event implementations. Still, it's worth understanding what's happening behind the scenes, so I'm going to cover the W3C model here before showing examples for various popular libraries.

Listening to Events

Events revolve around a function called `addEventListener()`, which takes three arguments: `type` (e.g., *click*), `listener` (i.e., callback), and `useCapture` (we'll cover `useCapture` later). Using the first two arguments, we can attach a function to a DOM element, which is invoked when that particular event, such as *click*, is triggered on the element:

```
var button = document.getElementById("createButton");

button.addEventListener("click", function(){ /* ... */ }, false);
```

We can remove the listener using `removeEventListener()`, passing the same arguments we gave `addEventListener()`. If the listener function is anonymous and there's no reference to it, it can't be removed without destroying the element:

```
var div = document.getElementById("div");

var listener = function(event) { /* ... */ };
div.addEventListener("click", listener, false);
div.removeEventListener("click", listener, false);
```

As its first argument, the listener function is passed an **event** object, which you can use to get information about the event, such as timestamp, coordinates, and target. It also contains various functions to stop the event propagation and prevent the default action.

As for event types, the supported ones vary from browser to browser, but all modern browsers have the following:

- *click*
- *dblclick*
- *mousemove*
- *mouseover*
- *mouseout*
- *focus*
- *blur*
- *change* (for form inputs)
- *submit* (for forms)

Check out Quirksmode (*http://www.quirksmode.org/dom/events/index.html*), which has a full event compatibility table.

Event Ordering

Before we go any further, it's important to discuss event ordering. If an element and one of its ancestors have an event handler for the same event type, which one should fire first when the event is triggered? Well, you won't be surprised to hear that Netscape and Microsoft had different ideas.

Netscape 4 supported event *capturing*, which triggers event listeners from the top-most ancestor to the element in question—i.e., from the outside in.

Microsoft endorsed event *bubbling*, which triggers event listeners from the element, propagating up through its ancestors—i.e., from the inside out.

Event bubbling makes more sense to me, and it is likely to be the model used in day-to-day development. The W3C compromised and stipulated support for both event models in their specification. Events conforming to the W3C model are first captured until they reach the target element; then, they bubble up again.

You can choose the type of event handler you want to register, capturing or bubbling, which is where the useCapture argument to addEventListener() comes into the picture. If the last argument to addEventListener() is true, the event handler is set for the capturing phase; if it is false, the event handler is set for the bubbling phase:

```
// Use bubbling by passing false as the last argument
button.addEventListener("click", function(){ /* ... */ }, false);
```

The vast majority of the time, you'll probably be using event bubbling. If in doubt, pass false as the last argument to addEventListener().

Canceling Events

When the event is bubbling up, you can stop its progress with the stopPropagation() function, located on the event object. Any handlers on ancestor elements won't be invoked:

```
button.addEventListener("click", function(e){
  e.stopPropagation();
  /* ... */
}, false);
```

Additionally, some libraries like jQuery support a stopImmediatePropagation() function, preventing any further handlers from being called at all—even if they're on the same element.

Browsers also give default actions to events. For example, when you click on a link, the browser's default action is to load a new page, or when you click on a checkbox, the browser checks it. This default action happens after all the event propagation phases and can be canceled during any one of those. You can prevent the default action with the preventDefault() function on the event object. Alternatively, you can just return false from the handler:

```
form.addEventListener("submit", function(e){
  /* ... */
  return confirm("Are you super sure?");
}, false);
```

If the call to confirm() returns false—i.e., the user clicks cancel in the confirmation dialog—the event callback function will return false, canceling the event and form submission.

The Event Object

As well as the aforementioned functions—stopPropagation() and preventDefault()—the event object contains a lot of useful properties. Most of the properties in the W3C specification are documented below; for more information, see the full specification (http://www.w3.org/TR/DOM-Level-2-Events/).

Type of event:

bubbles
> A boolean indicating whether the event bubbles up through the DOM

Properties reflecting the environment when the event was executed:

button
: A value indicating which, if any, mouse button(s) was pressed

ctrlKey
: A boolean indicating whether the Ctrl key was pressed

altKey
: A boolean indicating whether the Alt key was pressed

shiftKey
: A boolean indicating whether the Shift key was pressed

metaKey
: A boolean indicating whether the Meta key was pressed

Properties specific to keyboard events:

isChar
: A boolean indicating whether the event has a key character

charCode
: A unicode value of the pressed key (for *keypress* events only)

keyCode
: A unicode value of a noncharacter key

which
: A unicode value of the pressed key, regardless of whether it's a character

Where the event happened:

pageX, pageY
: The event coordinates relative to the page (i.e., viewport)

screenX, screenY
: The event coordinates relative to the screen

Elements associated with the event:

currentTarget
: The current DOM element within the event bubbling phase

target, originalTarget
: The original DOM element

relatedTarget
: The other DOM element involved in the event, if any

These properties vary in browsers, especially among those that are not W3C-compliant. Luckily, libraries like jQuery and Prototype will smooth out any differences.

Event Libraries

In all likelihood you'll end up using a JavaScript library for event management; otherwise, there are just too many browser inconsistencies. I'm going to show you how to use jQuery's event management API, although there are many other good choices, such as Prototype (*http://www.prototypejs.org*), MooTools (*http://mootools.net*), and YUI (*http://developer.yahoo.com/yui*). Refer to their respective APIs for more in-depth documentation.

jQuery's API has a `bind()` function for adding cross-browser event listeners. Call this function on jQuery instances, passing in an event name and handler:

```
jQuery("#element").bind(eventName, handler);
```

For example, you can register a click handler on an element like so:

```
jQuery("#element").bind("click", function(event) {
  // ...
});
```

jQuery has some shortcuts for event types like *click*, *submit*, and *mouseover*. It looks like this:

```
$("#myDiv").click(function(){
  // ...
});
```

It's important to note that the element must exist before you start adding events to it—i.e., you should do so after the page has loaded. All you need to do is listen for the window's *load* event, and then start adding listeners:

```
jQuery(window).bind("load", function() {
  $("#signinForm").submit(checkForm);
});
```

However, there's a better event to listen for than the window's *load*, and that's *DOMContentLoaded*. It fires when the DOM is ready, but before the page's images and stylesheets have downloaded. This means the event will always fire before users can interact with the page.

The *DOMContentLoaded* event isn't supported in every browser, so jQuery abstracts it with a `ready()` function that has cross-browser support:

```
jQuery.ready(function($){
  $("#myForm").bind("submit", function(){ /* ... */ });
});
```

In fact, you can skip the `ready()` function and pass the handler straight to the jQuery object:

```
jQuery(function($){
  // Called when the page is ready
});
```

Context Change

One thing that's often confusing about events is how the context changes when the handler is invoked. When using the browser's native `addEventListener()`, the context is changed from the local one to the targeted HTML element:

```
new function(){
  this.appName = "wem";

  document.body.addEventListener("click", function(e){
    // Context has changed, so appName will be undefined
    alert(this.appName);
  }, false);
};
```

To preserve the original context, wrap the handler in an anonymous function, keeping a reference to it. We covered this pattern in Chapter 1, where we used a proxy function to maintain the current context. It's such a common pattern that jQuery includes a `proxy()` function—just pass in the function and context in which you want it to be invoked:

```
$("signinForm").submit($.proxy(function(){ /* ... */ }, this));
```

Delegating Events

It may have occurred to you that since events bubble up, we could just add a listener on a parent element, checking for events on its children. This is exactly the technique that frameworks like SproutCore (*http://www.sproutcore.com*) use to reduce the number of event listeners in the application:

```
// Delegating events on a ul list
list.addEventListener("click", function(e){
  if (e.currentTarget.tagName == "li") {
    /* ... */
    return false;
  }
}, false);
```

jQuery has a great way of doing this; simply pass the `delegate()` function a child selector, event type, and handler. The alternative to this approach would be to add a *click* event to every `li` element. However, by using `delegate()`, you're reducing the number of event listeners, improving performance:

```
// Don't do this! It adds a listener to every 'li' element (expensive)
$("ul li").click(function(){ /* ... */ });

// This only adds one event listener
$("ul").delegate("li", "click", /* ... */);
```

Another advantage to event delegation is that any children added dynamically to the element would still have the event listener. So, in the above example, any li elements added to the list after the page loaded would still invoke the click handler.

Custom Events

Beyond events that are native to the browser, you can trigger and bind them to your own custom events. Indeed, it's a great way of architecting libraries—a pattern a lot of jQuery plug-ins use. The W3C spec for custom events has been largely ignored by the browser vendors; you'll have to use libraries like jQuery or Prototype for this feature.

jQuery lets you fire custom events using the `trigger()` function. You can namespace event names, but namespaces are separated by full stops and reversed. For example:

```
// Bind custom event
$(".class").bind("refresh.widget", function(){});

// Trigger custom event
$(".class").trigger("refresh.widget");
```

And to pass data to the event handler, just pass it as an extra parameter to `trigger()`. The data will be sent to callbacks as extra arguments:

```
$(".class").bind("frob.widget", function(event, dataNumber){
  console.log(dataNumber);
});

$(".class").trigger("frob.widget", 5);
```

Like native events, custom events will propagate up the DOM tree.

Custom Events and jQuery Plug-Ins

Custom events, often used to great effect in jQuery plug-ins, are a great way to architect any piece of logic that interacts with the DOM. If you're unfamiliar with jQuery plug-ins, skip ahead to Appendix B, which includes a jQuery primer.

If you're adding a piece of functionality to your application, always consider whether it could be abstracted and split out in a plug-in. This will help with decoupling and could leave you with a reusable library.

For example, let's look at a simple jQuery plug-in for tabs. We're going to have a ul list that will respond to click events. When the user clicks on a list item, we'll add an *active* class to it and remove the *active* class from the other list items:

```
<ul id="tabs">
  <li data-tab="users">Users</li>
  <li data-tab="groups">Groups</li>
</ul>

<div id="tabsContent">
```

```
<div data-tab="users"> ... </div>
  <div data-tab="groups"> ... </div>
</div>
```

In addition, we have a `tabsContent` div that contains the actual contents of the tabs. We'll also be adding and removing the *active* class from the div's children, depending on which tab was clicked. The actual displaying and hiding of the tabs will be done by CSS—our plug-in just toggles the *active* class:

```
jQuery.fn.tabs = function(control){
  var element = $(this);
  control = $(control);

  element.find("li").bind("click", function(){
    // Add/remove active class from the list-item
    element.find("li").removeClass("active");
    $(this).addClass("active");

    // Add/remove active class from tabContent
    var tabName = $(this).attr("data-tab");
    control.find(">[data-tab]").removeClass("active");
    control.find(">[data-tab='" + tabName + "']").addClass("active");
  });

  // Activate first tab
  element.find("li:first").addClass("active");

  // Return 'this' to enable chaining
  return this;
};
```

The plug-in is on jQuery's `prototype`, so it can be called on jQuery instances:

```
$("ul#tabs").tabs("#tabContent");
```

What's wrong with the plug-in so far? Well, we're adding a *click* event handler onto all the list items, which is our first mistake. Instead, we should be using the `delegate()` function covered earlier in this chapter. Also, that click handler is massive, so it's difficult to see what's going on. Furthermore, if another developer wanted to extend our plug-in, he'd probably have to rewrite it.

Let's see how we can use custom events to clean up our code. We'll fire a *change.tabs* event when a tab is clicked, and bind several handlers to change the *active* class as appropriate:

```
jQuery.fn.tabs = function(control){
  var element = $(this);
  control = $(control);

  element.delegate("li", "click", function(){
    // Retrieve tab name
    var tabName = $(this).attr("data-tab");

    // Fire custom event on tab click
    element.trigger("change.tabs", tabName);
```

```
  });

  // Bind to custom event
  element.bind("change.tabs", function(e, tabName){
    element.find("li").removeClass("active");
    element.find(">[data-tab='" + tabName + "']").addClass("active");
  });

  element.bind("change.tabs", function(e, tabName){
    control.find(">[data-tab]").removeClass("active");
    control.find(">[data-tab='" + tabName + "']").addClass("active");
  });

  // Activate first tab
  var firstName = element.find("li:first").attr("data-tab");
  element.trigger("change.tabs", firstName);

  return this;
};
```

See how much cleaner the code is with custom event handlers? It means we can split up the tab change handlers, and it has the added advantage of making the plug-in much easier to extend. For example, we can now programmatically change tabs by firing our *change.tabs* event on the observed list:

```
$("#tabs").trigger("change.tabs", "users");
```

We could also tie up the tabs with the window's hash, adding back button support:

```
$("#tabs").bind("change.tabs", function(e, tabName){
  window.location.hash = tabName;
});

$(window).bind("hashchange", function(){
  var tabName = window.location.hash.slice(1);
  $("#tabs").trigger("change.tabs", tabName);
});
```

The fact that we're using custom events gives other developers a lot of scope when extending our work.

Non-DOM Events

Event-based programming is very powerful because it decouples your application's architecture, leading to better self-containment and maintainability. Events aren't restricted to the DOM though, so you can easily write your own event handler library. The pattern is called Publish/Subscribe (*http://en.wikipedia.org/wiki/Publish/sub scribe*), and it's a good one to be familiar with.

Publish/Subscribe, or Pub/Sub, is a messaging pattern with two actors, publishers, and subscribers. Publishers publish messages to a particular channel, and subscribers subscribe to channels, receiving notifications when new messages are published. The key here is that publishers and subscribers are completely decoupled—they have no idea of each other's existence. The only thing the two share is the channel name.

The decoupling of publishers and subscribers allows your application to grow without introducing a lot of interdependency and coupling, improving the ease of maintenance, as well as adding extra features.

So, how do you actually go about using Pub/Sub in an application? All you need to do is record handlers associated with an event name and then have a way of invoking them. Here's an example PubSub object, which we can use for adding and triggering event listeners:

```
var PubSub = {
  subscribe: function(ev, callback) {
    // Create _callbacks object, unless it already exists
    var calls = this._callbacks || (this._callbacks = {});

    // Create an array for the given event key, unless it exists, then
    // append the callback to the array
    (this._callbacks[ev] || (this._callbacks[ev] = [])).push(callback);
    return this;
  },

  publish: function() {
    // Turn arguments object into a real array
    var args = Array.prototype.slice.call(arguments, 0);

    // Extract the first argument, the event name
    var ev   = args.shift();

    // Return if there isn't a _callbacks object, or
    // if it doesn't contain an array for the given event
    var list, calls, i, l;
    if (!(calls = this._callbacks)) return this;
    if (!(list  = this._callbacks[ev])) return this;

    // Invoke the callbacks
    for (i = 0, l = list.length; i < l; i++)
      list[i].apply(this, args);
    return this;
  }
};

// Example usage
PubSub.subscribe("wem", function(){
  alert("Wem!");
});

PubSub.publish("wem");
```

You can namespace events by using a separator, such as a colon (:).

```
PubSub.subscribe("user:create", function(){ /* ... */ });
```

If you're using jQuery, there's an even easier library (*https://gist.github.com/799721/c119783954e1b10551c4afef53b2c04fefcb7465*) by Ben Alman (*http://benalman.com*). It's so simple, in fact, that we can put it inline:

```
/*!
 * jQuery Tiny Pub/Sub - v0.3 - 11/4/2010
 * http://benalman.com/
 *
 * Copyright (c) 2010 "Cowboy" Ben Alman
 * Dual licensed under the MIT and GPL licenses.
 * http://benalman.com/about/license/
 */

(function($){
  var o = $({});

  $.subscribe = function() {
    o.bind.apply( o, arguments );
  };

  $.unsubscribe = function() {
    o.unbind.apply( o, arguments );
  };

  $.publish = function() {
    o.trigger.apply( o, arguments );
  };
})(jQuery);
```

The API takes the same arguments as jQuery's `bind()` and `trigger()` functions. The only difference is that the functions reside directly on the `jQuery` object, and they are called `publish()` and `subscribe()`:

```
$.subscribe( "/some/topic", function( event, a, b, c ) {
  console.log( event.type, a + b + c );
});

$.publish( "/some/topic", "a", "b", "c" );
```

We've been using Pub/Sub for global events, but it's just as easy to scope it. Let's take the `PubSub` object we created previously and scope it to an object:

```
var Asset = {};

// Add PubSub
jQuery.extend(Asset, PubSub);

// We now have publish/subscribe functions
Asset.subscribe("create", function(){
  // ...
});
```

We're using jQuery's extend() to copy PubSub's properties onto our Asset object. Now, all calls to publish() and subscribe() are scoped by Asset. This is useful in lots of scenarios, including events in an object-relational mapping (ORM), changes in a state machine, or callbacks once an Ajax request has finished.

## CHAPTER 3

Models and Data

One of the challenges with moving state to the client side is data management. Traditionally, you could fetch data directly from the database during the page request, interoperating the result directly into the page. However, data management in stateful JavaScript applications is a completely different process. There's no request/response model, and you don't have access to server-side variables. Instead, data is fetched remotely and stored temporarily on the client side.

Although making this transition can be a hassle, there are a few advantages. For example, client-side data access is practically instantaneous, as you're just fetching it from memory. This can make a real difference to your application's interface; any interaction with the application gives immediate feedback, often dramatically improving the user's experience.

How you architect data storage on the client side requires some thought. This is an area riddled with pitfalls and potential traps, often tripping up less-experienced developers—especially as their applications get larger. In this chapter, we'll cover how best to make that transition, and I'll give you some recommended patterns and practices.

MVC and Namespacing

Ensuring that there's a clear separation between your application's views, state, and data is crucial to keeping its architecture uncluttered and sustainable. With the MVC pattern, data management happens in models (the "M" of MVC). Models should be decoupled from views and controllers. Any logic associated with data manipulation and behavior should reside in models and be namespaced properly.

In JavaScript, you can namespace functions and variables by making them properties of an object. For example:

```
var User = {
  records: [ /* ... */ ]
};
```

The array of users is namespaced properly under User.records. Functions associated with users can also be namespaced under the User model. For example, we can have a fetchRemote() function for fetching user data from a server:

```
var User = {
  records: [],
  fetchRemote: function(){ /* ... */ }
};
```

Keeping all of a model's properties under a namespace ensures that you don't get any conflicts and that it's MVC-compliant. It also prevents your code from spiraling down into a tangled mess of functions and callbacks.

You can take namespacing a step further and keep any functions specific to user instances on the actual user objects. Let's say we had a destroy() function for user records; it refers to specific users, so it should be on User instances:

```
var user = new User;
user.destroy()
```

To achieve that, we need to make User a class, rather than a plain object:

```
var User = function(atts){
  this.attributes = atts || {};
};

User.prototype.destroy = function(){
  /* ... */
};
```

Any functions and variables that don't relate to specific users can be properties directly on the User object:

```
User.fetchRemote = function(){
  /* ... */
};
```

For more information about namespacing, visit Peter Michaux's blog, where he's written an excellent article (*http://michaux.ca/articles/javascript-namespacing*) on the subject.

Building an ORM

Object-relational mappers, or ORMs, are typically used in languages other than JavaScript. However, they're a very useful technique for data management as well as a great way of using models in your JavaScript application. With an ORM, for example, you can tie up a model with a remote server—any changes to model instances will send background Ajax requests to the server. Or, you could tie up a model instance with an HTML element—any changes to the instance will be reflected in the view. I'll elaborate on those examples later, but for now, let's look at creating a custom ORM.

Essentially, an ORM is just an object layer wrapping some data. Typically, ORMs are used to abstract SQL databases, but in our case, the ORM will just be abstracting JavaScript data types. The advantage of this extra layer is that we can enhance the basic data with more functionality by adding our own custom functions and properties. This lets us add things like validation, observers, persistence, and server callbacks while still being able to reuse a lot of code.

Prototypal Inheritance

We're going to use `Object.create()` to construct our ORM, which is a little different from the class-based examples we covered in Chapter 1. This will allow us to use prototype-based inheritance, rather than using constructor functions and the `new` keyword.

`Object.create()` takes one argument, a prototype object, and returns a new object with the specified prototype object. In other words, you give it an object, and it returns a new one, inheriting from the one you specified.

`Object.create()` was recently added to ECMAScript, 5th Edition, so it isn't implemented in some browsers, such as IE. However, this doesn't pose a problem since we can easily add support if needed:

```
if (typeof Object.create !== "function")
    Object.create = function(o) {
        function F() {}
        F.prototype = o;
        return new F();
    };
```

The example above was taken from Douglas Crockford's article on Prototypal Inheritance (*http://javascript.crockford.com/prototypal.html*). Check it out if you want a more in-depth explanation behind JavaScript prototypes and inheritance.

We're going to create a `Model` object, which will be in charge of creating new models and instances:

```
var Model = {
  inherited: function(){},
  created: function(){},

  prototype: {
    init: function(){}
  },

  create: function(){
    var object = Object.create(this);
    object.parent = this;
    object.prototype = object.fn = Object.create(this.prototype);

    object.created();
    this.inherited(object);
    return object;
```

```
      },

      init: function(){
        var instance = Object.create(this.prototype);
        instance.parent = this;
        instance.init.apply(instance, arguments);
        return instance;
      }
    };
```

If you're unfamiliar with `Object.create()`, this may look daunting, so let's break it down. The `create()` function returns a new object, inheriting from the `Model` object; we'll use this for creating new models. The `init()` function returns a new object, inheriting from `Model.prototype`—i.e., an instance of the `Model` object:

```
    var Asset = Model.create();
    var User  = Model.create();

    var user = User.init();
```

Adding ORM Properties

Now, if we add properties to `Model`, they'll be available on all inherited models:

```
    // Add object properties
    jQuery.extend(Model, {
      find: function(){}
    });

    // Add instance properties
    jQuery.extend(Model.prototype, {
      init: function(atts) {
        if (atts) this.load(atts);
      },

      load: function(attributes){
        for(var name in attributes)
          this[name] = attributes[name];
      }
    });
```

`jQuery.extend()` is just a shorthand way of using a `for` loop to copy over properties manually, which is similar to what we're doing in the `load()` function. Now, our object and instance properties are propagating down to our individual models:

```
    assertEqual( typeof Asset.find, "function" );
```

In fact, we're going to be adding a lot of properties, so we might as well make `extend()` and `include()` part of the `Model` object:

```
    var Model = {
      /* ... snip ... */

      extend: function(o){
        var extended = o.extended;
```

```
    jQuery.extend(this, o);
    if (extended) extended(this);
  },

  include: function(o){
    var included = o.included;
    jQuery.extend(this.prototype, o);
    if (included) included(this);
  }
};

// Add object properties
Model.extend({
  find: function(){}
});

// Add instance properties
Model.include({
  init: function(atts) { /* ... */ },
  load: function(attributes){ /* ... */ }
});
```

Now, we can create new assets and set some attributes:

```
var asset = Asset.init({name: "foo.png"});
```

Persisting Records

We need a way of persisting records—i.e., of saving a reference to created instances so we can access them later. We'll do that using a records object, set on the Model. When we're saving an instance, we'll add it to that object; when deleting instances, we'll remove them from the object:

```
// An object of saved assets
Model.records = {};

Model.include({
  newRecord: true,

  create: function(){
    this.newRecord = false;
    this.parent.records[this.id] = this;
  },

  destroy: function(){
    delete this.parent.records[this.id];
  }
});
```

What about updating an existing instance? Easy—just update the object reference:

```
Model.include({
  update: function(){
    this.parent.records[this.id] = this;
```

```
    }
});
```

Let's create a convenience function to save an instance, so we don't have to check to see whether the instance was saved previously, or whether it needs to be created:

```
// Save the object to the records hash, keeping a reference to it
Model.include({
  save: function(){
    this.newRecord ? this.create() : this.update();
  }
});
```

And what about implementing that find() function, so we can find assets by their ID?

```
Model.extend({
  // Find by ID, or raise an exception
  find: function(id){
    return this.records[id] || throw("Unknown record");
  }
});
```

Now that we've succeeded in creating a basic ORM, let's try it out:

```
var asset  = Asset.init();
asset.name = "same, same";
asset.id   = 1
asset.save();

var asset2 = Asset.init();
asset2.name = "but different";
asset2.id   = 2;
asset2.save();

assertEqual( Asset.find(1).name, "same, same" );

asset2.destroy();
```

Adding ID Support

At the moment, every time we save a record we have to specify an ID manually. This sucks, but fortunately, it's something we can automate. First, we need a way of generating IDs, which we can do with a Globally Unique Identifier (GUID) generator. Well, technically, JavaScript can't generate official, bona fide 128-bit GUIDs for API reasons—it can only generate pseudorandom numbers. Generating truly random GUIDs is a notoriously difficult problem, and operating systems calculate them using the MAC address, mouse position, and BIOS checksums, or by measuring electrical noise or radioactive decay—and even lava lamps! However, JavaScript's native Math.random(), although pseudorandom, will be enough for our needs.

Robert Kieffer has written an easy and succinct GUID generator that uses Math.ran dom() to generate pseudorandom GUIDs (*http://www.broofa.com/2008/09/javascript -uuid-function/*). It's so simple that we can put it inline:

```
Math.guid = function(){
  return 'xxxxxxxx-xxxx-4xxx-yxxx-xxxxxxxxxxxx'.replace(/[xy]/g, function(c) {
    var r = Math.random()*16|0, v = c == 'x' ? r : (r&0x3|0x8);
    return v.toString(16);
  }).toUpperCase();
};
```

Now that we have a function to generate GUIDs, integrating that into our ORM is simple; all we need to change is the create() function:

```
Model.extend({
  create: function(){
    if ( !this.id ) this.id = Math.guid();
    this.newRecord = false;
    this.parent.records[this.id] = this;
  }
});
```

Now, any newly created records have random GUIDs as their ID:

```
var asset = Asset.init();
asset.save();

asset.id //=> "54E52592-313E-4F8B-869B-58D61F00DC74"
```

Addressing References

If you've been observing closely, you might have spotted a bug relating to the references in our ORM. We're not cloning instances when they're returned by find() or when we're saving them, so if we change any properties, they're changed on the original asset. This is a problem because we only want assets to update when we call the update() function:

```
var asset = new Asset({name: "foo"});
asset.save();

// Assert passes correctly
assertEqual( Asset.find(asset.id).name, "foo" );

// Let's change a property, but not call update()
asset.name = "wem";

// Oh dear! This assert fails, as the asset's name is now "wem"
assertEqual( Asset.find(asset.id).name, "foo" );
```

Let's fix that by creating a new object during the find() operation. We'll also need to duplicate the object whenever we create or update the record:

```
Asset.extend({
  find: function(id){
    var record = this.records[id];
    if ( !record ) throw("Unknown record");
    return record.dup();
  }
```

```
});

Asset.include({
  create: function(){
    this.newRecord = false;
    this.parent.records[this.id] = this.dup();
  },

  update: function(){
    this.parent.records[this.id] = this.dup();
  },

  dup: function(){
    return jQuery.extend(true, {}, this);
  }
});
```

We have another problem—Model.records is an object shared by every model:

```
assertEqual( Asset.records, Person.records );
```

This has the unfortunate side effect of mixing up all the records:

```
var asset = Asset.init();
asset.save();

assert( asset in Person.records );
```

The solution is to set a new records object whenever we create a new model. Model.cre
ated() is the callback for new object creation, so we can set any objects that are specific
to the model in there:

```
Model.extend({
  created: function(){
    this.records = {};
  }
});
```

Loading in Data

Unless your web application is entirely restricted to the browser, you'll need to load in
remote data from a server. Typically, a subset of data is loaded when the application
starts, and more data is loaded after the interaction. Depending on the type of application and the amount of data, you may be able to load everything you need on the
initial page load. This is ideal, so users never have to wait for more data to be loaded.
However, this isn't feasible for a lot of applications because there's too much data to
fit comfortably in a browser's memory.

Preloading data is crucial to making your application feel slick and fast to your users,
keeping any waiting time to a minimum. However, there's a fine line between preloading data that's actually accessed and loading redundant data that's never used. You

need to predict what sort of data your users will want (or use metrics once your application is live).

If you're displaying a paginated list, why not preload the next page so transitions are instant? Or, even better, just display a long list and automatically load and insert data as the list is scrolled (the infinite scroll pattern). The less latency a user feels, the better.

When you do fetch new data, make sure the UI isn't blocked. Display some sort of loading indicator, but make sure the interface is still usable. There should be very few scenarios, if any, that require blocking the UI.

Data can be present inline in the initial page or loaded with separate HTTP requests through Ajax or JSONP. Personally, I would recommend the latter two technologies, as including a lot of data inline increases the page size, whereas parallel requests load faster. AJAX and JSON also let you cache the HTML page, rather than dynamically render it for every request.

Including Data Inline

I don't really advocate this approach for the reasons I outlined in the previous paragraph, but it can be useful in specific situations, especially for loading in a very small amount of data. This technique has the advantage of being really simple to implement.

All you need to do is render a JSON object directly into the page. For example, here's how you'd do it with Ruby on Rails:

```
<script type="text/javascript">
  var User = {};
  User.records = <%= raw @users.to_json %>;
</script>
```

We're using ERB tags to output a JSON interpretation of the user data. The `raw` method is simply to stop the JSON from being escaped. When the page is rendered, the resulting HTML looks like this:

```
<script type="text/javascript">
  var User = {};
  User.records = [{"first_name": "Alex"}];
</script>
```

JavaScript can just evaluate the JSON as-is because it has the same structure as a JavaScript object.

Loading Data with Ajax

This is probably the first method of loading remote data that springs to mind when you hear background requests, and for good reason: it's tried, tested, and supported in all modern browsers. That's not to say that Ajax is without its drawbacks—its unstandardized history has resulted in an inconsistent API and, due to browser security, loading data from different domains is tricky.

If you need a short primer on Ajax and the XMLHttpRequest class, read "Getting Started," a Mozilla Developer article (*https://developer.mozilla.org/en/Ajax/Getting_Started*). In all likelihood, though, you'll end up using a library like jQuery that abstracts Ajax's API, massaging out the differences among browsers. For that reason, we'll cover jQuery's API here, rather than the raw XMLHttpRequest class.

jQuery's Ajax API consists of one low-level function, jQuery.ajax(), and several higher-level abstractions of it, reducing the amount of code you need to write. jQuery .ajax() takes a hash of settings for request parameters, content type, and callbacks, among others. As soon as you call the function, the request is asynchronously sent in the background.

url
> The request url. The default is the current page.

success
> A function to be called if the request succeeds. Any data returned from the server is passed as a parameter.

contentType
> Sets the Content-Type header of the request. If the request contains data, the default is application/x-www-form-urlencoded, which is fine for most use cases.

data
> The data to be sent to the server. If it's not already a string, jQuery will serialize and URL-encode it.

type
> The HTTP method to use: GET, POST, or DELETE. The default is GET.

dataType
> The type of data you're expecting back from the server. jQuery needs to know this so it knows what to do with the result. If you don't specify a dataType, jQuery will do some intelligent guessing based on the MIME type of the response. Supported values are:
>
> text
> > Plain-text response; no processing is needed.
>
> script
> > jQuery evaluates the response as JavaScript.
>
> json
> > jQuery evaluates the response as JSON, using a strict parser.
>
> jsonp
> > For JSONP requests, which we'll cover in detail later.

For example, let's do a simple Ajax request, which alerts whatever data returned by the server:

```
jQuery.ajax({
  url: "/ajax/endpoint",
```

```
    type: "GET",
    success: function(data) {
      alert(data);
    }
  });
```

However, all those options are a bit verbose. Luckily, jQuery has a few shortcuts. `jQuery.get()` takes a URL and optional data and callback:

```
jQuery.get("/ajax/endpoint", function(data){
  $(".ajaxResult").text(data);
});
```

Or, if we want to send a few query parameters with the GET request:

```
jQuery.get("/ajax/endpoint", {foo: "bar"}, function(data){
  /* ... */
});
```

If we're expecting JSON back from the server, we need to call `jQuery.getJSON()` instead, which sets the request's `dataType` option to `"json"`:

```
jQuery.getJSON("/json/endpoint", function(json){
  /* ... */
});
```

Likewise, there's a `jQuery.post()` function, which also takes a URL, data, and callback:

```
jQuery.post("/users", {first_name: "Alex"}, function(result){
  /* Ajax POST was a success */
});
```

If you want to use other HTTP methods—DELETE, HEAD, and OPTIONS—you'll have to use the lower-level `jQuery.ajax()` function.

That was a brief overview of jQuery's Ajax API, but if you need more information, read the full documentation (*http://api.jquery.com/category/ajax*).

A limitation of Ajax is the *same origin policy*, which restricts requests to the same domain, subdomain, and port as the address of the page from which they're made. There's a good reason for this: whenever an Ajax request is sent, all that domain's cookie information is sent along with the request. That means, to the remote server, the request appears to be from a logged-in user. Without the same origin policy, an attacker could potentially fetch all your emails from Gmail, update your Facebook status, or direct message your followers on Twitter—quite a security flaw.

However, while the same origin policy is integral to the security of the Web, it's also somewhat inconvenient for developers trying to access legitimate remote resources. Other technologies like Adobe Flash and Java have implemented workarounds to the problem with cross-domain policy files, and now Ajax is catching up with a standard called *CORS* (*http://www.w3.org/TR/access-control*), or cross-origin resource sharing.

CORS lets you break out of the same origin policy, giving you access to authorized remote servers. The specification is well supported by the major browsers, so unless you're using IE6, you should be fine.

CORS support by browser:

- IE >= 8 (with caveats)
- Firefox >= 3
- Safari: full support
- Chrome: full support
- Opera: no support

Using CORS is trivially easy. If you want to authorize access to your server, just add a few lines to the HTTP header of returned responses:

```
Access-Control-Allow-Origin: example.com
Access-Control-Request-Method: GET,POST
```

The above header will authorize cross-origin GET and POST requests from *example.com*. You should separate multiple values with commas, as with the GET,POST values above. To allow access from additional domains, just list them comma-separated in the Access-Control-Allow-Origin header. Or, to give any domain access, just set the origin header to an asterisk (*).

Some browsers, like Safari, will first make an OPTIONS request to check whether the request is allowed. Firefox, on the other hand, will make the request and just raise a security exception if the CORS headers aren't set. You'll need to take account of this different behavior server side.

You can even authorize custom request headers using the Access-Control-Request-Headers header:

```
Access-Control-Request-Headers: Authorization
```

This means that clients can add custom headers to Ajax requests, such as signing the request with OAuth:

```
var req = new XMLHttpRequest();
req.open("POST", "/endpoint", true);
req.setRequestHeader("Authorization", oauth_signature);
```

Unfortunately, while CORS works with versions of Internet Explorer 8 and higher, Microsoft chose to ignore the spec and the working group (*http://lists.w3.org/Archives/ Public/public-webapps/2008AprJun/0168.html*). Microsoft created its own object, XDo mainRequest (*http://msdn.microsoft.com/en-us/library/cc288060%28VS.85%29.aspx*), which is to be used instead of XMLHttpRequest for cross-domain requests. While its interface is similar to XMLHttpRequest's, it has a number of restrictions and limitations (*http://blogs.msdn.com/b/ieinternals/archive/2010/05/13/xdomainrequest-restric tions-limitations-and-workarounds.aspx*). For example, only GET and POST methods work, no authentication or custom headers are supported, and finally, the kicker—

only the "Content-Type: text/plain" is supported. If you're prepared to work around those restrictions, then—with the correct `Access-Control` headers—you can get CORS working in IE.

JSONP

JSONP (*http://bob.pythonmac.org/archives/2005/12/05/remote-json-jsonp*), or JSON with padding, was created before CORS was standardized, and is another way of fetching data from remote servers. The idea is that you have a script tag that points to a JSON endpoint where returned data is wrapped in a function invocation. Script tags aren't subject to any cross-domain limitations, and this technique is supported in practically every browser.

So, here we have a script tag that points to our remote server:

```
<script src="http://example.com/data.json"> </script>
```

Then the endpoint, *data.json*, returns a JSON object wrapped in a function invocation:

```
jsonCallback({"data": "foo"})
```

We then define a globally accessible function. Once the script has loaded, this function will be called:

```
window.jsonCallback = function(result){
  // Do stuff with the result
}
```

As it is, this is a fairly convoluted process. Luckily, jQuery wraps it in a succinct API:

```
jQuery.getJSON("http://example.com/data.json?callback=?", function(result){
  // Do stuff with the result
});
```

jQuery replaces the last question mark in the above URL with a random name of a temporary function it creates. Your server needs to read the `callback` parameter and use that as the name of the returned wrapping function.

Security with Cross-Domain Requests

If you're opening up your server to cross-origin requests or JSONP from any domain, you've got to really think about security. Usually the cross-origin domain policy stops an attacker from calling, say, Twitter's API, and fetching your personal data. CORS and JSONP change all of that. As with a normal Ajax request, all your session cookies are passed with the request, so you'll be logged into Twitter's API. Any potential attackers have full control over your account; security considerations are therefore paramount.

With this in mind, here are some key points to take into account when using CORS/JSONP if you're not controlling which domains can access your API:

- Don't reveal any sensitive information, such as email addresses.
- Don't allow any actions (like a Twitter "follow").

Or, alternatively, to mitigate those security issues, just have a whitelist of domains that can connect, or you can use OAuth authentication exclusively.

Populating Our ORM

Populating our ORM with data is pretty straightforward. All we need to do is fetch the data from the server and then update our model's records. Let's add a `populate()` function to the `Model` object, which will iterate over any values given, create instances, and update the `records` object:

```
Model.extend({
  populate: function(values){
    // Reset model & records
    this.records = {};

    for (var i=0, il = values.length; i < il; i++) {
      var record = this.init(values[i]);
      record.newRecord = false;
      this.records[record.id] = record;
    }
  }
});
```

Now, we can use the `Model.populate()` function with the result of our request for data:

```
jQuery.getJSON("/assets", function(result){
  Asset.populate(result);
});
```

Any records the server returned will now be available in our ORM.

Storing Data Locally

In the past, local data storage was a pain in the neck. The only options available to use were cookies and plug-ins like Adobe Flash. Cookies had an antiquated API, couldn't store much data, and sent all the data back to the server on every request, adding unnecessary overhead. As for Flash, well, let's try and steer clear of plug-ins if possible.

Fortunately, support for local storage was included in HTML5 and is implemented in the major browsers. Unlike cookies, data is stored exclusively on the client side and is never sent to servers. You can also store a great deal more data—the maximum amount differs per browser (and version number, as listed below), but they all offer at least 5 MB per domain:

- IE >= 8
- Firefox >= 3.5
- Safari >= 4
- Chrome >= 4
- Opera >= 10.6

HTML5 storage comes under the HTML5 Web Storage specification (*http://www.w3 .org/TR/webstorage*), and consists of two types: *local storage* and *session storage*. Local storage persists after the browser is closed; session storage persists only for the lifetime of the window. Any data stored is scoped by domain and is only accessible to scripts from the domain that originally stored the data.

You can access and manipulate local storage and session storage using the local Storage and sessionStorage objects, respectively. The API is very similar to setting properties on a JavaScript object and, apart from the two objects, is identical for both local and session storage:

```
// Setting a value
localStorage["someData"] = "wem";
```

There are a few more features to the WebStorage API:

```
// How many items are stored
var itemsStored = localStorage.length;

// Set an item (aliased to a hash syntax)
localStorage.setItem("someData", "wem");

// Get a stored item, returning null if unknown
localStorage.getItem("someData"); //=> "wem";

// Delete an item, returning null if unknown
localStorage.removeItem("someData");

// Clear all items
localStorage.clear();
```

Data is stored as strings, so if you intend on saving any objects or integers, you'll have to do your own conversion. To do this using JSON, serialize the objects into JSON before you save them, and deserialize the JSON strings when fetching them:

```
var object = {some: "object"};

// Serialize and save an object
localStorage.setItem("seriData", JSON.stringify(object));

// Load and deserialize an object
var result = JSON.parse(localStorage.getItem("seriData"));
```

If you go over your storage quota (usually 5 MB per host), a QUOTA_EXCEEDED_ERR will be raised when saving additional data.

Adding Local Storage to Our ORM

Let's add local storage support to our ORM so that records can be persisted between page refreshes. To use the `localStorage` object, we need to serialize our records into a JSON string. The problem is that, at the moment, serialized objects look like this:

```
var json = JSON.stringify(Asset.init({name: "foo"}));
json //=> "{"parent":{"parent":{"prototype":{}},"records":[]},"name":"foo"}"
```

So, we need to override JSON's serialization of our models. First, we need to determine which properties need to be serialized. Let's add an `attributes` array to the `Model` object, which individual models can use to specify their attributes:

```
Model.extend({
  created: function(){
    this.records = {};
    this.attributes = [];
  }
});

Asset.attributes = ["name", "ext"];
```

Because every model has different attributes—and therefore can't share the same array reference—the `attributes` property isn't set directly on the Model. Instead, we're creating a new array when a model is first created, similar to what we're doing with the `records` object.

Now, let's create an `attributes()` function, which will return an object of attributes to values:

```
Model.include({
  attributes: function(){
    var result = {};
    for(var i in this.parent.attributes) {
      var attr = this.parent.attributes[i];
      result[attr] = this[attr];
    }
    result.id = this.id;
    return result;
  }
});
```

Now, we can set an array of attributes for every model:

```
Asset.attributes = ["name", "ext"];
```

And the `attributes()` function will return an object with the correct properties:

```
var asset = Asset.init({name: "document", ext: ".txt"});
asset.attributes(); //=> {name: "document", ext: ".txt"};
```

As for the overriding of `JSON.stringify()`, all that's needed is a `toJSON()` method on model instances. The JSON library will use that function to find the object to serialize, rather than serializing the `records` object as-is:

```
Model.include({
  toJSON: function(){
    return(this.attributes());
  }
});
```

Let's try serializing the records again. This time, the resultant JSON will contain the correct properties:

```
var json = JSON.stringify(Asset.records);
json //= "{"7B2A9E8D...":"{"name":"document","ext":".txt","id":"7B2A9E8D..."}"}"
```

Now that we've got JSON serializing working smoothly, adding local storage support to our models is trivial. We'll add two functions onto our Model: saveLocal() and loadLocal(). When saving, we'll convert the Model.records object into an array, serialize it, and send it to localStorage:

```
var Model.LocalStorage = {
  saveLocal: function(name){
    // Turn records into an array
    var result = [];
    for (var i in this.records)
      result.push(this.records[i])

    localStorage[name] = JSON.stringify(result);
  },

  loadLocal: function(name){
    var result = JSON.parse(localStorage[name]);
    this.populate(result);
  }
};

Asset.extend(Model.LocalStorage);
```

It's probably a good idea for the records to be read from the local storage when the page loads and to be saved when the page is closed. That, however, will be left as an exercise for the reader.

Submitting New Records to the Server

Earlier, we covered how to use jQuery's post() function to send data to the server. The function takes three arguments: the endpoint URL, request data, and a callback:

```
jQuery.post("/users", {first_name: "Alex"}, function(result){
  /* Ajax POST was a success */
});
```

Now that we have an attributes() function, creating records to the server is simple—just POST the record's attributes:

```
jQuery.post("/assets", asset.attributes(), function(result){
  /* Ajax POST was a success */
});
```

If we're following REST conventions, we'll want to do an HTTP POST when creating a record and a PUT request when updating the record. Let's add two functions to Model instances—createRemote() and updateRemote()—which will send the correct HTTP request type to our server:

```
Model.include({
  createRemote: function(url, callback){
    $.post(url, this.attributes(), callback);
  },

  updateRemote: function(url, callback){
    $.ajax({
      url:     url,
      data:    this.attributes(),
      success: callback,
      type:    "PUT"
    });
  }
});
```

Now if we call createRemote() on an Asset instance, its attributes will be POSTed to the server:

```
// Usage:
Asset.init({name: "jason.txt"}).createRemote("/assets");
```

## CHAPTER 4

Controllers and State

Historically, state was managed server side with session cookies. So, whenever users navigated to a new page, the previous page's state was lost—only the cookies persisted. JavaScript applications, however, are confined to a single page, which means we can now store state on the client's memory.

One of the major advantages to storing state on the client is a really responsive interface. A user gets immediate feedback when interacting with the page, rather than waiting a few seconds for the next page to load. Speed greatly improves the user experience, making many JavaScript applications a real pleasure to use.

However, storing state on the client causes challenges as well. Where exactly should it be stored? In local variables? Perhaps in the DOM? This is where a lot of developers get led astray, which is an unfortunate state of affairs because storing state properly is one of the most critical areas to get right.

First, you should avoid storing data or state in the DOM. That's just a slippery slope leading to an entangled mess and anarchy! In our case—since we're using the tried and tested MVC architecture—state is stored inside our application's controllers.

What exactly is a controller? Well, you can think of it as the glue between the application's views and models. It's the only component aware of the application's views and models, tying them together. When the page loads, your controller attaches event handlers to views and processes callbacks appropriately, interfacing with models as necessary.

You don't need any libraries to create controllers, although they can be useful. The only essential part is that controllers are modular and independent. Ideally, they shouldn't be defining any global variables, instead functioning as fairly decoupled components. An excellent way of ensuring this is with the module pattern.

Module Pattern

The module pattern is a great way to encapsulate logic and prevent global namespace pollution. It's all made possible by anonymous functions, which are arguably the single best feature of JavaScript. We'll just create an anonymous function and execute it immediately. All the code residing within the function runs inside a closure, providing a local and private environment for our application's variables:

```
(function(){
  /* ... */
})();
```

We have to surround the anonymous function with braces () before we can execute it. JavaScript requires this so it can interpret the statement correctly.

Global Import

Variable definitions inside the module are local, so they can't be accessed outside in the global namespace. However, the application's global variables are all still available, and they can be readily accessed and manipulated inside the module. It's often not obvious which global variables are being used by a module, especially when your modules get larger.

In addition, implied globals are slower to resolve because the JavaScript interpreter has to walk up the scope chain to resolve them. Local variable access will always be faster and more efficient.

Luckily, our modules provide an easy way to resolve these problems. By passing globals as parameters to our anonymous function, we can import them into our code, which is both clearer and faster than implied globals:

```
(function($){
  /* ... */
})(jQuery);
```

In the example above, we're importing the global variable jQuery into our module and aliasing it to $. It's obvious which global variables are being accessed inside the module, and their lookup is quicker. In fact, this is the recommended practice (*http://docs.jquery .com/Plugins/Authoring#Getting_Started*) whenever you want to use jQuery's $ shortcut, which ensures that your code won't conflict with any other libraries.

Global Export

We can use a similar technique when it comes to exporting global variables. Ideally, you should be using as few global variables as possible, but there's always the odd occasion when they're needed. We can import the page's window into our module, setting properties on it directly, thereby exposing variables globally:

```
(function($, exports){

  exports.Foo = "wem";

})(jQuery, window);

assertEqual( Foo, "wem" );
```

The fact that we're using a variable called exports to set any global variables means the code is clearer, making it obvious which global variables a module is creating.

Adding a Bit of Context

Using a local context is a useful way of structuring modules, especially when it comes to registering callbacks to events. As it stands, the context inside our module is global—this is equal to window:

```
(function(){
  assertEqual( this, window );
})();
```

If we want to scope the context, we need to start adding functions onto an object. For example:

```
(function(){
  var mod = {};

  mod.contextFunction = function(){
    assertEqual( this, mod );
  };

  mod.contextFunction();
})();
```

The context inside contextFunction() is now local to our mod object. We can start using this without worrying about creating global variables. To give you a better indication of how it would be used in practice, let's further flesh out that example:

```
(function($){

  var mod = {};

  mod.load = function(func){
    $($.proxy(func, this));
  };

  mod.load(function(){
    this.view = $("#view");
  });

  mod.assetsClick = function(e){
    // Process click
  };
```

```
  mod.load(function(){
    this.view.find(".assets").click(
      $.proxy(this.assetsClick, this)
    );
  });

})(jQuery);
```

We're creating a `load()` function that takes a callback, executing it when the page has loaded. Notice that we're using `jQuery.proxy()` to ensure that the callback is invoked in the correct context.

Then, when the page loads, we're adding a click handler onto an element, giving it a local function, `assetsClick()`, as a callback. Creating a controller doesn't need to be any more complicated than that. What's important is that all of the controller's state is kept local and encapsulated cleanly into a module.

Abstracting into a Library

Let's abstract that library out so we can reuse it with other modules and controllers. We'll include the existing `load()` function and add new ones like `proxy()` and `include()`:

```
(function($, exports){
  var mod = function(includes){
    if (includes) this.include(includes);
  };
  mod.fn = mod.prototype;

  mod.fn.proxy = function(func){
    return $.proxy(func, this);
  };

  mod.fn.load = function(func){
    $(this.proxy(func));
  };

  mod.fn.include = function(ob){
    $.extend(this, ob);
  };

  exports.Controller = mod;
})(jQuery, window);
```

`proxy()` ensures that functions are executed in the local context, which is a useful pattern for event callbacks. The `include()` function is just a shortcut for adding properties onto the controller, saving some typing.

We're adding our library to the `exports` object, exposing it as the global `Controller` variable. Inside the module we can instantiate a `Controller` object using its constructor function. Let's go through a simple example that toggles an element's class depending on whether the mouse is over the element:

```
(function($, Controller){

  var mod = new Controller;

  mod.toggleClass = function(e){
    this.view.toggleClass("over", e.data);
  };

  mod.load(function(){
    this.view = $("#view");
    this.view.mouseover(this.proxy(this.toggleClass), true);
    this.view.mouseout(this.proxy(this.toggleClass), false);
  });

})(jQuery, Controller);
```

When the page loads, we're creating a `view` variable and attaching some event listeners. They in turn call `toggleClass()` when the mouse moves over the element, toggling the element's class. You can see the full example in this book's accompanying files, in *assets/ch04/modules.html*.

Granted, using context rather than local variables means there is probably more code to write, what with all the usage of `this`. However, the technique gives us much greater scope for reusing code and including mixins. For example, we could add a function onto every `Controller` instance by setting a property on its `prototype`:

```
Controller.fn.unload = function(func){
  jQuery(window).bind("unload", this.proxy(func));
};
```

Or, we could extend an individual controller by using the `include()` function we defined earlier, passing it an object:

```
var mod = new Controller;
mod.include(StateMachine);
```

The `StateMachine` object, in this example, could be reused over and over again with our other modules, preventing us from duplicating code and keeping things DRY (don't repeat yourself).

Loading Controllers After the Document

As it stands, some parts of our controllers are being loaded before the DOM, and other parts are in callbacks to be invoked after the page's document has loaded. This can be confusing because the controller's logic is being executed under different states, resulting in a lot of document load callbacks.

We can solve this in one fell swoop by loading controllers *after* the DOM. I personally advocate this approach because it ensures that you don't need to think constantly about what state the page's DOM is in when accessing elements.

Let's first take advantage and clear up our library, making our controllers a bit cleaner. The Controller class doesn't need to be a constructor function because the context switch needed when generating subcontrollers is unnecessary here:

```
// Use global context, rather than the window
// object, to create global variables
var exports = this;

(function($){
  var mod = {};

  mod.create = function(includes){
    var result = function(){
      this.init.apply(this, arguments);
    };

    result.fn = result.prototype;
    result.fn.init = function(){};

    result.proxy    = function(func){ return $.proxy(func, this); };
    result.fn.proxy = result.proxy;

    result.include = function(ob){ $.extend(this.fn, ob); };
    result.extend  = function(ob){ $.extend(this, ob); };
    if (includes) result.include(includes)

    return result;
  };

  exports.Controller = mod;
})(jQuery);
```

Now we can use our new Controller.create() function to create controllers, passing in an object literal of instance properties. Notice that the entire controller is wrapped in jQuery(function(){ /* ... */ }). This is an alias for jQuery.ready(), and it ensures that the controller is loaded only after the page's DOM has fully initialized:

```
jQuery(function($){
  var ToggleView = Controller.create({
    init: function(view){
      this.view = $(view);
      this.view.mouseover(this.proxy(this.toggleClass), true);
      this.view.mouseout(this.proxy(this.toggleClass), false);
    },

    this.toggleClass: function(e){
      this.view.toggleClass("over", e.data);
    }
  });

  // Instantiate controller, calling init()
  new ToggleView("#view");
});
```

The other significant change we've made is passing in the view element to the controller upon instantiation, rather than hardcoding it inside. This is an important refinement because it means we can start reusing controllers with different elements, keeping code repetition to a minimum.

Accessing Views

A common pattern is to have one controller per view. That view has an ID, so it can be passed to controllers easily. Elements inside the view then use classes, rather than IDs, so they don't conflict with elements in other views. This pattern provides a good structure for a general practice, but it should not be conformed to rigidly.

So far in this chapter we've been accessing views by using the jQuery() selector, storing a local reference to the view inside the controller. Subsequent searches for elements inside the view are then scoped by that view reference, speeding up their lookup:

```
// ...
init: function(view){
  this.view = $(view);
  this.form = this.view.find("form");
}
```

However, it does mean that controllers fill up with a lot of selectors, requiring us to query the DOM constantly. We can clean this up somewhat by having one place in the controller where selectors are mapped to variables names, like so:

```
elements: {
  "form.searchForm": "searchForm",
  "form input[type=text]": "searchInput"
}
```

This ensures that the variables this.searchForm and this.searchInput will be created on the controller when it's instantiated, set to their respective elements. These are normal jQuery objects, so we can manipulate them as usual, setting event handlers and fetching attributes.

Let's implement support for that elements mapping inside our controllers, iterating over all the selectors and setting local variables. We'll do this inside our init() function, which is called when our controller is instantiated:

```
var exports = this;

jQuery(function($){
  exports.SearchView = Controller.create({
    // Map of selectors to local variable names
    elements: {
      "input[type=search]": "searchInput",
      "form": "searchForm"
    },

    // Called upon instantiation
    init: function(element){
```

```
          this.el = $(element);
          this.refreshElements();
          this.searchForm.submit(this.proxy(this.search));
        },

        search: function(){
          console.log("Searching:", this.searchInput.val());
        },

        // Private

        $: function(selector){
          // An `el` property is required, and scopes the query
          return $(selector, this.el);
        },

        // Set up the local variables
        refreshElements: function(){
          for (var key in this.elements) {
            this[this.elements[key]] = this.$(key);
          }
        }
      });

      new SearchView("#users");
    });
```

refreshElements() expects every controller to have a current element property, el, which will scope any selectors. Once refreshElements() is called, the this.search Form and this.searchInput properties will be set on the controller and are subsequently available for event binding and DOM manipulation.

You can see a full example of this in this book's accompanying files, in *assets/ch04/ views.html*.

Delegating Events

We can also take a stab at cleaning up all that event binding and proxying by having an events object that maps event types and selectors to callbacks. This is going to be very similar to the elements object, but instead will take the following form:

```
events: {
  "submit form": "submit"
}
```

Let's go ahead and add that to our SearchView controller. Like refreshElements(), we'll have a delegateEvents() function that will be called when the controller is instantiated. This will parse the controller's events object, attaching event callbacks. In our Search View example, we want the search() function to be invoked whenever the view's <form /> is submitted:

```
var exports = this;
```

```
jQuery(function($){
  exports.SearchView = Controller.create({
    // Map all the event names,
    // selectors, and callbacks
    events: {
      "submit form": "search"
    },

    init: function(){
      // ...
      this.delegateEvents();
    },

    search: function(e){ /* ... */ },

    // Private

    // Split on the first space
    eventSplitter: /^(\w+)\s*(.*)$/,

    delegateEvents: function(){
      for (var key in this.events) {
        var methodName = this.events[key];
        var method     = this.proxy(this[methodName]);

        var match      = key.match(this.eventSplitter);
        var eventName  = match[1], selector = match[2];

        if (selector === '') {
          this.el.bind(eventName, method);
        } else {
          this.el.delegate(selector, eventName, method);
        }
      }
    }
  });
});
```

Notice we're using the delegate() function inside delegateEvents(), as well as the bind() function. If the event selector isn't provided, the event will be placed straight on el. Otherwise, the event will be delegated (*http://api.jquery.com/delegate*), and it will be triggered if the event type is fired on a child matching the selector. The advantage of delegation is that it often reduces the amount of event listeners required—i.e., listeners don't have to be placed on every element selected because events are caught dynamically when they bubble up.

We can push all those controller enhancements upstream to our Controller library so they can be reused in every controller. Here's the finished example; you can find the full controller library in *assets/ch04/finished_controller.html*:

```
var exports = this;

jQuery(function($){
  exports.SearchView = Controller.create({
    elements: {
```

```
      "input[type=search]": "searchInput",
      "form": "searchForm"
    },

    events: {
      "submit form": "search"
    },

    init: function(){ /* ... */ },

    search: function(){
      alert("Searching: " + this.searchInput.val());
      return false;
    },
  });

  new SearchView({el: "#users"});
});
```

State Machines

State machines—or to use their proper term, *Finite State Machines* (FSMs)—are a great way to program UIs. Using state machines, you can easily manage multiple controllers, showing and hiding views as necessary. So, what exactly is a state machine? At its core, a state machine consists of two things: states and transitions. It has only one active state, but it has a multitude of passive states. When the active state switches, transitions between the states are called.

How does this work in practice? Well, consider having a few application views that need to be displayed independently—say, a view for showing contacts and a view for editing contacts. These two views need to be displayed exclusively—when one is shown, the other view needs to be hidden. This is a perfect scenario to introduce a state machine because it will ensure that only one view is active at any given time. Indeed, if we want to add additional views, such as a settings view, using a state machine makes this trivial.

Let's flesh out a practical example that will give you a good idea of how state machines can be implemented. The example is simple and doesn't cater to different transition types, but it is sufficient for our needs. First, we're going to create an Events object that will use jQuery's event API (as discussed in Chapter 2) to add the ability to bind and trigger events on our state machine:

```
var Events = {
  bind: function(){
    if ( !this.o ) this.o = $({});
    this.o.bind.apply(this.o, arguments);
  },

  trigger: function(){
    if ( !this.o ) this.o = $({});
    this.o.trigger.apply(this.o, arguments);
```

```
    }
};
```

The Events object is essentially extending jQuery's existing event support outside the DOM so that we can use it in our own library. Now let's set about creating the State Machine class, which will have one main function, add():

```
var StateMachine = function(){};
StateMachine.fn  = StateMachine.prototype;

// Add event binding/triggering
$.extend(StateMachine.fn, Events);

StateMachine.fn.add = function(controller){
  this.bind("change", function(e, current){
    if (controller == current)
      controller.activate();
    else
      controller.deactivate();
  });

  controller.active = $.proxy(function(){
    this.trigger("change", controller);
  }, this);
};
```

The state machine's add() function adds the passed controller to the list of states and creates an active() function. When active() is called, the active state will transition to the controller. The state machine will call activate() on the active controller and deactivate() on all the other controllers. We can see how this works by creating two example controllers, adding them to the state machine, and then activating one of them:

```
var con1 = {
  activate:   function(){ /* ... */ },
  deactivate: function(){ /* ... */ }
};

var con2 = {
  activate:   function(){ /* ... */ },
  deactivate: function(){ /* ... */ }
};

// Create a new StateMachine and add states
var sm = new StateMachine;
sm.add(con1);
sm.add(con2);

// Activate first state
con1.active();
```

The state machine's add() function works by creating a callback for the *change* event, calling the activate() or deactivate() function, depending on which is appropriate. Although the state machine gives us an active() function, we can also change the state by manually triggering the *change* event:

```
sm.trigger("change", con2);
```

Inside our controller's `activate()` function, we can set up and display its view, adding and showing elements. Likewise, inside the `deactivate()` function, we can tear down anything that is hiding the view. CSS classes offer a good way of hiding and showing views. Simply add a class—say, `.active`—when the view is active, and remove it upon deactivation:

```
var con1 = {
  activate: function(){
    $("#con1").addClass("active");
  },
  deactivate: function(){
    $("#con1").removeClass("active");
  }
};

var con2 = {
  activate: function(){
    $("#con2").addClass("active");
  },
  deactivate: function(){
    $("#con2").removeClass("active");
  }
};
```

Then, in your stylesheets, make sure that the views have a `.active` class; otherwise, they're hidden:

```
#con1, #con2 { display: none; }
#con1.active, #con2.active { display: block; }
```

You can see the full examples in *assets/ch04/state_machine.html*.

Routing

Our application is now running from a single page, which means its URL won't change. This is a problem for our users because they're accustomed to having a unique URL for a resource on the Web. Additionally, people are used to navigating the Web with the browser's back and forward buttons.

To resolve this, we want to tie the application's state to the URL. When the application's state changes, so will the URL. The reverse is true, too—when the URL changes, so will the application's state. During the initial page load, we'll check the URL and set up the application's initial state.

Using the URL's Hash

However, the page's base URL can't be changed without triggering a page refresh, which is something we're trying to avoid. Luckily, there are a few solutions. The traditional way to manipulate the URL was to change its hash. The hash is never sent to the server, so it can be changed without triggering a page request. For example, here's the URL for my Twitter page, the hash being #!/maccman:

```
http://twitter.com/#!/maccman
```

You can retrieve and alter the page's hash using the location object:

```
// Set the hash
window.location.hash = "foo";
assertEqual( window.location.hash , "#foo" );

// Strip "#"
var hashValue = window.location.hash.slice(1);
assertEqual( hashValue, "foo" );
```

If the URL doesn't have a hash, location.hash is an empty string. Otherwise, loca tion.hash equals the URL's hash fragment, prefixed with the # character.

Setting the hash too often can really hurt performance, especially on mobile browsers. So, if you're setting it frequently—say, as a user scrolls through a list—you may want to consider throttling.

Detecting Hash Changes

Historically, changes to the hash were detected rather crudely with a polling timer. Things are improving, though, and modern browsers support the *hashchange* event. This is fired on the window, and you can listen for it in order to catch changes to the hash:

```
window.addEventListener("hashchange", function(){ /* ... */ }, false);
```

Or with jQuery:

```
$(window).bind("hashchange", function(event){
  // hash changed, change state
});
```

When the hashchange event fires, we can make sure the application is in the appropriate state. The event has good cross-browser support, with implementations in all the latest versions of the major browsers:

- IE >= 8
- Firefox >= 3.6
- Chrome
- Safari >= 5
- Opera >= 10.6

The event isn't fired on older browsers; however, there's a useful jQuery plug-in (*http: //benalman.com/projects/jquery-hashchange-plugin/*) that adds the *hashchange* event to legacy browsers.

It's worth noting that this event isn't fired when the page initially loads, only when the hash changes. If you're using hash routing in your application, you may want to fire the event manually on page load:

```
jQuery(function(){
  var hashValue = location.hash.slice(1);
  if (hashValue)
    $(window).trigger("hashchange");
});
```

Ajax Crawling

Because they don't execute JavaScript, search engine crawlers can't see any content that's created dynamically. Additionally, none of our hash routes will be indexed; as in the eyes of the crawlers, they're all the same URL—the hash fragment is never sent to the server.

This is obviously a problem if we want our pure JavaScript applications to be indexable and available on search engines like Google. As a workaround, developers would create a "parallel universe" of content. Crawlers would be sent to special static HTML snapshots of the content, while normal browsers would continue to use the dynamic JavaScript version of the application. This resulted in a lot more work for developers and entailed practices like browser sniffing, something best avoided. Luckily, Google has provided an alternative: the Ajax Crawling specification (*http://code.google.com/web/ajaxcrawling/index.html*).

Let's take a look at my Twitter profile address again (notice the exclamation mark after the hash):

```
http://twitter.com/#!/maccman
```

The exclamation mark signifies to Google's crawlers that our site conforms to the Ajax Crawling spec. Rather than request the URL as-is—excluding the hash, of course—the crawler translates the URL into this:

```
http://twitter.com/?_escaped_fragment_=/maccman
```

The hash has been replaced with the _escaped_fragment_ URL parameter. In the specification, this is called an *ugly* URL, and it's something users will never see. The crawler then goes ahead and fetches that ugly URL. Since the hash fragment is now a URL parameter, your server knows the specific resource the crawler is requesting—in this case, my Twitter page.

The server can then map that ugly URL to whatever resource it represented and respond with a pure HTML or text fragment, which is then indexed. Since Twitter still has a static version of their site, they just redirect the crawler to that.

```
curl -v http://twitter.com/?_escaped_fragment_=/maccman
  302 redirected to http://twitter.com/maccman
```

Because Twitter is using a temporary redirect (302) rather than a permanent one (301), the URL shown in the search results will typically be the hash address—i.e., the dynamic JavaScript version of the site (`http://twitter.com/#!/maccman`). If you don't have a static version of your site, just serve up a static HTML or text fragment when URLs are requested with the `_escaped_fragment_` parameter.

Once you've added support for the Ajax Crawling spec to your site, you can check whether it's working using the Fetch as Googlebot tool (*http://www.google.com/support/webmasters/bin/answer.py?hl=en&answer=158587*). If you choose not to implement the scheme on your site, pages will remain indexed as-is, with a good likelihood of not being properly represented in search results. In the long term, however, it's likely that search engines like Google will add JavaScript support to their crawlers, making schemes like this one unnecessary.

Using the HTML5 History API

The History API is part of the HTML5 spec and essentially allows you to replace the current location with an arbitrary URL. You can also choose whether to add the new URL to the browser's history, giving your application "back button" support. Like setting the location's hash, the key is that the page won't reload—its state will be preserved.

Supported browsers are:

- Firefox >= 4.0
- Safari >= 5.0
- Chrome >= 7.0
- IE: no support
- Opera >= 11.5

The API is fairly straightforward, revolving mostly around the `history.pushState()` function. This takes three arguments: a data object, a title, and the new URL:

```
// The data object is arbitrary and is passed with the popstate event
var dataObject = {
    createdAt: '2011-10-10',
    author:    'donnamoss'
};

var url = '/posts/new-url';
history.pushState(dataObject, document.title, url);
```

The three arguments are all optional, but they control what's pushed onto the browser's history stack:

The data *object*
This is completely arbitrary—you specify any custom object you want. It'll be passed along with a *popstate* event (which we'll cover in depth later).

The `title` *argument*

> This is currently ignored by a lot of browsers, but according to the spec will change the new page's title and appear in the browser's history.

The `url` *argument*

> This is a string specifying the URL to replace the browser's current location. If it's relative, the new URL is calculated relative to the current one, with the same domain, port, and protocol. Alternatively, you can specify an absolute URL, but for security reasons, it's restricted to the same domain as the current location.

The issue with using the new History API in JavaScript applications is that every URL needs a real HTML representation. Although the browser won't request the new URL when you call `history.pushState()`, it will be requested if the page is reloaded. In other words, every URL you pass to the API needs to exist—you can't just make up fragments like you can with hashes.

This isn't a problem if you already have a static HTML representation of your site, but it is if your application is pure JavaScript. One solution is to always serve up the JavaScript application regardless of the URL called. Unfortunately, this will break 404 (page not found) support, so every URL will return a successful response. The alternative is to actually do some server-side checking to make sure the URL and requested resource is valid before serving up the application.

The History API contains a few more features. `history.replaceState()` acts exactly the same as `history.pushState()`, but it doesn't add an entry to the history stack. You can navigate through the browser's history using the `history.back()` and `history.for ward()` functions.

The *popstate* event mentioned earlier is triggered when the page is loaded or when `history.pushState()` is called. In the case of the latter, the `event` object will contain a `state` property that holds the data object given to `history.pushState()`:

```
window.addEventListener("popstate", function(event){
  if (event.state) {
    // history.pushState() was called
  }
});
```

You can listen to the event and ensure that your application's state stays consistent with the URL. If you're using jQuery, you need to bear in mind that the event is normalized. So, to access the state object, you'll need to access the original event:

```
$(window).bind("popstate", function(event){
  event = event.originalEvent;
  if (event.state) {
    // history.pushState() was called
  }
});
```

## CHAPTER 5

Views and Templating

Views are the interface to your application; they're what the end user actually interacts with and sees. In our case, views are logicless HTML fragments managed by the application's controllers, which deal with event handlers and interpolating data. This is where it can be quite tempting to break the MVC abstraction by including logic directly into your views. Don't succumb to that temptation! You'll end up with senseless spaghetti code.

One of the biggest architectural changes you'll have to make when moving server-side applications to the client side is with views. Traditionally, you could just interpolate server-side data with HTML fragments, creating new pages. However, views in JavaScript applications are somewhat different.

First, you have to transfer any data needed for the view to the client because you don't have access to server-side variables. This is generally done with an Ajax call, returning a JSON object, which is then loaded by your application's models. You shouldn't be prerendering any HTML on the server side, but rather delegating all of that to the client. This will ensure that your client-side application isn't reliant on the server for rendering views, keeping its interface snappy.

You then load that data into your views, either by creating the DOM elements dynamically with JavaScript or by using templates. I'll elaborate on those two options below.

Dynamically Rendering Views

One way to create views is pragmatically via JavaScript. You can create DOM elements using `document.createElement()`, setting their contents and appending them to the page. When it's time to redraw the view, just empty the view and repeat the process:

```
var views = document.getElementById("views");
views.innerHTML = ""; // Empty the element

var container = document.createElement("div");
container.id = "user";
```

```
var name = document.createElement("span");
name.innerHTML = data.name;

container.appendChild(name);
views.appendChild(container);
```

Or, for a more succinct API with jQuery:

```
$("#views").empty();

var container = $("<div />").attr({id: "user"});
var name     = $("<span />").text(data.name);

$("#views").append(container.append(name));
```

I'd only advocate this if the view you need to render is very small, perhaps just a couple of elements. Placing view elements in your controllers or states compromises the application's MVC architecture.

Instead of creating the elements from scratch, I advise including the static HTML in the page—hiding and showing it when necessary. This will keep any view-specific code in your controllers to an absolute minimum, and you can just update the element's contents when necessary.

For example, let's create an HTML fragment that will serve as our view:

```
<div id="views">
  <div class="groups"> ... </div>
  <div class="user">
    <span></span>
  </div>
</div>
```

Now, we can use jQuery selectors to update the view and to toggle the display of the various elements:

```
$("#views div").hide();

var container = $("#views .user");
container.find("span").text(data.name);
container.show();
```

This method is preferable to generating the elements because it keeps the view and controller as separate as possible.

Templates

If you're used to interpolating server variables in HTML, templating will be familiar. There are a variety of templating libraries out there—your choice will probably depend on which DOM library you're using. However, most of them share a similar syntax, which I'll describe below.

The gist of JavaScript templates is that you can take an HTML fragment interpolated with template variables and combine it with a JavaScript object, replacing those template variables with values from the object. Overall, JavaScript templating works in much the same way as templating libraries in other languages, such as PHP's Smarty, Ruby's ERB, and Python's string formatting.

We're going to use the jQuery.tmpl (*http://api.jquery.com/category/plugins/templates/*) library as the basis for the templating examples. If you aren't using jQuery, or if you want to use a different templating library, the examples should still be useful; the templating syntax for most libraries is very similar, if not identical. If you want a good alternative, check out Mustache (*http://mustache.github.com*), which has implementations in a lot of languages, including JavaScript.

Created by Microsoft, jQuery.tmpl is a templating plug-in based on John Resig's original work (*http://ejohn.org/blog/javascript-micro-templating/*). It's a well-maintained library and is fully documented on the jQuery site (*http://api.jquery.com/jquery.tmpl*). The library has one main function, jQuery.tmpl(), to which you can pass a template and some data. It renders a template element that you can append to the document. If the data is an array, the template is rendered once for every data item in the array; otherwise, a single template is rendered:

```
var object = {
  url: "http://example.com",
  getName: function(){ return "Trevor"; }
};

var template = '<li><a href="${url}">${getName()}</a></li>';

var element = jQuery.tmpl(template, object);
// Produces: <li><a href="http://example.com">Trevor</a></li>

$("body").append(element);
```

So, you can see we're interpolating variables using the ${} syntax. Whatever is inside the brackets is evaluated in the context of the object passed to jQuery.tmpl(), regardless of whether it is a property or a function.

However, templates are much more powerful than mere interpolation. Most templating libraries have advanced features like conditional flow and iteration. You can control flow by using if and else statements, the same as with pure JavaScript. The difference here is that we need to wrap the keyword with double brackets so that the templating engine can pick them up:

```
{{if url}}
  ${url}
{{/if}}
```

The if block will be executed if the specified attribute value doesn't evaluate to false, 0, null, "", Nan, or undefined. As you can see, the block is closed with a {{/if}}, so don't forget to include that! A common pattern is to display a message when an array—say, of chat messages—is empty:

```
{{if messages.length}}
  <!-- Display messages... -->
{{else}}
  <p>Sorry, there are no messages</p>
{{/if}}
```

No templating library can afford to be without iteration. With JS templating libraries, you can iterate over any JavaScript type—Object or Array—using the {{each}} keyword. If you pass an Object to {{each}}, it will iterate a block over the object's properties. Likewise, passing an array results in the block iterating over every index in the array.

When inside the block, you can access the value currently being iterated over using the $value variable. Displaying the value is the same as the interpolation example above, which uses ${$value}. Consider this object:

```
var object = {
  foo: "bar",
  messages: ["Hi there", "Foo bar"]
};
```

Then, use the following template to iterate through the messages array, displaying each message. Additionally, the current iteration's index is also exposed using the $index variable.

```
<ul>
  {{each messages}}
    <li>${$index + 1}: <em>${$value}</em></li>
  {{/each}}
</ul>
```

As you can see, the jQuery.tmpl templating API is very straightforward. As I mentioned earlier, most of the alternative templating libraries have a similar API, although many offer more advanced features, such as lambdas, partials, and comments.

Template Helpers

Sometimes it's useful to use generic helper functions inside the view, perhaps to format a date or a number. However, it's important to keep your MVC architecture in mind, rather than arbitrarily inserting functions directly into the view. For example, let's replace links in some plain text with <a></a> tags. This would certainly be the wrong way to go about doing it:

```
<div>
  ${ this.data.replace(
/((http|https|ftp):\/\/[\w?=&.\/-;#~%-]+(?![\w\s?&.\/;#~%"=-]*>)))/g,
  '<a target="_blank" href="$1">$1</a> ') }
</div>
```

Rather than injecting the function straight into the view, we should abstract and namespace it, keeping logic separate from views. In this case, we're going to create a separate *helpers.js* file, containing all our application's helpers, such as the `autoLink()` function. Then, we can tidy up the view with our helper:

```
// helper.js
var helper = {};
helper.autoLink = function(data){
  var re = /((http|https|ftp):\/\/[\w?=&.\/-;#~%-]+(?![\w\s?&.\/;#~%"=-]*>))/g;
  return(data.replace(re, '<a target="_blank" href="$1">$1</a> ') );
};

// template.html
<div>
  ${ helper.autoLink(this.data) }
</div>
```

There's an added advantage: the `autoLink()` function is now generic and can be reused elsewhere inside the application.

Template Storage

When it comes to storing view templates, there are a few options:

- Inline in the JavaScript
- Inline in a custom script tag
- Loaded remotely
- Inline in the HTML

Some of these, however, are better at respecting the MVC architecture. I personally advocate storing templates inline in custom script tags for the reasons outlined below.

You can store templates inside your JavaScript files. This isn't really recommended, though, because it entails putting view code inside the controller, violating the MVC architecture.

By sending an Ajax call, you can dynamically load in templates when they're needed. The advantage of this is that the initial page load is smaller; the disadvantage is that you could slow the UI down while templates are loading. One of the main reasons to build JavaScript apps is for their enhanced speed, so you should be careful about squandering this advantage when loading in remote resources.

You can store templates inline, inside the page's HTML. The advantage to this approach is that it doesn't have the slow loading problem that fetching remote templates has. The source code is much more obvious—templates are inline where they're being displayed and used. The obvious disadvantage is that it results in a large page size. To be honest, though, this speed difference should be negligible—especially if you're using page compression and caching.

I recommend using custom script tags and referencing them by ID from JavaScript. This is a convenient way of storing templates, especially if you want to use them in multiple places. Custom script tags also have the advantage of not being rendered by the browser, which just interprets their contents as text.

If the template is defined inline in the page, you can use `jQuery.fn.tmpl(data)`—i.e., call `tmpl()` on a jQuery element:

```
<script type="text/x-jquery-tmpl" id="someTemplate">
  <span>${getName()}</span>
</script>

<script>
  var data = {
    getName: function(){ return "Bob" }
  };
  var element = $("#someTemplate").tmpl(data);
  element.appendTo($("body"));
</script>
```

Behind the scenes, jQuery.tmpl makes sure that the compiled template, once generated, is cached. This speeds things up because the template doesn't have to be recompiled when you next use it. Notice we're generating the element before appending it to the page; this method performs better than manipulating elements already attached to the page, making it a recommended practice.

Even if you're rendering all the templates inline into the page, it doesn't mean your server side should be structured like that. Try to keep each template in a separate file (or partial), and then concatenate them into the one document when the page is requested. Some of the dependency-management tools covered in Chapter 6, like RequireJS, will do this for you.

Binding

Binding is where you start to see the real benefits of view rendering on the client side. Essentially, binding hooks together a view element and a JavaScript object (usually a model). When the JavaScript object changes, the view automatically updates to reflect the newly modified object. In other words, once you've got your views and models bound together, the views will rerender automatically when the application's models are updated.

Binding is a really big deal. It means your controllers don't have to deal with updating views when changing records, because it all happens automatically in the background. Structuring your application using binders also paves the way for real-time applications, which we'll cover in depth in Chapter 8.

So, in order to bind JavaScript objects and views, we need to get a callback that instructs the view to update when an object's property changes. The trouble is that JavaScript doesn't provide a native method for doing that. The language doesn't have any method_missing functionality like in Ruby or Python, and it isn't yet possible to emulate the behavior using JavaScript getters and setters (*http://ejohn.org/blog/javascript-getters -and-setters*). However, because JavaScript is a very dynamic language, we can roll our own change callback:

```
var addChange = function(ob){
  ob.change = function(callback){
    if (callback) {
      if ( !this._change ) this._change = [];
      this._change.push(callback);
    } else {
      if ( !this._change ) return;
      for (var i=0; i < this._change.length; i++)
        this._change[i].apply(this);
    }
  };
};
```

The addChange() function adds a change() function onto any object it's passed. The change() function works exactly the same as the *change* event in jQuery. You can add callbacks by invoking change() with a function, or trigger the event by calling change() without any arguments. Let's see it in practice:

```
var object = {};
object.name = "Foo";

addChange(object);

object.change(function(){
  console.log("Changed!", this);
  // Potentially update view
});

object.change();

object.name = "Bar";
object.change();
```

So, you see we've added a change() callback to the object, allowing us to bind and trigger *change* events.

Binding Up Models

Now let's take that binding example a step further and apply it to models. Whenever a model record is created, updated, or destroyed, we'll trigger a *change* event, rerendering the view. In the example below, we're creating a basic User class, setting up event binding and triggering, and finally listening to the *change* event, rerendering the view whenever it's triggered:

```
<script>
  var User = function(name){
    this.name = name;
  };
```

```
User.records = []

User.bind = function(ev, callback) {
  var calls = this._callbacks || (this._callbacks = {});
  (this._callbacks[ev] || (this._callbacks[ev] = [])).push(callback);
};

User.trigger = function(ev) {
  var list, calls, i, l;
  if (!(calls = this._callbacks)) return this;
  if (!(list  = this._callbacks[ev])) return this;
  jQuery.each(list, function(){ this() })
};

User.create = function(name){
  this.records.push(new this(name));
  this.trigger("change")
};

jQuery(function($){
  User.bind("change", function(){
    var template = $("#userTmpl").tmpl(User.records);

    $("#users").empty();
    $("#users").append(template);
  });
});
</script>

<script id="userTmpl" type="text/x-jquery-tmpl">
  <li>${name}</li>
</script>

<ul id="users">
</ul>
```

Now, whenever we alter User's records, the User model's *change* event will be triggered, invoking our templating callback and redrawing the list of users. This is pretty useful, as we can go about creating and updating users without having to worry about updating the view, which will happen automatically. For example, let's create a new User:

```
User.create("Sam Seaborn");
```

The User's *change* event will be invoked and our template will rerender, automatically updating the view and showing our new user. You can see the full model-binding example in *assets/ch05/model.html*.

## CHAPTER 6

Dependency Management

One of the things that's held JavaScript back as a language has been the lack of dependency management and a module system. Unlike other languages, namespacing and modules aren't something traditionally emphasized when people are learning JavaScript. Indeed, popular libraries like jQuery don't enforce any application structure; there's definitely an onus on the developer to resolve this himself. Too often, I see spaghetti-styled JavaScript, with a crazy amount of indentation and anonymous functions. Does this look familiar?

```
function() {
  function() {
    function() {
      function() {

      }
    }
  }
}
```

The usage of modules and namespacing is one thing, but the lack of native dependency systems is becoming an increasing concern when building larger applications. For a long time, a `script` tag was deemed sufficient, as the amount of JavaScript present on the page didn't justify anything further. However, when you start writing complex JavaScript applications, a dependency system is absolutely critical. It's completely impractical to keep track of dependencies yourself by adding script tags to the page manually. You'll often end up with a mess like this:

```
<script src="jquery.js" type="text/javascript" charset="utf-8"></script>
<script src="jquery.ui.js" type="text/javascript" charset="utf-8"></script>
<script src="application.utils.js" type="text/javascript" charset="utf-8"></script>
<script src="application.js" type="text/javascript" charset="utf-8"></script>
<script src="models/asset.js" type="text/javascript" charset="utf-8"></script>
<script src="models/activity.js" type="text/javascript" charset="utf-8"></script>
<script src="states/loading.js" type="text/javascript" charset="utf-8"></script>
<script src="states/search.js" type="text/javascript" charset="utf-8"></script>
<!-- ... -->
```

It's not just the practicalities of the situation that warrant a specific dependency management system—there are performance aspects as well. Your browser needs to make an HTTP request for each of these JavaScript files, and—although it can do this asynchronously—there's a huge cost to making so many connections. Each connection has the overhead of HTTP headers, like cookies, and has to initiate another TCP handshake. The situation is exacerbated if your application is served using SSL.

CommonJS

As JavaScript has moved to the server side, several proposals have been put forward for dependency management. SpiderMonkey (*http://www.mozilla.org/js/spidermonkey/*) and Rhino (*http://www.mozilla.org/rhino/*) offer a `load()` function, but they do not have any specific patterns for namespacing. Node.js (*http://nodejs.org/*) has the `require()` function for loading in extra source files, as well as its own module system. The code wasn't interchangeable, though, so what happens when you want to run your Rhino code on Node.js?

It became obvious that a standard was needed to ensure code interoperability, which all JavaScript implementations could abide by, allowing us to use libraries across all the environments. Kevin Dangoor started the CommonJS initiative to do just that. It began with a blog post (*http://www.blueskyonmars.com/2009/01/29/what-server-side -javascript-needs*) in which Kevin advocated a shared standard for JavaScript interpreters and for developers to band together and write some specs:

> JavaScript needs a standard way to include other modules and for those modules to live in discreet namespaces. There are easy ways to do namespaces, but there's no standard programmatic way to load a module (once!).

> [This] is not a technical problem. It's a matter of people getting together and making a decision to step forward and start building up something bigger and cooler together.

A mailing list (*http://groups.google.com/group/commonjs*) was set up, and CommonJS (*http://www.commonjs.org*) was born. It quickly gathered momentum with support from the major players. It is now the de facto module format for JavaScript with a growing set of standards, including IO interfaces, Socket streams, and Unit tests.

Declaring a Module

Declaring a CommonJS module is fairly straightforward. Namespacing is baked directly in; modules are separated into different files, and they expose variables publicly by adding them to an interpreter-defined `exports` object:

```
// maths.js
exports.per = function(value, total) {
  return( (value / total) * 100 );
};

// application.js
```

```
var Maths = require("./maths");
assertEqual( Maths.per(50, 100), 50 );
```

To use any functions defined in a module, simply `require()` the file, saving the result in a local variable. In the example above, any functions exported by *maths.js* are available on the `Maths` variable. The key is that modules are namespaced and will run on all CommonJS-compliant JavaScript interpreters, such as Narwhal (*http://narwhaljs.org*) and Node.js.

Modules and the Browser

So, how does this relate to client-side JS development? Well, lots of developers saw the implications of using modules on the client side—namely, that the standard, as it currently stood, required CommonJS modules to be loaded in synchronously. This is fine for server-side JavaScript, but it can be very problematic in the browser because it locks up the UI and requires eval-based compilation of scripts (always something to be avoided). The CommonJS team developed a specification, the module transport format (*http://wiki.commonjs.org/wiki/Modules/Transport*), to address this issue. This transport format wraps CommonJS modules with a callback to allow for asynchronous loading on clients.

Let's take our module example above. We can wrap it in the transport format to allow asynchronous loading, making it palatable for the browser:

```
// maths.js
require.define("maths", function(require, exports){

  exports.per = function(value, total) {
    return( (value / total) * 100 );
  };

});

// application.js
require.define("application", function(require, exports){

  var per = require("./maths").per;
  assertEqual( per(50, 100), 50 );

}), ["./maths"]); // List dependencies (maths.js)
```

Our modules can then be required by a module loader library and executed in the browser. This is a really big deal. Not only have we split up our code into separate module components, which is the secret to good application design, but we've also got dependency management, scope isolation, and namespacing. Indeed, the same modules can be run on browsers, servers, in desktop apps, and in any other CommonJS-compliant environment. In other words, it's now possible to share the same code between server and client!

Module Loaders

To use CommonJS modules on the client side, we need to use a module loader library. There is a variety of options, each with its own strengths and weaknesses. I'll cover the most popular ones and you can choose which one best suits your needs.

The CommonJS module format is still in flux, with various proposals under review. As it stands, there's no officially blessed transport format, which unfortunately complicates things. The two main module implementations in the wild are Transport C (*http://wiki.commonjs.org/wiki/Modules/AsynchronousDefinition*) and Transport D (*http://wiki.commonjs.org/wiki/Modules/Transport/D*). If you use any of the wrapping tools mentioned in the sections below, you'll have to make sure it generates wrapped modules in a format your loader supports. Fortunately, many module loaders also come with compatible wrapping tools, or they specify supported ones in their documentation.

Yabble

Yabble (*https://github.com/jbrantly/yabble*) is an excellent and lightweight module loader. You can configure Yabble to either request modules with XHR or to use script tags. The advantage to fetching modules with XHR is that they don't need wrapping in the transport format. However, the disadvantage is that modules have to be executed using `eval()`, making debugging more difficult. Additionally, there are cross-domain issues, especially if you're using a CDN. Ideally, you should only use the XHR option for quick and dirty development, certainly not in production:

```
<script src="https://github.com/jbrantly/yabble/raw/master/lib/yabble.js"> </script>
<script>
  require.setModuleRoot("javascripts");

  // We can use script tags if the modules
  // are wrapped in the transport format
  require.useScriptTags();

  require.ensure(["application"], function(require) {
    // Application is loaded
  });
</script>
```

The above example will fetch our wrapped `application` module and then load its dependencies, *utils.js*, before running the module. We can load modules using the `require()` function:

```
<script>
  require.ensure(["application", "utils"], function(require) {
    var utils = require("utils");
    assertEqual( utils.per( 50, 200 ), 25 );
  });
</script>
```

Although `utils` is required twice—once by the inline `require.ensure()` function, and once by the `application` module—our script is clever enough to fetch the module only once. Make sure any dependencies your module needs are listed in the transport wrapping.

RequireJS

A great alternative to Yabble is RequireJS (*http://requirejs.org*), one of the most popular loaders. RequireJS has a slightly different take on loading modules—it follows the Asynchronous Module Definition (*http://wiki.commonjs.org/wiki/Modules/Asynchro nousDefinition*) format, or AMD. The main difference you need to be concerned with is that the API evaluates dependencies eagerly, rather than lazily. In practice, RequireJS is completely compatible with CommonJS modules, requiring only different wrapping transport.

To load JavaScript files, just pass their paths to the `require()` function, specifying a callback that will be invoked when the dependencies are all loaded:

```
<script>
  require(["lib/application", "lib/utils"], function(application, utils) {
    // Loaded!
  });
</script>
```

As you can see in the example above, the `application` and `utils` modules are passed as arguments to the callback; they don't have to be fetched with the `require()` function.

It's not just modules that you can require—RequireJS also supports ordinary JavaScript libraries as dependencies, specifically jQuery and Dojo. Other libraries will work, but they won't be passed correctly as arguments to the required callback. However, any library that has dependencies is required to use the module format:

```
require(["lib/jquery.js"], function($) {
  // jQuery loaded
  $("#el").show();
});
```

Paths given to `require()` are relative to the current file or module, unless they begin with a /. To help with optimization, RequireJS encourages you to place your initial script loader in a separate file. The library even provides shorthand to do this: the `data-main` attribute:

```
<script data-main="lib/application" src="lib/require.js"></script>
```

Setting the `data-main` attribute instructs RequireJS to treat the script tag like a `require()` call and load the attribute's value. In this case, it would load the *lib/application.js* script, which would in turn load the rest of our application:

```
// Inside lib/application.js
require(["jquery", "models/asset", "models/user"], function($, Asset, User) {
```

```
  //...
});
```

So, we've covered requiring modules, but what about actually defining them? Well, as stated previously, RequireJS uses a slightly different syntax for modules. Rather than using `require.define()`, just use the plain `define()` function. As long as modules are in different files, they don't need explicit naming. Dependencies come first, as an array of strings, and then comes a callback function containing the actual module. As in the RequireJS `require()` function, dependencies are passed as arguments to the callback function:

```
define(["underscore", "./utils"], function(_, Utils) {
  return({
    size: 10
  })
});
```

By default, there's no `exports` variable. To expose variables from inside the module, just return data from the function. The benefit to RequireJS modules is that they're already wrapped up, so you don't have to worry about transport formats for the browser. However, the caveat to this API is that it's not compatible with CommonJS modules—i.e., you couldn't share modules between Node.js and the browser. All is not lost, though; RequireJS has a compatibility layer for CommonJS modules—just wrap your existing modules with the `define()` function:

```
define(function(require, exports) {
  var mod = require("./relative/name");

  exports.value = "exposed";
});
```

The arguments to the callbacks need to be exactly as shown above—i.e., `require` and `exports`. Your modules can then carry on using those variables as usual, without any alterations.

Wrapping Up Modules

At this stage, we've got dependency management and namespacing, but there's still the original problem: all those HTTP requests. Any module we depend on has to be loaded in remotely, and even though this happens asynchronously, it's still a big performance overhead, slowing the startup of our application.

We're also hand-wrapping our modules in the transport format which, while necessary for asynchronous loading, is fairly verbose. Let's kill two birds with one stone by using a server-side step to concatenate the modules into one file. This means the browser has to fetch only one resource to load all the modules, which is much more efficient. The build tools available are intelligent, too—they don't just bundle the modules arbitrarily, but statically analyze them to resolve their dependencies recursively. They'll also take care of wrapping the modules up in the transport format, saving some typing.

In addition to concatenation, many module build tools also support minification, further reducing the request size. In fact, some tools—such as rack-modulr (*https://github.com/maccman/rack-modulr*) and Transporter (*http://github.com/kriszyp/transporter*)—integrate with your web server, handling module processing automatically when they're first requested.

For example, here's a simple Rack (*http://rack.rubyforge.org*) CommonJS module server using rack-modulr:

```
require "rack/modulr"

use Rack::Modulr, :source => "lib", :hosted_at => "/lib"
run Rack::Directory.new("public")
```

You can start the server with the `rackup` command. Any CommonJS modules contained inside the *lib* folder are now concatenated automatically with all their dependencies and are wrapped in a transport callback. Our script loader can then request modules when they're needed, loading them into the page:

```
>> curl "http://localhost:9292/lib/application.js"
    require.define("maths"....
```

If Ruby's not your thing, there is a multitude of other options from which to choose. FlyScript (*http://www.flyscript.org*) is a CommonJS module wrapper written in PHP, Transporter is one for JSGI (*http://jackjs.org*) servers, and Stitch (*https://github.com/sstephenson/stitch*) integrates with Node.js servers.

Module Alternatives

You may decide not to go the module route, perhaps because you've already got a lot of existing code and libraries to support that can't be easily converted. Luckily, there are some great alternatives, such as Sprockets (*http://getsprockets.org*). Sprockets adds synchronous `require()` support to your JavaScript. Comments beginning with //= act as directives to the Sprockets preprocessor. For example, the //= `require` directive instructs Sprockets to look in its load path for the library, fetch it, and include it inline:

```
//= require <jquery>
//= require "./states"
```

In the example above, *jquery.js* is in Sprockets' load path, and *states.js* is required relative to the current file. Sprockets is clever enough to include a library only once, regardless of the amount of time required. As with all the CommonJS module wrappers, Sprockets supports caching and minification. During development, your server can parse and concatenate files on demand in the course of the page load. When the site is live, the JavaScript files can be preconcatenated and served statically, increasing performance.

Although Sprockets is a command-line tool, there are some great integrations to Rack and Rails, such as rack-sprockets (*https://github.com/kelredd/rack-sprockets*). There are even some PHP implementations (*https://github.com/stuartloxton/php-sprockets*). The downside to Sprockets—and indeed all these module wrappers—is that all your Java-Script files need to be preprocessed, either by the server or via the command-line tool.

LABjs

LABjs (*http://www.labjs.com*) is one of the simplest dependency management solutions out there. It doesn't require any server-side involvement or CommonJS modules. Loading your scripts with LABjs reduces resource blocking during page load, which is an easy and effective way to optimize your site's performance. By default, LABjs will load and execute scripts in parallel as fast as possible. However, you can easily specify the execution order if some scripts have dependencies:

```
<script>
  $LAB
  .script('/js/json2.js')
  .script('/js/jquery.js').wait()
  .script('/js/jquery-ui.js')
  .script('/js/vapor.js');
</script>
```

In the above example, all the scripts load in parallel, but LABjs ensures *jquery.js* is executed before *jquery-ui.js* and *vapor.js*. The API is incredibly simple and succinct, but if you want to learn about LABjs' more advanced features, such as support for inline scripts, check out the documentation (*http://labjs.com/documentation.php*).

FUBCs

One thing to watch out for with any of these script loaders is that during the page load, users may see a flash of unbehaviored content (FUBC)—i.e., a glimpse at the raw page before any JavaScript is executed. This won't be a problem if you're not relying on JavaScript to style or manipulate the initial page. But if you are, address this issue by setting some initial styles in CSS, perhaps hiding a few elements, or by displaying a brief loading splash screen.

## CHAPTER 7

Working with Files

Traditionally, file access and manipulation was within the realm of desktop apps, with the Web limited to functionality provided by plug-in technologies like Adobe Flash. However, all of that is changing with HTML5, which gives developers a lot more scope for dealing with files, further blurring the boundaries between desktop and the Web. With modern browsers, users can drag and drop files onto the page, paste structured data, and see real-time progress bars as files upload in the background.

Browser Support

Support for the new HTML5 file APIs is not universal, but certainly enough browsers have implementations that it's worth your while to integrate them.

- Firefox >= 3.6
- Safari >= 6.0
- Chrome >= 7.0
- IE: no support
- Opera >= 11.1

As there's no IE support yet, you'll have to use progressive enhancement. Give users the option of a traditional file input for uploading, as well as allowing the more advanced drag/dropping of files. Detecting support is simple—just check whether the relevant objects are present:

```
if (window.File && window.FileReader && window.FileList) {
  // API supported
}
```

Getting Information About Files

The main security consideration behind HTML5's file handling is that only files selected by the user can be accessed. This can be done by dragging the file onto the browser, selecting it in a file input, or pasting it into a web application. Although there has been some work to expose a filesystem to JavaScript (*http://www.html5rocks.com/en/tutorials/file/filesystem/*), access has always been sandboxed. Obviously, it would be a tremendous security flaw if JavaScript could read and write arbitrary files on your system.

Files are represented in HTML5 by `File` objects, which have three attributes:

name
: The file's name as a read-only string

size
: The file's size as a read-only integer

type
: The file's MIME type as a read-only string, or an empty string ("") if the type couldn't be determined

For security reasons, a file's path information is never exposed.

Multiple files are exposed as `FileList` objects, which you can essentially treat as an array of `File` objects.

File Inputs

File inputs, which have been around since the dawn of the Web, are the traditional way of letting users upload files. HTML5 improves on them, reducing some of their drawbacks. One of the long-standing bugbears for developers was allowing multiple file uploads. In the past, developers had to resort to a mass of file inputs or rely on a plugin like Adobe Flash. HTML5 addresses this with the `multiple` attribute. By specifying `multiple` on a file input, you're indicating to the browser that users should be allowed to select multiple files. Older browsers that don't support HTML5 will simply ignore the attribute:

```
<input type="file" multiple>
```

The UI isn't perfect, though; to select multiple files, users need to hold down the Shift key. You may want to show users a message to this effect. For example, Facebook found that 85% of users who uploaded a photo would upload only one photo (*http://www.zurb.com/article/515/podcast-of-julie-zhuos-talk-on-how-facebo*). By adding a tip that explains how to select multiple photos to the uploading process, as shown in Figure 7-1, the metrics dropped from 85% to 40%.

Another problem for developers was not having any information about which files had been selected. Often, it's useful to validate the selected files, making sure they're a certain type or not above a certain size. HTML5 makes this possible now by giving you access to the input's selected files, using the `files` attribute.

The read-only `files` attribute returns a `FileList`, which you can iterate through, performing your validation, and then informing the user of the result:

```
var input = $("input[type=file]");

input.change(function(){
  var files = this.files;

  for (var i=0; i < files.length; i++)
    assert( files[i].type.match(/image.*/) )
});
```

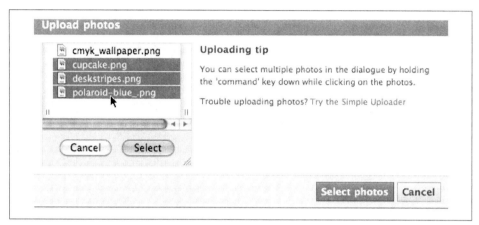

Figure 7-1. Uploading multiple files on Facebook

Having access to the selected files doesn't limit you to validation, though. For example, you could read the file's contents, displaying an upload preview. Or, rather than having the UI block as the files are uploaded, you could upload them in the background using Ajax, displaying a live progress bar. All this and more is covered in the subsequent sections.

Drag and Drop

Drag and drop support was originally "designed" and implemented by Microsoft back in 1999 for Internet Explorer 5.0, and IE has supported it ever since. The HTML5 specification has just documented what was already there, and now Safari, Firefox, and Chrome have added support, emulating Microsoft's implementation. However, to put it kindly, the specification is rather a mess (*http://www.quirksmode.org/blog/archives/2009/09/the_html5_drag.html*), and it requires a fair bit of hoop-jumping to satisfy its often pointless requirements.

There are no less than seven events associated with drag and drop: *dragstart*, *drag*, *dragover*, *dragenter*, *dragleave*, *drop*, and *dragend*. I'll elaborate on each in the sections below.

Even if your browser doesn't support the HTML5 file APIs, it's likely that you can still use the drag and drop APIs. Currently, the browser requirements are:

- Firefox >= 3.5
- Safari >= 3.2
- Chrome >= 7.0
- IE >= 6.0
- Opera: no support

Dragging

Dragging is fairly straightforward. To make an element draggable, set its `draggable` attribute to true.

```
<div id="dragme" draggable="true">Drag me!</div>
```

Now we have to associate that draggable element with some data. We can do this by listening to the *dragstart* event and calling the event's `setData()` function:

```
var element = $("#dragme");

element.bind("dragstart", function(event){
  // We don't want to use jQuery's abstraction
  event = event.originalEvent;

  event.dataTransfer.effectAllowed = "move";
  event.dataTransfer.setData("text/plain", $(this).text());
  event.dataTransfer.setData("text/html", $(this).html());
  event.dataTransfer.setDragImage("/images/drag.png", -10, -10);
});
```

jQuery provides an abstraction of the event, which doesn't contain the `dataTransfer` object we need. Conveniently, the abstracted event has an `originalEvent` attribute, which we can use to access the drag/drop APIs.

As demonstrated above, the event has a `dataTransfer` object, which has the various drag and drop functions we need. The `setData()` function takes a mimetype and string data. In this case, we're setting some `text` and `text/html` data on the *drag* event. When the element is dropped, and a *drop* event is triggered, we can read this data. Likewise, if the element is dragged outside the browser, other applications can handle the dropped data according to which file types they support.

When dragging text, use the `text/plain` type. It's recommended to always set this as a fallback for applications or drop targets that don't support any of the other formats. Dragged links should have two formats: `text/plain` and `text/uri-list`. To drag multiple links, join each link with a new line:

```
// Dragging links
event.dataTransfer.setData("text/uri-list", "http://example.com");
event.dataTransfer.setData("text/plain", "http://example.com");

// Multiple links are separated by a new line
```

```
event.dataTransfer.setData("text/uri-list", "http://example.com\nhttp://google.com");
event.dataTransfer.setData("text/plain", "http://example.com\nhttp://google.com");
```

The optional setDragImage() function controls what is displayed under the cursor during drag operations. It takes an image source and x/y coordinates, the position of the image relative to the cursor. If it's not supplied, you just get a ghostly clone of the dragged element. An alternative to setDragImage() is addElement(element, x, y), which uses the given element to update the drag feedback. In other words, you can provide a custom element to be displayed during drag operations.

You can also allow users to drag files out of the browser by setting the DownloadURL type. You can specify a URL to the file's location, which the browser will subsequently download. Gmail uses this to great effect by allowing users to drag and drop email attachments straight out of the browser onto the desktop.

The bad news is that this is currently only supported by Chrome, and it is rather undocumented. It can't hurt to use it, though, and hopefully other browsers will add support in the future. The DownloadURL format's value is a colon (:)-separated list of file information: the mime, name, and location.

```
$("#preview").bind("dragstart", function(e){
  e.originalEvent.dataTransfer.setData("DownloadURL", [
    "application/octet-stream",    // MIME type
    "File.exe",                    // File name
    "http://example.com/file.png"  // File location
  ].join(":"));
});
```

You can see the full example of HTML5's drag/drop API in this book's accompanying assets, in *assets/ch07/drag.html*.

Dropping

The drag/drop API lets you listen to *drop* events, which can respond to dropped files and other elements. This is where we start to see some of the drag/drop API craziness; for the *drop* event to fire at all, you have to cancel the defaults of both the *dragover* and the *dragenter* events! For example, here's how to cancel the two events:

```
var element = $("#dropzone");

element.bind("dragenter", function(e){
  // Cancel event
  e.stopPropagation();
  e.preventDefault();
});

element.bind("dragover", function(e){
  // Set the cursor
  e.originalEvent.dataTransfer.dropEffect = "copy";

  // Cancel event
  e.stopPropagation();
```

```
    e.preventDefault();
  });
```

You can also set a dropEffect—i.e., the cursor appearance—in the *dragover* event, as demonstrated above. By listening to the *dragenter* and *dragleave* events and toggling classes for the targeted element, you can give a visual indication to users that a certain area accepts dropped files.

Only once we've canceled *dragenter* and *dragover*'s events can we start listening to *drop* events. The *drop* event will trigger when a dragged element or file is dropped over the target element. The *drop* event's dataTransfer object has a files attribute, which returns a FileList of all dropped files:

```
element.bind("drop", function(event){
  // Cancel redirection
  event.stopPropagation();
  event.preventDefault();

  event = event.originalEvent;

  // Access dragged files
  var files = event.dataTransfer.files;

  for (var i=0; i < files.length; i++)
    alert("Dropped " + files[i].name);
});
```

You can access data other than files using the dataTransfer.getData() function, passing the format you support. If that format isn't available, the function will just return undefined.

```
var text = event.dataTransfer.getData("Text");
```

The dataTransfer object has a read-only types attribute, which returns a DOMString List (essentially an array) of the mime formats that were set on the *dragstart* event. Additionally, if any files are being dragged, one of the types will be the string "Files".

```
var dt = event.dataTransfer
for (var i=0; i < dt.types.length; i++)
  console.log( dt.types[i], dt.getData(dt.types[i]) );
```

See the full drop example in *assets/ch07/drop.html*.

Cancel Default Drag/Drop

By default, dragging a file onto a web page makes the browser navigate to that file. We want to prevent that behavior because we don't want users navigating away from our web application if they miss the drop area. This is easily accomplished—just cancel the body's *dragover* event.

```
$("body").bind("dragover", function(e){
  e.stopPropagation();
  e.preventDefault();
```

```
    return false;
});
```

Copy and Paste

In addition to drag-and-drop desktop integration, some browsers have support for copying and pasting. The API hasn't been standardized, and it isn't part of the HTML5 spec, so you'll need to determine how to cater to the various browsers.

Again, funnily enough, IE is the pioneer here, with support dating back to IE 5.0. WebKit has taken Microsoft's API and improved it somewhat, bringing it inline with the drag-and-drop API. Both are virtually identical, except for the different objects: `clipboardData` rather than `dataTransfer`.

Firefox has no support yet, and although it has a proprietary API for accessing the clipboard, it's unwieldy to say the least. WebKit (Safari/Chrome) has good support, and I imagine the W3C will eventually standardize its take on clipboard APIs. Browser support is as follows:

- Safari >= 6.0
- Chrome (only pasting)
- Firefox: no support
- IE >= 5.0 (different API)

Copying

There are two events associated with copying, and two events with cutting:

- *beforecopy*
- *copy*
- *beforecut*
- *cut*

As the name suggests, *beforecopy* and *beforecut* are triggered before any clipboard operations, allowing you to cancel them if necessary. When the user copies some selected text, the *copy* event fires, giving you a `clipboardData` object that can be used to set custom clipboard data. Like the `dataTransfer` object, `clipboardData` has a `setData()` function, which takes a mime format and string value. If you're planning on calling this function, you should cancel the original *copy* event, preventing the default action.

Rather than on the event, IE sets the `clipboardData` object on `window`. You'll need to check to see whether the object is present on the event, and if not, whether it's present on the window.

Firefox will actually fire the *copy* event, but it won't give you access to the `clipboardData` object. Chrome will give you the object, but it will ignore any data you set on it.

```
$("textarea").bind("copy", function(event){
  event.stopPropagation();
  event.preventDefault();

  var cd = event.originalEvent.clipboardData;

  // For IE
  if ( !cd ) cd = window.clipboardData;

  // For Firefox
  if ( !cd ) return;

  cd.setData("text/plain", $(this).text());
});
```

At the rate browsers are innovating, it's quite likely support will be standardized soon. If you want to add copy/paste support to your application, you should take a look at the current situation yourself.

Pasting

There are two events associated with pasting, *beforepaste* and *paste*. The *paste* event is triggered when the user initiates a paste, but before any data has been pasted. Again, different browsers have different implementations. Chrome triggers the event, even if no element has focus. Both IE and Safari require an actively focused element.

The API is very similar to the *drop* event API. The event has a `clipboardData` property, which gives you access to the pasted data using the `getData()` function, passing in a mime format. Unfortunately, from my tests, the `types` property is always `null`, so you can't see which mime types are available on the clipboard data. Unless you cancel the event, the paste process will carry on as normal, and the data will be pasted into the focused element:

```
$("textarea").bind("paste", function(event){
  event.stopPropagation();
  event.preventDefault();

  event = event.originalEvent;

  var cd = event.clipboardData;

  // For IE
  if ( !cd ) cd = window.clipboardData;

  // For Firefox
  if ( !cd ) return;

  $("#result").text(cd.getData("text/plain"));

  // Safari event support file pasting
  var files = cd.files;
});
```

The nightly versions of WebKit (*http://nightly.webkit.org*) give you access to a `files` property on `clipboardData`, allowing you to support file pasting into your application. I expect other browsers will follow suit once the specification is standardized.

So, is there any possibility of getting this to work cross-browser? Well, yes, there are actually a few workarounds. Cappuccino (*http://cappuccino.org*), for example, bypasses the *oncopy* family of events completely, and simply captures key inputs. When the key combination Command/Ctrl + v is detected, it then focuses a hidden input field, which gets filled with the pasted data. This works in every browser, but obviously for pastes initiated by the keyboard only—not the menu.

Reading Files

Once you've obtained a `File` reference, you can instantiate a `FileReader` object to read its contents into memory. Files are read asynchronously—you provide a callback to the `FileReader` instance, which will be invoked when the file is ready.

`FileReader` gives you four functions to read file data. Which you use depends on which data format you want returned.

`readAsBinaryString(Blob|File)`
> Returns the file/blob's data as a binary string. Every byte is represented by an integer in the range 0 to 255.

`readAsDataURL(Blob|File)`
> Returns the file/blob's data encoded as a data URL (*http://en.wikipedia.org/wiki/Data_URI_scheme*). For example, this can be used as the `src` attribute value for an image.

`readAsText(Blob|File, encoding='UTF-8')`
> Returns the file/blob's data as a text string. By default, the string is decoded as UTF-8.

`readAsArrayBuffer(Blob|File)`
> Returns the file/blob's data as an `ArrayBuffer` object. This is unimplemented in most browsers.

`FileReader` instances have a number of events that are triggered when one of the above read functions is called. The main ones with which you need to be concerned are:

onerror
> Called when an error occurs

onprogress
> Called periodically while the data is being read

onload
> Called when the data is available

To use `FileReader`, just instantiate an instance, add the events, and use one of the read functions. The *onload* event contains a `result` attribute, specifying read data in the appropriate format:

```
var reader = new FileReader();
reader.onload = function(e) {
  var data = e.target.result;
};
reader.readAsDataURL(file);
```

For example, we can use the `data` variable above as an image source, displaying a thumbnail of the specified file:

```
var preview = $("img#preview")

// Check to see whether file is an image type, and isn't
// so big a preview that it would cause the browser problems
if (file.type.match(/image.*/) &&
      file.size < 50000000) {

  var reader = new FileReader();
  reader.onload = function(e) {
    var data    = e.target.result;
    preview.attr("src", data);
  };
  reader.readAsDataURL(file);
}
```

Blobs and Slices

Sometimes it's preferable to read a slice of the file into memory, rather than the entire thing. The HTML5 file APIs conveniently support a `slice()` function. This takes a starting byte as the first argument, and a byte offset (or slice length) as its second. It returns a `Blob` object, which we can interchange with methods that support the `File` object, such as `FileReader`. For example, we could buffer the file reading like this:

```
var bufferSize = 1024;
var pos = 0;

var onload = function(e){
  console.log("Read: ", e.target.result);
};

var onerror = function(e){
  console.log("Error!", e);
};

while (pos < file.size) {
  var blob = file.slice(pos, bufferSize);

  var reader = new FileReader();
  reader.onload  = onload;
  reader.onerror = onerror;
  reader.readAsText(blob);
```

```
    pos += bufferSize;
  }
```

As you can see above, you can use a `FileReader` instance only once; after that, you'll need to instantiate a new one.

You can check out the full example in *assets/ch07/slices.html*. One thing to watch out for is that the file can't be read if the sandbox is local. In other words, if *slices.html* is being read from the disk, rather than hosted, the read will fail and the *onerror* event will be triggered.

Custom Browse Buttons

Opening a file-browsing dialog programmatically is a common use case. In other words, a styled Browse or Attachment button immediately brings up a browse dialog when clicked, without the user having to interact with a traditional file input. However, for security reasons, this is trickier than it sounds. File inputs have no browse function, and, with the exception of Firefox, you can't just trigger a custom *click* event on a file input.

The current solution may sound like a hack, but it works rather well. When a user mouses over a browse button, overlay a transparent file input that has the same position and dimensions as the button. The transparent file input will catch any click events, opening a browse dialog.

Inside this book's *assets/ch07* folder, you'll find *jquery.browse.js*, a jQuery plug-in that does just that. To create a custom browse button, just call the `browseElement()` function on a jQuery instance. The function will return a file input that you can add a *change* event listener to, detecting when the user has selected some files.

```
var input = $("#attach").browseElement();

input.change(function(){
  var files = $(this).attr("files");
});
```

It's got full cross-browser support, and it couldn't be easier!

Uploading Files

Part of the XMLHttpRequest Level 2 specification (*http://www.w3.org/TR/XMLHttpRequest2*) was the ability to upload files. File uploads have long been a painful experience for users. Once they've browsed and selected a file, the page reloads and they have to wait for ages while it uploads, with no indication of progress or feedback—quite the usability nightmare. Luckily for us, XHR 2 solves this problem. It allows us to upload files in the background, and it even gives us progress events so that we can provide the user with a real-time progress bar. It's generally well supported by the major browsers:

- Safari >= 5.0
- Firefox >= 4.0
- Chrome >= 7.0
- IE: no support
- Opera: no support

File uploads can be done via the existing XMLHttpRequest API, using the send() function, or alternatively by using a FormData instance. A FormData instance just represents the contents of a form in an easy-to-manipulate interface. You can build a FormData object from scratch, or by passing in an existing form element when instantiating the object:

```
var formData = new FormData($("form")[0]);

// You can add form data as strings
formData.append("stringKey", "stringData");

// And even add File objects
formData.append("fileKey", file);
```

Once you've finished with the FormData, you can POST it to your server using XMLHttpRequest. If you're using jQuery for Ajax requests, you'll need to set the proc essData option to false so that jQuery doesn't try to serialize the supplied data. Don't set the Content-Type header because the browser will set it automatically to multipart/form-data, along with a multipart boundary:

```
jQuery.ajax({
  data: formData,
  processData: false,
  url: "http://example.com",
  type: "POST"
})
```

The alternative to using FormData is to pass the file directly to the XHR object's send() function:

```
var req = new XMLHttpRequest();
req.open("POST", "http://example.com", true);
req.send(file);
```

Or, with jQuery's Ajax API, you can upload files like this:

```
$.ajax({
  url: "http://example.com",
  type: "POST",
  success: function(){ /* ... */ },
  processData: false,
  data: file
});
```

It's worth noting that this upload is a bit different from the traditional multipart/form-data one. Usually, information about the file, such as the name, would be included in the upload. Not so in this case—the upload is pure file data. To pass information about the file, we can set custom headers, such as X-File-Name. Our servers can read these headers and process the file properly:

```
$.ajax({
  url: "http://example.com",
  type: "POST",
  success: function(){ /* ... */ },
  processData: false,
  contentType: "multipart/form-data",

  beforeSend: function(xhr, settings){
    xhr.setRequestHeader("Cache-Control", "no-cache");
    xhr.setRequestHeader("X-File-Name", file.fileName);
    xhr.setRequestHeader("X-File-Size", file.fileSize);
  },

  data: file
});
```

Unfortunately, many servers will have trouble receiving the upload because pure data is a more unfamiliar format than multipart or URL-encoded form parameters. Using this method, you may have to parse the request manually. For this reason, I advocate using FormData objects, and sending the upload serialized as a multipart/form-data request. In the *assets/ch07* folder, you'll find *jquery.upload.js*, a jQuery plug-in that abstracts file uploading into a simple $.upload(url, file) interface.

Ajax Progress

The XHR Level 2 specification adds support for *progress* events, both for download and upload requests. This allows for a real-time file upload progress bar, giving users an estimated duration before the upload is complete.

To listen to the progress event on the download request, add it directly on the XHR instance:

```
var req = new XMLHttpRequest();

req.addEventListener("progress", updateProgress, false);
req.addEventListener("load", transferComplete, false);
req.open();
```

For the upload progress event, add it to the upload attribute of the XHR instance:

```
var req = new XMLHttpRequest();

req.upload.addEventListener("progress", updateProgress, false);
req.upload.addEventListener("load", transferComplete, false);
req.open();
```

The *load* event will fire once the upload request has completed, but before the server has issued a response. We can add it to jQuery because the XHR object and settings are passed to the `beforeSend` callback. The full example, including custom headers, looks like this:

```
$.ajax({
  url: "http://example.com",
  type: "POST",
  success: function(){ /* ... */ },
  processData: false,
  dataType: "multipart/form-data",

  beforeSend: function(xhr, settings){
    var upload = xhr.upload;

    if (settings.progress)
      upload.addEventListener("progress", settings.progress, false);

    if (settings.load)
      upload.addEventListener("load", settings.load, false);

    var fd = new FormData;

    for (var key in settings.data)
      fd.append(key, settings.data[key]);

    settings.data = fd;
  },

  data: file
});
```

The *progress* event contains the `position` of the upload (that is, how many bytes have uploaded) and the `total` (the size of the upload request in bytes). You can use these two properties to calculate a progress percentage:

```
var progress = function(event){
  var percentage = Math.round((event.position / event.total) * 100);
  // Set progress bar
}
```

In fact, the event has a timestamp, so if you record the time you started the upload, you can create a rudimentary estimated time of completion (ETA):

```
var startStamp = new Date();
var progress = function(e){
  var lapsed = startStamp - e.timeStamp;
  var eta    = lapsed * e.total / e.position - lapsed;
};
```

However, this estimation is unlikely to be accurate with smaller (and therefore quicker) uploads. In my opinion, it's only worth showing an ETA if the upload will take longer than four minutes or so. A percentage bar is usually sufficient, as it gives users a clear and visual indication of how much longer an upload will take.

jQuery Drag and Drop Uploader

So, let's put all that knowledge into practice by building a drag-and-drop file uploader. We're going to need several libraries: *jquery.js* for the backbone, *jquery.ui.js* for the progress bar, *jquery.drop.js* to abstract the drag-and-drop APIs, and *jquery.upload.js* for the Ajax upload. All our logic will go inside `jQuery.ready()`, so it will be run when the DOM is ready:

```
//= require <jquery>
//= require <jquery.ui>
//= require <jquery.drop>
//= require <jquery.upload>

jQuery.ready(function($){
  /* ... */
});
```

Creating a Drop Area

We want users to be able to drag and drop files onto the `#drop` element, so let's turn it into a drop area. We need to bind to the *drop* event, canceling it and retrieving any dropped files, which are then passed to the `uploadFile()` function:

```
var view = $("#drop");
view.dropArea();

view.bind("drop", function(e){
  e.stopPropagation();
  e.preventDefault();

  var files = e.originalEvent.dataTransfer.files;
  for ( var i = 0; i < files.length; i++)
    uploadFile(files[i]);

  return false;
});
```

Uploading the File

And now for the `uploadFile()` function—where the magic happens. We're going use the `$.upload()` function in jquery.upload.js to send an Ajax upload request to the server. We'll listen to progress events on the request and update a jQuery UI progress bar. Once the upload is complete, we'll notify the user and remove the element:

```
var uploadFile = function(file){
  var element = $("<div />");
  element.text(file.fileName);

  var bar = $("<div />");
  element.append(bar);
  $("#progress").append(element);
```

```
var onProgress = function(e){
  var per = Math.round((e.position / e.total) * 100);
  bar.progressbar({value: per});
};

var onSuccess = function(){
  element.text("Complete");
  element.delay(1000).fade();
};

$.upload("/uploads", file, {upload: {progress: onProgress}, success: onSuccess});
};
```

That's pretty straightforward! To see the full example, check out *assets/ch07/dragdro-pupload.html.*

## CHAPTER 8

The Real-Time Web

Why is the real-time Web so important? We live in a real-time world, so it's only natural that the Web is moving in that direction. Users clamor for real-time communication, data, and search. Our expectations for how quickly the Internet should deliver us information have changed—delays of minutes in breaking news stories are now unacceptable. Major companies like Google, Facebook, and Twitter have been quick to catch onto this, offering real-time functionality in their services. This is a growing trend that's only going to get bigger.

Real Time's History

Traditionally, the Web was built around the request/response model of HTTP: a client requests a web page, the server delivers it, and nothing happens again until the client requests another page. Then, Ajax came along and made web pages feel a bit more dynamic—requests to the server could now be made in the background. However, if the server had additional data for clients, there was no way of notifying them after the page was loaded; live data couldn't be pushed to clients.

Lots of solutions were devised. The most basic was polling: just asking the server over and over again for any new information. This gave users the perception of real time. In practice, it introduced latency and performance problems because servers had to process a huge number of connections a second, with both TCP handshake and HTTP overheads. Although polling is still used, it's by no means ideal.

Then, more advanced transports were devised under the umbrella term Comet. These techniques consisted of iframes (forever frames), xhr-multipart, htmlfiles, and long polling. With long polling, a client opens an XMLHttpRequest (XHR) connection to a server that never closes, leaving the client hanging. When the server has new data, it's duly sent down the connection, which then closes. The whole process then repeats itself, essentially allowing server push.

Comet techniques were unstandardized hacks, and as such, browser compatibility was a problem. On top of that, there were performance issues. Every connection to the server contained a full set of HTTP headers, so if you needed low latency, this could be quite a problem. That's not to knock Comet, though—it was a valid solution when there were no other alternatives.

Browser plug-ins, such as Adobe Flash and Java, were also used for server push. These would allow raw TCP socket connections with servers, which could be used for pushing real-time data out to clients. The caveat was that these plug-ins weren't guaranteed to be installed, and they often suffered from firewall issues, especially on corporate networks.

There are now alternative solutions as part of the HTML5 specification. However, it will be a while before all the browsers, particularly Internet Explorer, are up to speed with the current developments. Until then, Comet will remain a useful tool in any frontend developer's arsenal.

WebSockets

WebSockets (*http://dev.w3.org/html5/websockets*) are part of the HTML5 specification (*http://www.w3.org/TR/html5*), providing bidirectional, full-duplex sockets over TCP. This means that servers can push data to clients without developers resorting to long polling or browser plug-ins, which is quite an improvement. Although a number of browsers have implemented support, the protocol (*http://tools.ietf.org/html/draft -hixie-thewebsocketprotocol-76*) is still in flux due to security issues. However, that shouldn't put you off; the teething problems will soon get ironed out and the spec will be finalized. In the meantime, browsers that don't support WebSockets can fall back to legacy methods like Comet or polling.

WebSockets have significant advantages over previous server push transports because they are full-duplex, aren't over HTTP, and persist once opened. The real drawback to Comet was the overhead of HTTP—every request also had a full set of HTTP headers. Then there was the overhead of multiple extraneous TCP handshakes, which was significant at high levels of requests.

With WebSockets, once a handshake is completed between client and server, messages can be sent back and forth without the overhead of HTTP headers. This greatly reduces bandwidth usage, thus improving performance. Since there is an open connection, servers can reliably push updates to clients as soon as new data becomes available (no polling is required). In addition, the connection is duplex, so clients can also send messages back to the server, again without the overhead of HTTP.

This is what Google's Ian Hickson, the HTML5 specification lead, said about Web-Sockets:

> Reducing kilobytes of data to 2 bytes...and reducing latency from 150ms to 50ms is far more than marginal. In fact, these two factors alone are enough to make WebSockets seriously interesting to Google.

So, let's look at WebSocket support in the browsers:

- Chrome >= 4
- Safari >= 5
- iOS >= 4.2
- Firefox >= 4*
- Opera >= 11*

Although Firefox and Opera have WebSocket implementations, it's currently disabled due to recent security scares. This will all get sorted out though, probably by the time this book goes to print. In the meantime, you can gracefully degrade with older technologies like Comet and Adobe Flash. IE support is nowhere on the map at the moment, and it probably won't be added until after IE9.

Detecting support for WebSockets is very straightforward:

```
var supported = ("WebSocket" in window);
if (supported) alert("WebSockets are supported");
```

From a browser perspective, the WebSocket API is clear and logical. You instantiate a new socket using the WebSocket class, passing the socket server endpoint—in this case, ws://example.com:

```
var socket = new WebSocket("ws://example.com");
```

Then, we can add some event listeners to the socket:

```
// The connection has connected
socket.onopen = function(){ /* ... */ }

// The connection has some new data
socket.onmessage = function(data){ /* ... */ }

// The connection has closed
socket.onclose = function(){ /* ... */ }
```

When the server sends some data, *onmessage* will be called. Clients, in turn, can call the send() function to transmit data back to the server. Clearly, we should call that only after the socket has connected and the *onopen* event has fired:

```
socket.onmessage = function(msg){
  console.log("New data - ", msg);
};

socket.onopen = function(){
  socket.send("Why, hello there").
};
```

When sending and receiving messages, only strings are supported. However, it's simple enough to serialize and deserialize the message strings into JSON, creating your own protocol:

```
var rpc = {
  test: function(arg1, arg2) { /* ... */ }
};

socket.onmessage = function(data){
  // Parse JSON
  var msg = JSON.parse(data);

  // Invoke RPC function
  rpc[msg.method].apply(rpc, msg.args);
};
```

Above, we've created a remote procedure call (RPC) script. Our server can send some simple JSON, like the following, to invoke functions on the client side:

```
{"method": "test", "args": [1, 2]}
```

Notice we're restricting invocation to the rpc object. This is important for security reasons—we don't want to expose clients to hackers by evaluating arbitrary JavaScript.

To terminate the connection, just call the close() function:

```
var socket = new WebSocket("ws://localhost:8000/server");
```

You'll notice when instantiating a WebSocket that we're using the WebSocket scheme, ws://, rather than http://. WebSockets also allow encrypted connections via TLS using the wss:// schema. By default, WebSockets will use port 80 for nonencrypted connections and port 443 for encrypted ones. You can override this by providing a custom port in the URL. Keep in mind that not all ports are available to clients; firewalls may block the more uncommon ones.

At this stage, you may be thinking, "I can't possibly use this in production—the standard's a moving target and there's no IE support." Well, those are valid concerns, but luckily there's a solution. Web-socket-js (*https://github.com/gimite/web-socket-js*) is a WebSocket implementation powered by Adobe Flash. You can use this library to provide legacy browsers a WebSocket fallback to Flash, a plug-in that's almost ubiquitously available. It mirrors the WebSocket API exactly, so when WebSockets have better penetration, you'll only need to remove the library—not change the code.

Although the client-side API is fairly straightforward, things aren't quite so simple server side. The WebSocket protocol has been through several incompatible iterations: drafts 75 (*http://tools.ietf.org/html/draft-hixie-thewebsocketprotocol-75*) and 76 (*http://tools.ietf.org/html/draft-hixie-thewebsocketprotocol-76*). Servers need to take account of both drafts by detecting the type of handshake clients use.

WebSockets work by first performing an HTTP "upgrade" request to your server. If your server has WebSocket support, it will perform the WebSocket handshake and a connection will be initiated. Included in the upgrade request is information about the origin domain (where the request is coming from). Clients can make WebSocket connections to any domain—it's the server that decides which clients can connect, often by using a whitelist of allowed domains.

From conception, WebSockets were designed to work well with firewalls and prox-ies, using popular ports and HTTP headers for the initial connection. However, things rarely work out so simply in the wild Web. Some proxies change the WebSockets up-grade headers, breaking them. Others don't allow long-lived connections and will time out after a while. In fact, the most recent update to the protocol draft (version 76) unintentionally broke compatibility with reverse-proxies and gateways. There are a few steps you can take to give your WebSockets the best chance of success:

- Use secured WebSocket connections (wss). Proxies won't meddle with encrypted connections, and you get the added advantage that the data is safe from eaves-droppers.
- Use a TCP load balancer in front of your WebSocket servers, rather than an HTTP one. Consider an HTTP balancer only if it actively advertises WebSocket support.
- Don't assume that if a browser has WebSocket support, it will work. Instead, time out connections if they aren't established quickly, gracefully degrading to a differ-ent transport like Comet or polling.

So, what server options are there? Luckily, there is a multitude of implementations in languages like Ruby, Python, and Java. Make sure any implementation supports at least draft 76 of the protocol, as this is most common in clients.

- Node.js
  —node-Websocket-server (*http://github.com/miksago/node-websocket-server*)
  —Socket.IO (*http://socket.io*)
- Ruby
  —EventMachine (*http://github.com/igrigorik/em-websocket*)
  —Cramp (*https://github.com/lifo/cramp*)
  —Sunshowers (*http://rainbows.rubyforge.org/sunshowers/*)
- Python
  —Twisted (*http://github.com/rlotun/txWebSocket*)
  —Apache module (*http://code.google.com/p/pywebsocket*)
- PHP
  —php-Websocket (*https://github.com/nicokaiser/php-websocket*)
- Java
  —Jetty (*http://www.eclipse.org/jetty*)
- Google Go
  —native (*http://code.google.com/p/go*)

Node.js and Socket.IO

Node.js (*http://nodejs.org*) is the newest kid on the block, but one of the most exciting. Node.js is an evented JavaScript server, powered by Google's V8 JS engine (*http://code .google.com/p/v8*). As such, it's incredibly fast and is great for services that have a large number of connected clients, like a WebSocket server.

Socket.IO (*http://socket.io*) is a Node.js library for WebSockets. What's interesting, though, is that it goes far beyond that. Here's a blurb from its site:

> Socket.IO aims to make real-time apps possible in every browser and mobile device, blurring the differences between the different transport mechanisms.

Socket.IO will try and use WebSockets if they're supported, but it will fall back to other transports if necessary. The list of supported transports is very comprehensive and offers a lot of browser compatibility.

- WebSocket
- Adobe Flash Socket
- ActiveX HTMLFile (IE)
- XHR with multipart encoding
- XHR with long-polling
- JSONP polling (for cross-domain)

Socket.IO's browser support is brilliant. Server push can be notoriously difficult to implement, but the Socket.IO team has gone through all that pain for you, ensuring compatibility with most browsers. As such, it works in the following browsers:

- Safari >= 4
- Chrome >= 5
- IE >= 6
- iOS
- Firefox >= 3
- Opera >= 10.61

Although the server side to Socket.IO was initially written for Node.js, there are now implementations in other languages, like Ruby (Rack) (*http://github.com/markjeee/ Socket.IO-rack*), Python (Tornado) (*https://github.com/MrJoes/tornadio*), Java (*http:// code.google.com/p/socketio-java*), and Google Go (*http://github.com/madari/go-socket .io*).

A quick look at the API will demonstrate how simple and straightforward it is. The client-side API looks very similar to the WebSocket one:

```
var socket = new io.Socket();

socket.on("connect", function(){
```

```
  socket.send('hi!');
});

socket.on("message", function(data){
  alert(data);
});

socket.on("disconnect", function(){});
```

Behind the scenes, Socket.IO will work out the best transport to use. As written in its *readme* file, Socket.IO is "making creating real-time apps that work everywhere a snap."

If you're looking for something a bit higher level than Socket.IO, you may be interested in Juggernaut (*https://github.com/maccman/juggernaut*), which builds upon it. Juggernaut has a channel interface: clients can subscribe to channels and servers can publish to them, i.e.—the PubSub (*http://en.wikipedia.org/wiki/PubSub*) pattern. The library can manage scaling, publishing to specific clients, TLS, and more.

If you need hosted solutions, look no further than Pusher (*http://pusherapp.com*). Pusher lets you leave behind the hassle of managing your own server so that you can concentrate on the fun part: developing web applications. For clients, it is as simple as including a JavaScript file in the page and subscribing to a channel. When it comes to publishing messages, it's just a case of sending an HTTP request to their REST API (*http://pusherapp.com/docs*).

Real-Time Architecture

It's all very well being able to push data to clients in theory, but how does that integrate with a JavaScript application? Well, if your application is modeled correctly, it's actually remarkably straightforward. We're going to go through all the steps involved in making your application real time, specifically following the PubSub pattern. The first thing to understand is the process that updates go through to reach clients.

A real-time architecture is event-driven. Typically, events are driven by user interaction: a user changes a record and events are propagated throughout the system until data is pushed to connected clients, updating them. When you're thinking about making your application real time, you need to consider two things:

- Which models need to be real time?
- When those models' instances change, which users need notifying?

It may be that when a model changes, you want to send notifications to all connected clients. This would be the case for a real-time activity feed on the home page, for example, where every client saw the same information. However, the common use case is when you have a resource associated with a particular set of users. You need to notify those users of that resource change.

Let's consider an example scenario of a chat room:

1. A user posts a new message to the room.
2. An Ajax request is sent off to the server, and a Chat record is created.
3. Save callbacks fire on the Chat model, invoking our method to update clients.
4. We search for all users associated with the Chat record's room—these are the ones we need to notify.
5. An update detailing what's happened (Chat record created) is pushed to the relevant users.

The process details are specific to your chosen backend. However, if you're using Rails, Holla (*http://github.com/maccman/holla*) is a good example. When Message records are created, the JuggernautObserver updates relevant clients.

That brings us to the next question: how can we send notifications to specific users? Well, an excellent way of doing so is with the PubSub pattern: clients subscribe to particular channels and servers publish to those channels. A user just subscribes to a unique channel containing an identifier, perhaps the user's database ID; then, the server simply needs to publish to that unique channel to send notifications to that specific user.

For example, a particular user could subscribe to the following channel:

```
/observer/0765F0ED-96E6-476D-B82D-8EBDA33F4EC4
```

where the random set of digits is a unique identifier for the currently logged-in user. To send notifications to that particular user, the server just needs to publish to that same channel.

You may be wondering how the PubSub pattern works with transports like WebSockets and Comet. Fortunately, there are already a lot of solutions, such as Juggernaut and Pusher, both mentioned previously. PubSub is a common abstraction on top of Web-Sockets, and its API should be fairly similar to whatever service or library you end up choosing.

Once notifications have been pushed to clients, you'll see the real beauty of the MVC architecture. Let's go back to our chat example. The notification we sent out to clients could look like this.

```
{
  "klass":  "Chat",
  "type":   "create",
  "id":     "3",
  "record": {"body": "New chat"}
}
```

It contains the model that's changed, the type of change, and any relevant attributes. Using this, our client can create a new Chat record locally. As the client's models are bound to the UI, the interface is automatically updated to reflect the new chat message.

What's brilliant is that none of this is specific to the Chat model. If we want to make another model real time, it's just a case of adding another observer server side, making sure clients are updated when it changes. Our backend and client-side models are now tied together. Any changes to the backend models get automatically propagated to all the relevant clients, updating their UI. With this architecture, the application is truly real time. Any interaction a user makes is instantly broadcast to other users.

Perceived Speed

Speed is a critical but often neglected part of UI design because it makes a huge difference to the user experience (UX) and can have a direct impact on revenue. Companies, such as the following, are studying its implications all the time:

Amazon
100 ms of extra load time caused a 1% drop in sales (source: Greg Linden, Amazon).
Google
500 ms of extra load time caused 20% fewer searches (source: Marrissa Mayer, Google).
Yahoo!
400 ms of extra load time caused a 5–9% increase in the number of people who clicked "back" before the page even loaded (source: Nicole Sullivan, Yahoo!).

Perceived speed is just as important as actual speed because this is what users are going to notice. So, the key is to make users think an application is fast, even if in reality it isn't. The ability to do this is one of the benefits of JavaScript applications—UI doesn't block, even if a background request is taking a while.

Let's take the chat room scenario again. A user sends a new message, firing off an Ajax request to the server. We could wait until the message performs a roundtrip through the server and clients before appending it to the chat log. However, that would introduce a couple of seconds' latency between the time a user submitted a new message and when it appeared in her chat log. The application would seem slow, which would definitely hurt the user experience.

Instead, why not create the new message locally, thereby immediately adding it to the chat log? From a user's perspective, it seems like the message has been sent instantly. Users won't know (or care) that the message hasn't yet been delivered to other clients in the chat room. They'll just be happy with a fast and snappy user experience.

Aside from interactions, one of the slowest parts of Web applications is loading in new data. It's important to do intelligent preloading to try to[predict what a user will need before he actually asks for it. Then, cache the data in memory; if the user needs it subsequently, you shouldn't have to request it again from the server. Upon startup, the application should preload commonly used data. Users are more likely to be forgiving of slower initial load times than once the application's loaded.

You should always give users feedback when they interact with your application, usually with some sort of visual indicator. In business jargon this is called *expectation managment*, making sure clients are aware of a project's status and ETA. The same applies to UX—users will be more patient if they're given an indication that something's happening. While users are waiting for new data, show them a message or a spinner. If a file's being uploaded, show a progress bar and an estimated duration. All this gives a perception of speed, improving the user experience.

## CHAPTER 9

Testing and Debugging

All developers test, to some degree or another, when they're programming. Even just running the code manually is a form of testing. However, what we're going to cover here is automated testing in JavaScript—i.e., writing specific assertions that run automatically. Automated testing won't eliminate bugs from your code, but it is a measure to effectively reduce the number of defects and to prevent older bugs from creeping back into the codebase. There are lots of great resources out there justifying and explaining different types of testing. So, rather than creating an inferior rehash of those, this chapter will focus on the specifics of testing in JavaScript as opposed to other languages.

Testing in JavaScript isn't really ingrained into the culture, so many JavaScript developers don't write any tests for their code. I think the main reason is that automated JavaScript testing is difficult—it doesn't scale. Let's take jQuery for example. The library has hundreds of unit tests and about 10 different test suites to simulate the various environments it's expected to run in. Each test has to be run once in every suite. Now, take a look at the browsers jQuery supports:

- Safari: 3.2, 4, 5, nightly
- Chrome: 8, 9, 10, 11
- Internet Explorer: 6, 7, 8, 9
- Firefox: 2, 3, 3.5, 3.6, nightly
- Opera: 9.6, 10, 11

So, that's 5 browsers with about 20 versions among them, and each suite needs to be run on every browser version. You can see how the amount of tests that have to be run is expanding exponentially, and I haven't even gotten to platforms yet! It just doesn't scale.

Obviously, jQuery is a special case, an example designed to highlight the problem. You probably won't need to support half as many browsers as jQuery does, and you are not likely to have as many suites. However, you will have to choose which browsers your application will support, and then test for them.

Before we go any further, it's worth looking at the browser landscape, as this ultimately dictates the limitations imposed upon web developers. The landscape changes so quickly that this analysis is likely to be out of date by the time you read this. The general trends, though, should remain the same.

Browser adoption rates really depend on how you measure them. They change markedly between countries and continents, usually depending on how Internet-savvy the population is. For example, here are the *Statcounter.com* results for Europe in early 2011:

- Safari: 4%
- Chrome: 15%
- IE: 36%
- Firefox: 37%
- Opera: 2%

The general trend is that IE usage is decreasing, while Firefox and Chrome usage is increasing. Older browsers like IE6 are now relics of the past, with a percentage share of a few points. Unless you're developing for corporate or government clients with a lot of legacy users, you shouldn't have to worry about supporting these ancient browsers.

As they say, "There are three kinds of lies: lies, damned lies, and statistics." This applies doubly to browser stats. The stats for my blog, for example, show IE usage of about 5%, which is way below the national average. In other words, the traffic you'll see is greatly affected by your specific audience. If your site caters to a technical, early-adopter crowd, you'll get a high percentage of Firefox and Chrome users, whereas more mainstream sites will get visitors that better reflect the national average. When choosing which browsers your site needs to support, you should consider your specific audience rather than browser penetrations as a whole. However, as a rule of thumb, I generally test in the following browsers:

- IE 8, 9
- Firefox 3.6
- Safari 5
- Chrome 11

If you don't have stats for your existing services that show you which browsers your audience is using, you'll have to make an educated guess based on your target audience. Once you've chosen which browsers you're supporting, the next step is writing automated tests and making sure they pass in every supported browser.

Unit Testing

Manual testing is like integration testing, making sure that your application works from a high level. Unit testing is much more low level, ensuring that particular pieces of code behind the scenes are performing as expected. Unit testing is much more likely to reveal cross-browser issues, but it allows you to resolve them quickly, because you need to examine only small sections of code.

The other advantage to unit testing is that it paves the way for automation. We'll cover this in more detail later in this chapter, but unit tests make it possible to set up a continuous integration server, running the application's tests every time the code is committed. This is much quicker than running through your whole application manually, and making sure that changes to one piece of code aren't having any side effects elsewhere in the application.

There are lots of JavaScript libraries out there for unit testing, each with pros and cons. We're going to cover the most popular ones, but the general principles should apply to any you choose to use.

Assertions

Assertions are at the heart of testing; they determine which tests pass or fail. Assertions are statements that indicate the expected result of your code. If the assertion is incorrect, the test fails, and you know that something has gone wrong.

For example, here's the simple `assert()` function we've been using for the examples throughout this book:

```
var asset = function(value, msg) {
  if ( !value )
    throw(msg || (value + " does not equal true"));
};
```

This takes a value and an optional message. If the value doesn't evaluate to `true`, the assertion fails:

```
// Assertion fails
assert( false );
assert( "" );
assert( 0 );
```

JavaScript automatically type-converts `undefined`, `0`, and `null` to `false` during a Boolean check. In other words, the `assert` works for a `null` check, too:

```
// If the statement is null, the assertion fails
assert( User.first() );
```

Type conversion will really affect your testing, so it's worth checking out some of the weird and wonderful ways JavaScript behaves when converting types (*http://bonsaiden .github.com/JavaScript-Garden*).

Assert libraries aren't just limited to checking for the truth. Most libraries include a whole array of matchers, from comparing primitive objects to checking that a number is greater than another. They all include at least an `assertEqual()` function, which lets you compare two values:

```
var assertEqual = function(val1, val2, msg) {
  if (val1 !== val2)
    throw(msg || (val1 + " does not equal " + val2));
};

// Assertion passes
assertEqual("one", "one");
```

All the testing libraries we're going to cover consist of a set of assertions, with slightly differing APIs for defining them.

QUnit

QUnit (*http://docs.jquery.com/Qunit*) is one of the most popular and well-maintained libraries, originally developed to test jQuery. So, how do you set up a QUnit testing environment? The first step is to download the project files (*https://github.com/jquery/qunit/zipball/master*) locally, and then create a static test runner page:

```
<!DOCTYPE html>
<html>
<head>
    <title>QUnit Test Suite</title>
    <link rel="stylesheet" href="qunit/qunit.css" type="text/css" media="screen">
    <script type="text/javascript" src="qunit/qunit.js"></script>
    <!-- include tests here... -->
</head>
<body>
    <h1 id="qunit-header">QUnit Test Suite</h1>
    <h2 id="qunit-banner"></h2>
    <div id="qunit-testrunner-toolbar"></div>
    <h2 id="qunit-userAgent"></h2>
    <ol id="qunit-tests"></ol>
    <div id="qunit-fixture">test markup</div>
</body>
</html>
```

To create assertions, you should put them into a test case. For example, let's create a test suite for that ORM we built in Chapter 3:

```
test("load()", function(){
  var Asset = Model.setup();

  var a = Asset.init();
  a.load({
    local: true,
    name: "test.pdf"
  });
```

```
  ok(a.local, "Load sets properties");
  equals(a.name, "test.pdf", "load() sets properties (2)");

  var b = Asset.init({
    name: "test2.pdf"
  });

  equals(b.name, "test2.pdf", "Calls load() on instantiation");
});
```

We are defining a new case by calling `test()` and giving it the name of the test and the test callback (where the magic happens). Inside the callback we've got various assertions: `ok()` asserts that its first argument resolves to `true`, and `equals()` compares its two arguments. All the assertions take a last string argument, which is the name of the assertion, letting us easily see what passes and fails.

Let's add that test to the page and give it a refresh, as shown in Figure 9-1.

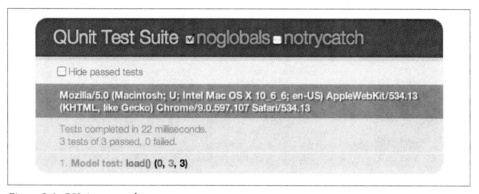

Figure 9-1. QUnit test results

That's pretty powerful! At a glance, we can see which tests have passed and failed—all it takes is a page refresh. We can now begin to test every browser our application supports, making sure our unit tests pass in all of them.

Tests are separated by the `module()` function, which takes a name and options. Let's clean up the first example by passing a `setup` option to `module()`, containing a callback that will be executed for every test that runs in the module. In this case, all our tests will need an **Asset** model, so we'll create that in the `setup`:

```
module("Model test", {
  setup: function(){
    this.Asset = Model.setup();
  }
});

test("load()", function(){
  var a = this.Asset.init();
  a.load({
    local: true,
```

```
    name: "test.pdf"
  });

  ok(a.local, "Load sets properties");
  equals(a.name, "test.pdf", "load() sets properties (2)");

  var b = this.Asset.init({
    name: "test2.pdf"
  });

  equals(b.name, "test2.pdf", "Calls load() on instantiation");
});
```

That's a bit cleaner, and it will be useful when adding further tests. module() also takes a teardown option, which is a callback that will be executed after every test in the module. Let's add another test to our suite:

```
test("attributes()", function(){
  this.Asset.attributes = ["name"];

  var a = this.Asset.init();
  a.name = "test.pdf";
  a.id   = 1;

  equals(a.attributes(), {
    name: "test.pdf",
    id: 1
  });
});
```

If you try this out, you'll see that the test has failed, like the page shown in Figure 9-2.

This is because the equals() function uses the == comparison operator, which will fail for objects and arrays. Instead, we need to use the same() function, which does a deep comparison, and our test suite will pass again:

```
test("attributes()", function(){
  this.Asset.attributes = ["name"];

  var a = this.Asset.init();
  a.name = "test.pdf";
  a.id   = 1;

  same(a.attributes(), {
    name: "test.pdf",
    id: 1
  });
});
```

QUnit includes a couple of other assertion types, such as notEqual() and raises(). For full examples of their usage, see *assets/ch09/qunit/model.test.js* or the QUnit docs (*http://docs.jquery.com/Qunit#API_documentation*).

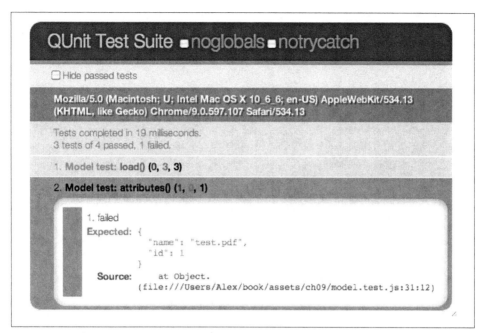

Figure 9-2. Failing tests in QUnit

Jasmine

Jasmine (*http://pivotal.github.com/jasmine*) is another popular testing library (and my personal favorite). Rather than unit tests, Jasmine has specs that describe the behavior of specific objects inside your application. In practice, they're similar to unit tests, just with a different terminology.

Jasmine's advantage is that it doesn't require any other libraries, or even a DOM. This means it can run in any JavaScript environment, such as on the server side with Node.js (*http://nodejs.org*).

As with QUnit, we need to set up a static HTML page that will load all the specs, run them, and display the result:

```
<!DOCTYPE HTML PUBLIC "-//W3C//DTD HTML 4.01 Transitional//EN"
  "http://www.w3.org/TR/html4/loose.dtd">
<html>
<head>
  <title>Jasmine Test Runner</title>
  <link rel="stylesheet" type="text/css" href="lib/jasmine.css">
  <script type="text/javascript" src="lib/jasmine.js"></script>
  <script type="text/javascript" src="lib/jasmine-html.js"></script>

  <!-- include source files here... -->
  <!-- include spec files here... -->
</head>
<body>
```

```
<script type="text/javascript">
  jasmine.getEnv().addReporter(new jasmine.TrivialReporter());
  jasmine.getEnv().execute();
</script>

</body>
</html>
```

Let's take a look at writing some Jasmine specs. We'll test some more of the ORM library from Chapter 3:

```
describe("Model", function(){
  var Asset;

  beforeEach(function(){
    Asset = Model.setup();
    Asset.attributes = ["name"];
  });

  it("can create records", function(){
    var asset = Asset.create({name: "test.pdf"});
    expect(Asset.first()).toEqual(asset);
  });

  it("can update records", function(){
    var asset = Asset.create({name: "test.pdf"});

    expect(Asset.first().name).toEqual("test.pdf");

    asset.name = "wem.pdf";
    asset.save();

    expect(Asset.first().name).toEqual("wem.pdf");
  });

  it("can destroy records", function(){
    var asset = Asset.create({name: "test.pdf"});

    expect(Asset.first()).toEqual(asset);

    asset.destroy();

    expect(Asset.first()).toBeFalsy();
  });
});
```

Specs are grouped into suites using the describe() function, which takes the name of the spec and an anonymous function. In the example above, we're using the beforeEach() function as a setup utility to be run before every function. Jasmine also includes a teardown function, afterEach(), which is called after every spec is run. We're defining the variable Asset outside the beforeEach() function, so it's local to the suite and can be accessed inside each spec.

A spec begins with the `it()` function, which gets passed the name of the spec and the anonymous function containing the assertions. Assertions are created by passing the relevant value to the `expect()` function, and then calling a matcher, such as one of the following:

`expect(x).toEqual(y)`
> Compares objects or primitives x and y, and passes if they are equivalent

`expect(x).toBe(y)`
> Compares objects or primitives x and y, and passes if they are the same object

`expect(x).toMatch(pattern)`
> Compares x to string or regular expression pattern, and passes if they match

`expect(x).toBeNull()`
> Passes if x is null

`expect(x).toBeTruthy()`
> Passes if x evaluates to true

`expect(x).toBeFalsy()`
> Passes if x evaluates to false

`expect(x).toContain(y)`
> Passes if array or string x contains y

`expect(fn).toThrow(e)`
> Passes if function `fn` throws exception e when executed

Jasmine includes lots of other matchers, and it even lets you write your own (*http://github.com/pivotal/jasmine/wiki/Matchers*) custom ones.

Figure 9-3 shows an overview of running the Jasmine Test Runner using the example specs above.

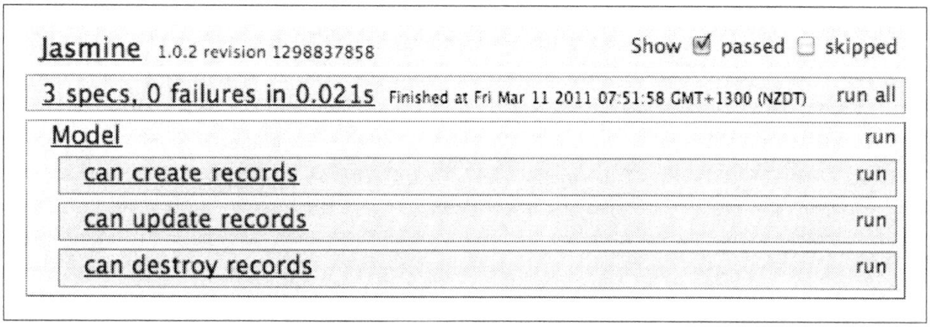

Figure 9-3. Jasmine test results

Drivers

Although by using a testing library we now have a degree of automation, there's still the problem of running your tests in lots of different browsers. It's not exactly productive having developers refresh the tests in five different browsers before every commit. Drivers were developed to solve exactly this problem. They're daemons that integrate with various browsers, running your JavaScript tests automatically and notifying you when they fail.

It can be quite a lot of work implementing a driver setup on every developer's machine, so most companies have a single continuous integration server, which will use a post-commit hook to run all the JavaScript tests automatically, making sure they all pass successfully.

Watir (*http://watir.com*), pronounced "water," is a Ruby driver library that integrates with Crome, Firefox, Safari, and Internet Explorer (dependent on the platform). After installation, you can give Watir some Ruby commands to drive the browser, clicking links and filling in forms the same as a person would. During this process, you can run a few test cases and assert that things are working as expected:

```ruby
# FireWatir drives Firefox
require "firewatir"

browser = Watir::Browser.new
browser.goto("http://bit.ly/watir-example")

browser.text_field(:name => "entry.0.single").set "Watir"
browser.button(:name => "logon").click
```

Due to limitations on which browsers can be installed on which operating systems, if you're testing with Internet Explorer, your continuous integration server will have to run a version of Windows. Likewise, to test in Safari, you'll also need a server running Mac OS X.

Another very popular browser-driving tool is Selenium (*http://seleniumhq.org*). The library provides a domain scripting language (DSL) to write tests in a number of programming languages, such as C#, Java, Groovy, Perl, PHP, Python, and Ruby. Selenium can run locally; typically, it runs in the background on a continuous integration server, keeping out of your way as you commit code, but notifying you when tests fail. Selenium's strengths lie in the number of languages it supports, as well as the Selenium IDE (*http://seleniumhq.org/projects/ide*), a Firefox plug-in that records and plays back actions inside the browser, greatly simplifying authoring tests.

In Figure 9-4, we're using the Selenium IDE tool to record clicking on a link, filling in a form, and finally submitting it. Once a session has been recorded, you can play it back using the green *play* button. The tool will emulate our recorded actions, navigating to and completing the test form.

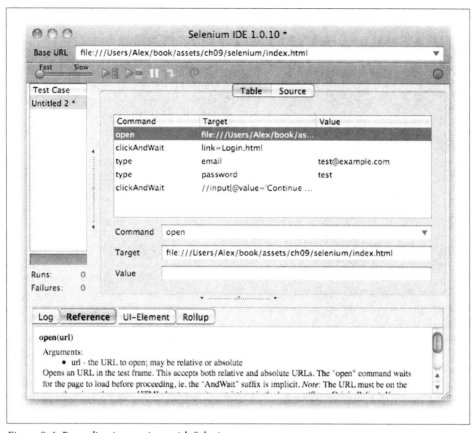

Figure 9-4. Recording instructions with Selenium

We can then export the recorded Test Case to a variety of formats, as shown in Figure 9-5.

For example, here's the exported Test Case as a Ruby Test::Unit case. As you can see, Selenium's IDE has conveniently generated all the relevant driver methods, greatly reducing the amount of work needed to test the page:

```ruby
class SeleniumTest < Test::Unit::TestCase
  def setup
    @selenium = Selenium::Client::Driver.new \
      :host => "localhost",
      :port => 4444,
      :browser => "*chrome",
      :url => "http://example.com/index.html",
      :timeout_in_second => 60

    @selenium.start_new_browser_session
  end

  def test_selenium
```

```
    @selenium.open "http://example.com/index.html"
    @selenium.click "link=Login.html"
    @selenium.wait_for_page_to_load "30000"
    @selenium.type "email", "test@example.com"
    @selenium.type "password", "test"
    @selenium.click "//input[@value='Continue →']"
    @selenium.wait_for_page_to_load "30000"
  end
end
```

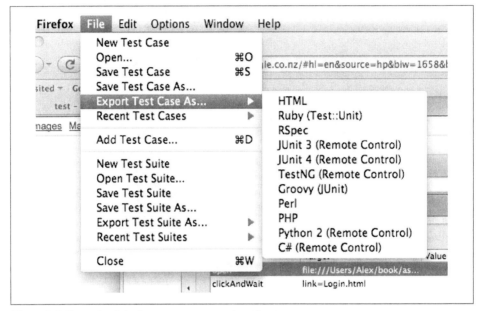

Figure 9-5. Exporting Selenium test cases to various formats

We can now make assertions on the @selenium object, such as ensuring that a particular bit of text is present:

```
def test_selenium
  # ...
  assert @selenium.is_text_present("elvis")
end
```

For more information about Selenium, visit the website and watch the introduction screencast (*http://seleniumhq.org/movies/intro.mov*).

Headless Testing

With the development of server-side JavaScript implementations such as Node.js and Rhino comes the possibility of running your tests outside the browser in a headless environment via the command line. This has the advantage of speed and ease of setup, as it does away with the multitude of browsers and the continuous integration environment. The disadvantage, of course, is that the tests aren't being run in a real-world environment.

This might not be as big a problem as it sounds, as you'll find that most of the JavaScript you write is application logic and not browser-dependent. In addition, libraries like jQuery have taken care of a lot of browser incompatibilities when it comes to the DOM and event management. For smaller applications, as long as you have a staging environment when deploying and some high-level cross-browser integration tests (whether manual or automated), you should be fine.

Envjs (*http://www.envjs.com*) is a library originally developed by John Resig, creator of the jQuery JavaScript framework. It offers an implementation of the browser and DOM APIs on top of Rhino, Mozilla's Java implementation of JavaScript. You can use the env.js library together with Rhino to run JavaScript tests on the command line.

Zombie

Zombie.js (*http://zombie.labnotes.org*) is a headless library designed to take advantage of the incredible performance and asynchronous nature of Node.js. Speed is a key feature: the less time you spend waiting for tests to complete, the more time you get to build new features and fix bugs.

Applications that use a lot of client-side JavaScript spend much of their time loading, parsing, and evaluating that JavaScript. Here, the sheer performance of Google's V8 JavaScript engine helps your tests run faster.

Although your test suite and client-side JavaScript both run on the same engine, Zombie uses another feature of V8—*contexts*—which keeps them separated so they do not mix the same global variables/state. It's similar to the way Chrome opens each tab in its own process.

Another benefit of contexts is being able to run multiple tests in parallel, each using its own `Browser` object. One test might be checking the DOM content while another test is waiting for a page request to come back, cutting down the time it takes to complete the entire test suite. You'll need to use an asynchronous test framework, such as the excellent Vows.js (*http://vowsjs.org*), and pay attention to which tests must run in parallel and which must run in sequence.

Zombie.js provides a `Browser` object that works much like a real web browser: it maintains state between pages (cookies, history, web storage) and provides access to the current window (and through it the loaded document). In addition, it provides you with methods for manipulating the current window, acting like a user (visiting pages, filling forms, clicking prompts, etc.) and inspecting the window contents (using XPath or CSS selectors).

For example, to fill in the username and password, submit a form and then test the contents of the title element:

```
// Fill email, password, and submit form.
browser.
  fill("email", "zombie@underworld.dead").
  fill("password", "eat-the-living").
  pressButton("Sign Me Up!", function(err, browser) {
  // Form submitted, new page loaded.
  assert.equal(browser.text("title"), "Welcome to Brains Depot");
  });
```

This example is incomplete. Obviously, you'll need to require the Zombie.js library, create a new Browser, and load the page before you can interact with it. You also want to take care of that err argument.

Just like a web browser, Zombie.js is asynchronous in nature: your code doesn't block waiting for a page to load, an event to fire, or a timer to timeout. Instead, you can either register listeners for events such as *loaded* and *error*, or pass a callback.

By convention, when you pass Zombie a callback, it will use it one of two ways. If the action was successful, it will pass null and some other value, most often a reference to the Browser object. If the action failed, it will pass a reference to the Error object. So, make sure to check the first argument to determine whether your request completed successfully, and whether there's anything interesting in the remaining arguments.

This convention is common to Node.js and many libraries written for it, including the aforementioned Vows.js test framework. Vows.js also uses callbacks, which it expects to be called with one argument that is error or null; if that argument is null, a second argument is passed along to the test case.

Here, for example, is a test case that uses Zombie.js and Vows.js. It visits a web page and looks for elements with the class *brains* (expecting to find none):

```
var zombie = require("zombie");

vows.describe("Zombie lunch").addBatch({
  "visiting home page": {
    topic: function() {
      var browser = new zombie.Browser;
      browser.cookies("localhost").update("session_id=5678");
      browser.visit("http://localhost:3003/", this.callback);
    },
    "should find no brains": function(browser) {
      assert.isEmpty(browser.css(".brains"));
    }
  }
});
```

There are many other things you can do with Zombie.js. For example, you can save the browser state (cookies, history, web storage, etc.) after running one test and use that state to run other tests (to start each test from the state of "new session and user logged in").

You can also fire DOM events—e.g., to simulate a mouse click—or respond to confirmation prompts and alerts. You can view the history of requests and responses, similar to the Resources tab in WebKit's Web Inspector. Although Zombie runs on Node.js, it can make HTTP requests to any web server, so you can certainly use it to test your Ruby or Python application.

Ichabod

The imaginatively named Ichabod (*http://github.com/maccman/ichabod*) library is another alternative for running tests headlessly, and it is a great solution if you're after simplicity and speed.

The advantage to Ichabod is that, rather than an emulation of the DOM and parser engine, it uses WebKit—the browser engine behind Safari and Chrome. However, Ichabod works only on OS X, as it requires MacRuby and the OS X WebView APIs.

Installation is pretty straightforward. First, install MacRuby, either off the project's site (*http://www.macruby.org*) or with rvm (*http://rvm.beginrescueend.com/interpreters/macruby/*). Then, install the Ichabod gem:

```
$ macgem install ichabod
```

Ichabod currently supports running Jasmine or QUnit tests, although additional libraries will be supported soon. Simply pass the test's endpoint to the ichabod executable:

```
$ ichabod --jasmine http://path/to/jasmine/specs.html
$ ichabod --qunit http://path/to/qunit/tests.html
```

The tests don't have to be hosted—you can also pass a local path:

```
$ ichabod --jasmine ./tests/index.html
...
Finished in 0.393 seconds
1 test, 5 assertions, 0 failures
```

Ichabod will load up all your tests and run them in a GUI-less version of WebKit, straight from the command line.

Distributed Testing

One solution to cross-browser testing is outsourcing the problem to a dedicated cluster of browsers. This is exactly the approach of TestSwarm (*http://swarm.jquery.org*):

> The primary goal of TestSwarm is to take the complicated, and time-consuming, process of running JavaScript test suites in multiple browsers and to grossly simplify it. It achieves this goal by providing all the tools necessary for creating a continuous integration workflow for your JavaScript project.

Rather than using plug-ins and extensions to integrate with browsers at a low level, TestSwarm takes the reverse approach. Browsers open up the TestSwarm endpoint, and automatically process tests pushed toward them. They can be located on any machine or operating system—all it takes to add a new browser is to navigate to the TestSwarm endpoint inside it.

This simple approach takes a lot of the pain and hassle out of running a continuous integration server. All that's involved is ensuring a decent number of browsers are connected to the swarm. Indeed, this is something you could outsource if you have an active community, achieving probably the most realistic testbed you could hope for, as shown in Figure 9-6.

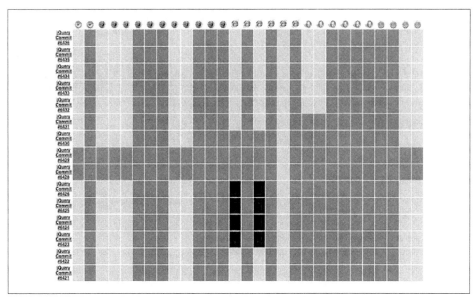

Figure 9-6. TestSwarm returns results to browsers as a grid of test suites

The alternative is to use a company like Sauce Labs (*http://saucelabs.com*) to manage and run all those browsers in the cloud. Simply upload any Selenium tests and their service will do the rest, running the tests on different browsers and platforms, making sure they all pass.

Providing Support

However many tests you write for your application, the likelihood is that there will always be bugs. The best thing to do is to accept this fact and prepare for users to come across bugs and errors. Provide an easy way for users to submit bug reports and set up a ticketing system to manage support requests.

Inspectors

JavaScript development and debugging has come a long way from the `alert()` calls of the past. Most of the major browsers now include powerful element inspectors and debuggers, which simplifies and improves web development dramatically. We're going to cover the two main inspectors next, but the general concepts should transfer over to any inspector you choose to use.

Web Inspector

Web Inspector is available on both the Safari and Google Chrome browsers. The inspector's interface differs slightly between the two browsers, but the functionality is fairly consistent.

In Safari, you have to enable it explicitly by checking the advanced preference, "Show Develop menu in menu bar," as shown in Figure 9-7.

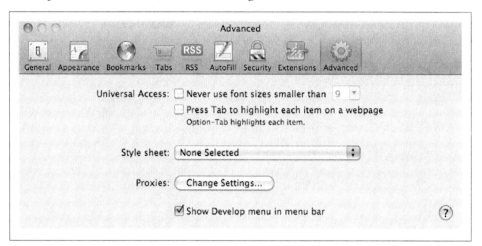

Figure 9-7. Enabling Safari Inspector

Chrome has a developer toolbar under the View toolbar, which you can use to enable the inspector. The alternative in both browsers is to right-click on an element and select "inspect".

Web Inspector, shown in Figure 9-8, is an incredibly useful tool, letting you inspect HTML elements, edit styles, debug JavaScript, and more. If it isn't the case already, the inspector should be part of your day-to-day JavaScript development.

We're going to cover more of its features in detail, but here's a basic overview of Web Inspector's components:

Elements
    Inspect HTML elements, edit styles

Resources
> Page resources and assets

Network
> HTTP requests

Scripts
> JavaScript files and debugger

Timeline
> Detailed view of browser rendering

Audits
> Code and memory auditor

Console
> Execute JavaScript and see logging

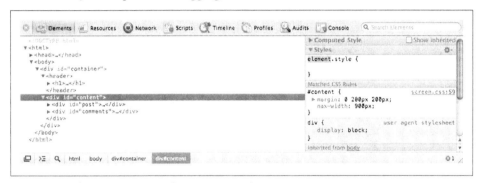

Figure 9-8. Safari's Web Inspector lets you inspect the DOM

Firebug

Firefox doesn't include a JavaScript inspector natively, but it has an excellent add-on to do the job: Firebug (*http://getfirebug.com/*). See Figure 9-9.

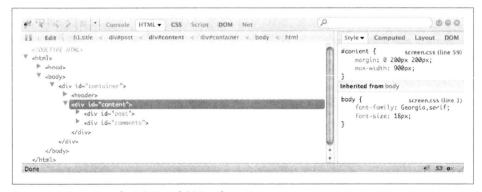

Figure 9-9. Inspecting the DOM and CSS with FireBug

You'll see that although the various components to Firebug have different names to their counterparts in Web Inspector, their functionality is very similar:

Console
> Execute JavaScript and see logging

HTML
> Inspect elements, edit styles

CSS
> See and edit the page's CSS

Script
> JavaScript files and debugger

DOM
> Global variable inspection

Net
> HTTP requests

Firebug's team has developed a Firefox-independent version, Firebug Lite (*http://get firebug.com/firebuglite*). It has the vast majority of features from Firebug, as well as the same look and feel, and it's compatible with all major browsers. Firebug Lite is especially useful for debugging Internet Explorer (it's rather superior to IE's built-in tools). Firebug Lite doesn't require any installation, and it can be added to a web page using a simple script tag:

```
<script type="text/javascript" src="https://getfirebug.com/firebug-lite.js"></script>
```

Alternatively, you can install the bookmarklet from the Firebug Lite (*http://getfirebug .com/firebuglite#Stable*) website.

The Console

The console lets you easily execute JavaScript and examine the pages' global variables. One of the major advantages to the console is that you can log directly to it, using the `console.log()` function. The call is asynchronous, can take multiple arguments, and inspects those arguments, rather than converting them to strings:

```
console.log("test");
console.log(1, 2, {3: "three"});
```

There are additional types of logging. You can use `console.warn()` and `console .error()` to elevate the logging level, giving an early indication that something might be going wrong:

```
console.warn("a diabolical warning");
console.error("something broke!");

try {
  // Raises something
```

```
    } catch(e) {
      console.error("App error!", e);
    }
```

It's also possible to namespace log calls by using a proxy function:

```
var App = {trace: true};
App.log = function(){
  if (!this.trace) return;
  if (typeof console == "undefined") return;
  var slice = Array.prototype.slice;
  var args  = slice.call(arguments, 0);
  args.unshift("(App)");
  console.log.apply(console, args);
};
```

The `App.log()` function prepends the string `"App"` to its arguments and then passes the call onto `console.log()`.

Keep in mind that when using the console for logging, the variable `console` may not be defined. In browsers that don't have support for the console—such as Internet Explorer or Firefox without Firebug—the `console` object won't be defined, causing errors if you try to use it. This is a good reason for using a proxy function like `App.log()` when logging inside your application.

You can output the scripts' current stack trace to the console using `console.trace()`. This is especially useful if you're trying to work out how a function is being called because it traces the stack back through the program:

```
// Log stack trace
console.trace();
```

The application's errors will also appear in the console and, unless the browser's JIT compiler has optimized the function call, the console will show a full stack trace.

Console Helpers

The console also includes a number of shortcuts and helper functions to save some typing. For example, the `$0` to `$4` variables contain the current and previous three selected nodes in Web Inspector or Firebug. Believe me, this is extremely useful when you want to access and manipulate elements:

```
// $0 is the currently selected element
$0.style.color = "green";

// Or, using jQuery
jQuery($0).css({background: "black"});
```

The `$()` function returns the element with the specified ID. It's essentially a shortcut to `document.getElementById()`. jQuery, Prototype, or a similar library that already uses `$` will override this:

```
$("user").addEventListener("click", function(){ /* ... */});
```

The $$() function returns the array of elements that match the given CSS selector. This is similar to document.querySelectorAll(). Again, if you use Prototype or MooTools, those libraries will override this:

```
// Select elements with a class of .users
var users = $$(".users");
users.forEach(function(){ /* ... */ });
```

The $x() function returns the array of elements that matches the given XPath expression:

```
// Select all forms
var checkboxes = $x("/html/body//form");
```

The clear() function clears the console:

```
clear();
```

dir() prints an interactive listing of all the object's properties:

```
dir({one: 1});
```

inspect() takes an element, database, or storage area as an argument, and automatically jumps to the appropriate panel to display the relevant information:

```
inspect($("user"));
```

keys() returns an array containing the names of all the object's properties:

```
// Returns ["two"]
keys({two: 2});
```

values() returns an array containing the values of all the object's properties—i.e., the opposite of keys():

```
// Returns [2]
values({two: 2});
```

Using the Debugger

The JavaScript debugger is one of the best-kept secrets in JavaScript development. It's a full-featured debugger that allows you to place breakpoints, watch expressions, examine variables, and work out exactly what's going on.

Placing a breakpoint is easy—just add the debugger statement inside the script at the point you want the debugger to pause execution:

```
var test = function(){
  // ...
  debugger
};
```

Alternatively, you can go to the Scripts panel in the inspector, select the relevant script, and click on the line number where you want to place the breakpoint. Figure 9-10 shows an example.

Figure 9-10. Setting a breakpoint with Safari's Web Inspector

The latter approach is probably preferable because you don't want to risk getting any debugger statements in production code. When the JavaScript execution reaches the breakpoint, it's paused, letting you examine the current scope, as shown in Figure 9-11.

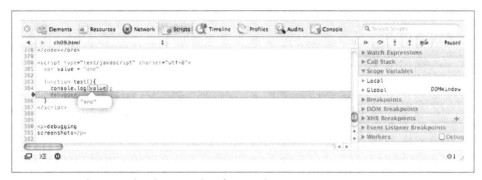

Figure 9-11. Debugging a breakpoint with Safari's Web Inspector

On the right of the inspector's Scripts panel, you can see the full call stack, the local and global variables, and other relevant debugging information. You can hover the mouse over any variable to see its current value. The console is even scoped to the breakpoint, allowing you to manipulate variables and call other functions.

You can continue code execution, step into or over the next function call, and navigate up the current stack using the Debugger toolbar on the right. The Debugger toolbar icons are specific to the browser, but you can determine each button's function by hovering the mouse over it, which displays a yellow information bubble.

It's important to remember that breakpoints remain between page reloads. If you want to remove a breakpoint, simply toggle its line number, or uncheck it in the breakpoint list. The JavaScript debugger is a wonderful alternative to console.log(), as it helps you work out exactly what's happening inside your application.

Analyzing Network Requests

As shown in Figure 9-12, the inspector's network section shows all the HTTP requests the page is making, how long they took, and when they completed.

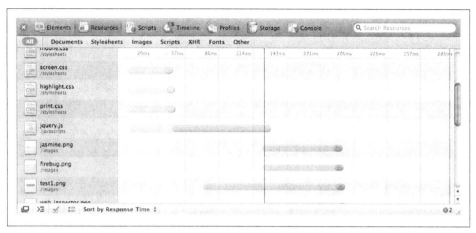

Figure 9-12. Analyzing network requests with Web Inspector

You can see the initial request's latency, which is a slightly transparent color. Then, when data starts getting received, the timeline's color goes opaque. In the example above, jQuery's file size is much bigger than the stylesheets', so although the initial request latency is similar, the script takes longer to download.

If you're not using the `async` or `defer` option with your scripts (see Chapter 10), you'll notice that JavaScript files are downloaded sequentially rather than in parallel. Scripts are requested only after the previous referenced script has been fully downloaded and executed. All other resources are downloaded in parallel.

The lines in the network timeline indicate the pages' load status. The blue line appears at the time the document's *DOMContentLoaded* event was fired or, in other words, when the DOM is ready. The red line appears once the window's *load* event is triggered, when all the page's images have been fully downloaded and the page has finished loading.

The network section also shows the full request and response headers for every request, which is especially useful for making sure any caching is being applied correctly. See Figure 9-13.

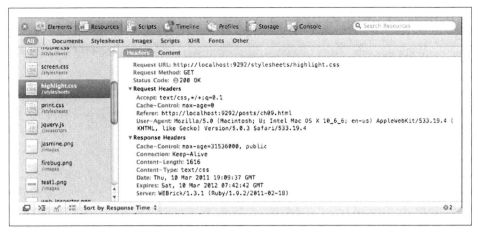

Figure 9-13. Viewing an in-depth analysis of network requests, such as request and response headers

Profile and Timing

When you're building large JavaScript apps, you need to keep an eye on performance, especially if you've got mobile clients. Both Web Inspector and Firebug include profiling and timing utilities that can help keep things ticking smoothly.

Profiling code is simple—just surround any code you want to profile with `console.pro file()` and `console.profileEnd()`:

```
console.profile();
// ...
console.profileEnd();
```

As soon as `profileEnd()` is called, a profile will be created, listing all the functions (and the time taken in each one) that were called between the two statements. See Figure 9-14 for an illustration.

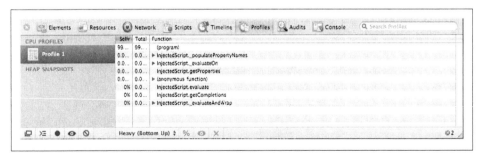

Figure 9-14. Profiling function execution rates with Web Inspector

Alternatively, you can use the *record* feature of the inspector's profiler, which is equivalent to wrapping code with the profile console statements. By seeing which functions are being called and which functions are taking longer to complete, you can discover and optimize bottlenecks in your code.

The profiler also allows you to take a *snapshot* of the page's current heap, as illustrated in Figure 9-15. This will show you how many objects have been allocated and the amount of memory the page is using. This is a great way of finding memory leaks because you can see whether any objects are being unwittingly stored, and are subsequently unable to be garbage collected.

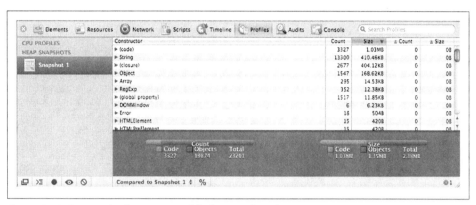

Figure 9-15. Seeing a bird's-eye view of the heap with Web Inspector

The console also lets you time how long it takes to execute some code. The API is similar to the profiler—simply wrap the code with `console.time(name)` and `console.time End(name)`. Unless you manage to fit everything on one line, you won't be able to time code from inside the JavaScript console accurately; instead, you will have to add the timing statements directly into your scripts:

```
console.time("timeName");
// ...
console.timeEnd("timeName");
```

When `timeEnd()` is called, the time taken between the two timing statements is sent to the console's log in milliseconds. Using the console's timing API, you could potentially incorporate benchmarking into your application's tests, ensuring that additional code wasn't significantly hurting the application's existing performance.

## CHAPTER 10

Deploying

Deploying your web application properly is just as important as actually developing it; there's no point in building the next Facebook if it loads too slowly for people to actually use it. Users want your site to be as reliable and fast as possible, with good uptime. Deploying JavaScript and HTML files sounds straightforward—they're static assets after all—but there's actually a fair amount to it. This is an often neglected part to web application building.

Luckily, there are a few tried-and-tested techniques that should apply to all JavaScript applications, and indeed serving any kind of static assets. If you follow the recommendations below, you should be well on your way to delivering speedy web apps.

Performance

One of the simplest ways of increasing performance is also the most obvious: minimize the amount of HTTP requests. Every HTTP request contains a lot of header information, as well as the TCP overhead. Keeping separate connections to an absolute minimum will ensure pages load faster for users. This clearly extends to the amount of data the server needs to transfer. Keeping a page and its assets' file size low will decrease any network time—the real bottleneck to any application on the Web.

Concatenating scripts into a single script and combining CSS into a single stylesheet will reduce the amount of HTTP connections needed to render the page. You can do this upon deployment or at runtime. If it's the latter, make sure any files generated are cached in production.

Use CSS sprites to combine images into one comprehensive image. Then, use the CSS `background-image` and `background-position` properties to display the relevant images in your page. You just have to scope the background position coordinates to cover the desired image.

Avoiding redirects also keeps the number of HTTP requests to a minimum. You may think these are fairly uncommon, but one of the most frequent redirect scenarios occurs when a trailing slash (/) is missing from a URL that should otherwise have one. For example, going to *http://facebook.com* currently redirects you to *http://facebook.com/*. If you're using Apache, you can fix this by using Alias or mod_rewrite.

It's also important to understand how your browser downloads resources. To speed up page rendering, modern browsers download required resources in parallel. However, the page can't start rendering until all the stylesheets and scripts have finished downloading. Some browsers go even further, blocking all other downloads while any JavaScript files are being processed.

However, most scripts need to access the DOM and add things like event handlers, which are executed after the page loads. In other words, the browser is needlessly restricting the page rendering until everything's finished downloading, decreasing performance. You can solve this by setting the defer attribute on scripts, letting the browser know the script won't need to manipulate the DOM until after the page has loaded:

```
<script src="foo.js" type="text/javascript" charset="utf-8" defer></script>
```

Scripts with the defer attribute set to "defer" will be downloaded in parallel with other resources and won't prevent page rendering. HTML5 has also introduced a new mode of script downloading and execution called async. By setting the async attribute, the script will be executed at the first opportunity after it's finished downloading. This means it's possible (and likely) that async scripts are not executed in the order in which they occur in the page, leaving an opportunity for dependency errors. If the script doesn't have any dependencies, though, async is a useful tool. Google Analytics, for example, takes advantage of it by default:

```
<script src="http://www.google-analytics.com/ga.js" async></script>
```

Caching

If it weren't for caching, the Web would collapse under network traffic. Caching stores recently requested resources locally so subsequent requests can serve them up from the disk, rather than downloading them again. It's important to explicitly tell browsers what you want cached. Some browsers like Chrome will make their own default decisions, but you shouldn't rely on that.

For static resources, make the cache "never" expire by adding a far future Expires header. This will ensure that the browser only ever downloads the resource once, and it should then be set on all static components, including scripts, stylesheets, and images.

```
Expires: Thu, 20 March 2015 00:00:00 GMT
```

You should set the expiry date in the far future relative to the current date. The example above tells the browser the cache won't be stale until March 20th, 2015. If you're using the Apache web server, you can set a relative expiration date easily using ExpiresDefault:

```
ExpiresDefault "access plus 5 years"
```

But what if you want to expire the resource before that time? A useful technique is to append the file's modified time (or mtime) as a query parameter on URLs referencing it. Rails, for example, does this by default. Then, whenever the file is modified, the resource's URL will change, clearing out the cache.

```
<link rel="stylesheet" href="master.css?1296085785" type="text/css">
```

HTTP 1.1. introduced a new class of headers, `Cache-Control`, to give developers more advanced caching and to address the limitations of `Expires`. The `Cache-Control` control header can take a number of options, separated by commas:

```
Cache-Control: max-age=3600, must-revalidate
```

To see the full list of options, visit the specification (*http://www.ietf.org/rfc/rfc2616 .txt*). The ones you're likely to use now are listed below:

`max-age`
Specifies the maximum amount of time, in seconds, that a resource will be considered fresh. Unlike `Expires`, which is absolute, this directive is relative to the time of the request.

`public`
Marks resources as cacheable. By default, if resources are served over SSL or if HTTP authentication is used, caching is turned off.

`no-store`
Turns off caching completely, which is something you'll want to do for dynamic content only.

`must-revalidate`
Tells caches they must obey any information you give them regarding resource freshness. Under certain conditions, HTTP allows caches to serve stale resources according to their own rules. By specifying this header, you're telling the cache that you want it to strictly follow your rules.

Adding a `Last-Modified` header to the served resource can also help caching. With subsequent requests to the resource, browsers can specify the `If-Modified-Since` header, which contains a timestamp. If the resource hasn't been modified since the last request, the server can just return a 304 (not modified) status. The browser still has to make the request, but the server doesn't have to include the resource in its response, saving network time and bandwidth:

```
# Request
GET /example.gif HTTP/1.1
Host:www.example.com
If-Modified-Since:Thu, 29 Apr 2010 12:09:05 GMT

# Response
HTTP/1.1 200 OK
Date: Thu, 20 March 2009 00:00:00 GMT
Server: Apache/1.3.3 (Unix)
Cache-Control: max-age=3600, must-revalidate
```

```
Expires: Fri, 30 Oct 1998 14:19:41 GMT
Last-Modified: Mon, 17 March 2009 00:00:00 GMT
Content-Length: 1040
Content-Type: text/html
```

There is an alternative to `Last-Modified`: ETags. Comparing ETags is like comparing the hashes of two files; if the ETags are different, the cache is stale and must be revalidated. This works in a similar way to the `Last-Modified` header. The server will attach an ETag to a resource with an `ETag` header, and a client will check ETags with an `If-None-Match` header:

```
# Request
GET /example.gif HTTP/1.1
Host:www.example.com
If-Modified-Since:Thu, 29 Apr 2010 12:09:05 GMT
If-None-Match:"48ef9-14a1-4855efe32ba40"

# Response
HTTP/1.1 304 Not Modified
```

ETags are typically constructed with attributes specific to the server—i.e., two separate servers will give different ETags for the same resource. With clusters becoming more and more common, this is a real issue. Personally, I advise you to stick with **Last-Modified** and turn off ETags altogether.

Minification

JavaScript minification reduces unnecessary characters from scripts without changing any functionality. These characters include whitespace, new lines, and comments. The better minifiers can interpret JavaScript. Therefore, they can safely shorten variables and function names, further reducing characters. Smaller file sizes are better because there's less data to transfer over the network.

It's not just JavaScript that can be minified. Stylesheets and HTML can also be processed. Stylesheets in particular tend to have a lot of redundant whitespace. Minification is something best done on deployment because you don't want to be debugging any minified code. If there's an error in production, try to reproduce it in a development environment first—you'll find it much easier to debug the problem.

Minification has the additional benefit of obscuring your code. It's true that a sufficiently motivated person could probably reconstruct it, but it's a barrier to entry for the casual observer.

There are a lot of minimizing libraries out there, but I advise you to choose one with a JavaScript engine that can actually interpret the code. YUI Compressor (*http://developer .yahoo.com/yui/compressor*) is my favorite because it is well maintained and supported. Created by Yahoo! engineer Julien Lecomte, its goal was to shrink JavaScript files even further than JSMin (*http://www.crockford.com/javascript/jsmin.html*) by applying smart optimizations to the source code. Suppose we have the following function:

```
function per(value, total) {
  return( (value / total) * 100 );
}
```

YUI Compressor will, in addition to removing whitespace, shorten the local variables, saving yet more characters:

```
function per(b,a){return((b/a)*100)};
```

Because YUI Compressor actually parses the JavaScript, it can usually replace variables—without introducing code errors. However, this isn't always the case; sometimes the compressor can't fathom your code, so it leaves it alone. The most common reason for this is the use of an `eval()` or `with()` statement. If the compressor detects you're using either of those, it won't perform variable name replacement. In addition, both `eval()` and `with()` can cause performance problems—the browser's JIT compiler has the same issue as the compressor. My advice is to stay well clear of either of these statements.

The simplest way to use YUI Compressor is by downloading the binaries (*http://yuili brary.com/downloads/#yuicompressor*), which require Java, and executing them on the command line:

```
java -jar yuicompressor-x.y.z.jar foo.js | foo.min.js
```

However, you can do this programmatically on deployment. If you're using a library like Sprockets (*http://getsprockets.org*) or Less (*http://lesscss.org*), they'll do this for you. Otherwise, there are several interface libraries to YUI Compressor, such as Sam Stephenson's Ruby-YUI-compressor gem (*https://github.com/sstephenson/ruby-yui-com pressor*) or the Jammit library (*http://documentcloud.github.com/jammit*).

Gzip Compression

Gzip is the most popular and supported compression method on the Web. It was developed by the GNU project, and support for it was added in HTTP/1.1. Web clients indicate their support for compression by sending an `Accept-Encoding` header along with the request:

```
Accept-Encoding: gzip, deflate
```

If the web server sees this header and supports any of the compression types listed, it may compress its response and indicate this via the `Content-Encoding` header:

```
Content-Encoding: gzip
```

Browsers can then decode the response properly. Obviously, compressing the data can reduce network time, but the true extent of this is often not realized. Gzip generally reduces the response size by 70%, a massive reduction that greatly speeds up the time it takes for your site to load.

Servers generally have to be configured over which file types should be gzipped. A good rule of thumb is to gzip any text response, such as HTML, JSON, JavaScript, and stylesheets. If the files are already compressed, such as images and PDFs, they shouldn't be served with gzip because the recompression doesn't reduce their size.

Configuring gzip depends on your web server, but if you use Apache 2.x or later, the module you need is mod_deflate (*http://httpd.apache.org/docs/2.0/mod/mod_deflate .html*). For other web servers, see their documentation.

Using a CDN

A content delivery network, or CDN, can serve static content on your behalf, reducing its load time. The user's proximity to the web server can have an impact on load times. CDNs can deploy your content across multiple geographically dispersed servers, so when a user requests a resource, it can be served up from a server near them (ideally in the same country). Yahoo! has found that CDNs can improve enduser response times by 20% or more (*http://developer.yahoo.com/performance/rules.html#cdn*).

Depending on how much you can afford to spend, there are lot of companies out there offering CDNs, such as Akamai Technologies (*http://www.akamai.com*), Limelight Networks (*http://www.limelightnetworks.com*), EdgeCast (*http://www.edgecast.com*), and Level 3 Communications (*http://www.level3.com*). Amazon Web Services (*http://aws.amazon.com*) has recently released an affordable option called Cloud Front (*http://aws.amazon.com/cloudfront*) that ties into its S3 service (*http://aws.amazon.com/s3*) closely and may be a good option for startups.

Google offers a free CDN and loading architecture for many popular open source Java-Script libraries, including jQuery and jQueryUI. One of the advantages of using Google's CDN is that many other sites use it too, increasing the likelihood that any Java-Script files you reference are already cached in a user's browser.

Check out the list of available libraries (*http://code.google.com/apis/libraries/devguide .html*). If, say, you want to include the jQuery library (*http://code.google.com/apis/libra ries/devguide.html#jquery*), you can either use Google's JavaScript loader library or, more simply, a plain old script tag:

```
<!-- minimized version of the jQuery library -->
<script src="//ajax.googleapis.com/ajax/libs/jquery/1.4.4/jquery.min.js"></script>

<!-- minimized version of the jQuery UI library -->
<script src="//ajax.googleapis.com/ajax/libs/jqueryui/1.8.6/jquery-ui.min.js">
</script>
```

You'll notice that in the example above we haven't specified a protocol; instead, // is used. This is a little-known trick that ensures the script file is fetched using the same protocol as the host page. In other words, if your page was loaded securely over HTTPS, the script file will be as well, eliminating any security warnings. A relative URL without a scheme is valid and compliant to the RTF spec. More importantly, it's got support across the board; heck, protocol-relative URLs even work in Internet Explorer 3.0.

Auditors

There are some really good tools to give you a quick heads up regarding your site's performance. YSlow (*http://developer.yahoo.com/yslow*) is an extension of Firebug, which is in turn a Firefox extension. You'll need to install all three to use it. Once it's installed, you can use it to audit web pages. The extension will run through a series of checks, including caching, minification, gzipping, and CDNs. It will give your site a grade, depending on how it fares, and then offer advice on how to improve your score.

Google Chrome and Safari also have auditors, but these are built right into the browser. As shown in Chrome in Figure 10-1, simply go to the Audits section of Web Inspector and click Run. This is a great way of seeing what things your site could improve on to increase its performance.

Figure 10-1. Auditing web page performance with Web Inspector

Resources

Both Yahoo! and Google have invested a huge amount into analyzing web performance. Increasing sites' render speed is obviously in their best interest, both for their own services and for the user experience of their customers when browsing the wider Web. Indeed, Google now takes speed into account with its Pagerank algorithm, which helps determine where sites are ranked for search queries. Both companies have excellent resources on improving performance, which you can find on the Google (*http://code .google.com/speed/page-speed/docs/payload.html*) and Yahoo! (*http://code.google.com/ speed/page-speed/docs/payload.html*) developer sites.

## CHAPTER 11

The Spine Library

Spine (*http://maccman.github.com/spine*) is a lightweight library for JavaScript application development that uses many of the concepts we've covered in this book, such as MVC, events, and classes. When I say lightweight, I mean lightweight—the library comes in at around 500 lines of JavaScript, which is about 2K minified and compressed. Don't get the wrong impression, though; Spine will let you build fully featured Java-Script applications while ensuring your code remains clean and decoupled.

I created Spine while writing this book because I couldn't find a client-side MVC framework that quite suited my needs. The library attempts to enshrine many of the best practices proposed in this book, and indeed the book's example application, Holla, is built using Spine.

Unlike widget-based libraries such as Cappuccino (*http://cappuccino.org*) and Sprout-Core (*http://sproutcore.com*), Spine doesn't make any decisions about how you display data to users. The emphasis is on flexibility and simplicity. Spine gives you the bare bones and gets out of your way so you get on with the fun stuff—developing awesome applications.

Spine includes a class library with inheritance support; `Spine.Class`; an events module, `Spine.Events`; an ORM, `Spine.Model`; and a controller class, `Spine.Controller`. Anything else you'll need, like templating support or a DOM library, is up to you, so use what you're most familiar with. Having said that, Spine includes specific support for jQuery and Zepto.js libraries, which complement it excellently.

Spine's weakness at the moment is its lack of documentation. But since it's still the early days of this library, the documentation situation is sure to improve. For now, this chapter should give you a pretty good introduction, and the sample applications will provide further explanation.

Setup

Simply download Spine from the project's repository (*http://github.com/maccman/spine*) and include it in your page; Spine has no dependencies:

```
<script src="spine.js" type="text/javascript" charset="utf-8"></script>
```

Spine is completely namespaced behind the Spine variable, so it shouldn't conflict with any other variables. You can safely include libraries like jQuery, Zepto, or Prototype without any complications.

Classes

Pretty much every object in Spine is encapsulated in a class. However, Spine's classes are constructed using Object.create() and pure prototypal inheritance, as covered in Chapter 3, which is different from how most class abstractions are constructed.

To create a new class, call Spine.Class.create([instanceProperties, classProperties]), passing an optional set of instance and class properties:

```
var User = Spine.Class.create({
  name: "Caroline"
});
```

In the example above, instances of User now have a default name property. Behind the scenes, create() is creating a new object whose prototype is set to Spine.Class —i.e., it's inheriting from it. If you want to create subsequent subclasses, simply call create() on their parent class:

```
var Friend = User.create();
```

Friend is now a subclass of User and will inherit all of its properties:

```
assertEqual( Friend.prototype.name, "Caroline" );
```

Instantiation

Because we're using pure prototypal objects and inheritance instead of constructor functions, we can't use the new keyword for instantiating instances. Rather, Spine uses the init() function:

```
var user = User.init();
assertEqual( user.name,  "Caroline" );

user.name = "Trish";
assertEqual( user.name, "Trish" );
```

Any arguments passed to init() will be sent to the instances initializer function, init():

```
var User = Spine.Class.create({
  init: function(name){
    this.name = name;
```

```
  }
});

var user = User.init("Martina");
assertEqual( user.name, "Martina" );
```

Extending Classes

As well as setting class and instance properties during creation, you can use `include` () and `extend()`, passing in an object literal:

```
User.include({
  // Instance properties
});

User.extend({
  // Class properties
});
```

`include()` and `extend()` pave the way for modules, which are reusable pieces of code that you can include multiple times:

```
var ORM = {
  extended: function(){
    // invoked when extended
    //   this === User
  },
  find:  function(){ /* ... */ },
  first: function(){ /* ... */ }
};

User.extend( ORM );
```

You can receive a callback when a module is included or extended. In the example above, the `extended` function will be invoked when `User.extend()` is called with a context of `User`. Likewise, if a module has an `included` property, it will be invoked when the module is included inside a class.

Because we're using prototypal-based inheritance, any properties we add onto classes will be reflected dynamically across subclasses at runtime:

```
var Friend = User.create();

User.include({
  email: "info@eribium.org"
});

assertEqual( Friend.init().email, "info@eribium.org" );
```

Properties in subclasses can be overridden without affecting the parent class. However, modifications to objects in subclasses, such as arrays, will be reflected across the whole inheritance tree. If you want an object to be specific to a class or instance, you'll need to create it when the class or instance is first initialized. You can do this in a `created` () function, which Spine will call when the class is first set up or instantiated:

```
// We want the records array to be specific to the class
var User = Spine.Class.create({
  // Called on instantiation
  init: function(){
    this.attributes = {};
  }
}, {
  // Called when the class is created
  created: function(){
    this.records = [];
  }
});
```

Context

Context changes are rife within JavaScript programs, so `Spine.Class` includes some utility methods for controlling scope. To demonstrate the problem, take this example:

```
var Controller = Spine.Class.create({
  init: function(){
    // Add event listener
    $("#destroy").click(this.destroy);
  },

  destroy: function(){
    // This destroy function is called with the wrong context,
    // so any references to `this` will cause problems
    // The following assertion will fail:
    assertEqual( this, Controller.fn );
  }
});
```

In the example above, when the event is invoked, the `destroy()` function will be called with the context of the element #destroy, rather than the Controller. To deal with this, you can proxy the context, forcing it to be a particular one you specify. Spine gives you the `proxy()` function to do that:

```
var Controller = Spine.Class.create({
  init: function(){
    $("#destroy").click(this.proxy(this.destroy));
  },

  destroy: function(){ }
});
```

If you find you're constantly proxying a function, you may want to rewrite it to always include a proxy. Spine includes a `proxyAll()` function to do just that:

```
var Controller = Spine.Class.create({
  init: function(){
    this.proxyAll("destroy", "render")
    $("#destroy").click(this.destroy);
  },

  // Functions are now always called with the correct context
```

```
    destroy: function(){ },
    render:  function(){ }
});
```

`proxyAll()` takes multiple function names, and when invoked, it will rewrite them, proxying the functions with the current scope. This will ensure that `destroy()` or `ren der()` will always be executed in the local context.

Events

Events are key to Spine, and they are frequently used internally. Spine's event functionality is contained inside the module `Spine.Events`, which can be included wherever it's needed. For example, let's add some event support to a Spine class:

```
var User = Spine.Class.create();
User.extend(Spine.Events);
```

`Spine.Events` gives you three functions for handling events:

- `bind(eventName, callback)`
- `trigger(eventName, [*data])`
- `unbind(eventName, [callback])`

If you've used jQuery's event API, this will look very familiar to you. For example, let's bind and trigger an event on our `User` class:

```
User.bind("create", function(){ /* ... */ });
User.trigger("create");
```

To bind multiple events with a single callback, just separate them with spaces:

```
User.bind("create update", function(){ /* ... */ });
```

`trigger()` takes an event name and passes optional arguments along to the event's callbacks:

```
User.bind("countChange", function(count){
  // `count` is passed by trigger
  assertEqual(count, 5);
});

User.trigger("countChange", 5);
```

You will most commonly use Spine's events with data binding, hooking up your application's models with its views. We'll cover that in detail later in the section "Building a Contacts Manager" on page 156.

Models

If you take a peek at Spine's source code (*https://github.com/maccman/spine/blob/mas ter/spine.js*), you'll see that the vast majority of it deals with models, and rightly so—models are the central part of any MVC application. Models deal with storing and manipulating your application's data, and Spine simplifies this by providing a full ORM.

Rather than use the create() function to make a new model, which is already reserved, use Spine.Model.setup(name, attrs), passing in the model name and an array of attribute names:

```
// Create the Task model.
var Task = Spine.Model.setup("Task", ["name", "done"]);
```

Use include() and extend() to add instance and class properties:

```
Task.extend({
  // Return all done tasks.
  done: function(){ /* ... */ }
});

Task.include({
  // Default name
  name: "Empty...",
  done: false,

  toggle: function(){
    this.done = !this.done;
  }
});
```

When instantiating a record, you can pass an optional object containing the record's initial properties:

```
var task = Task.init({name: "Walk the dog"});
assertEqual( task.name, "Walk the dog" );
```

Setting and retrieving attributes is the same as setting and getting properties on a normal object. In addition, the attributes() function returns an object literal containing all the record's attributes:

```
var task = Task.init();
task.name = "Read the paper";
assertEqual( task.attributes(), {name: "Read the paper"} );
```

Saving new or existing records is as simple as calling the save() function. When saving a record, an ID will be generated if it doesn't already exist; then, the record will be persisted locally in memory:

```
var task = Task.init({name: "Finish book"});
task.save();

task.id //=> "44E1DB33-2455-4728-AEA2-ECBD724B5E7B"
```

Records can be retrieved using the model's find() function, passing in the record's ID:

```
var task = Task.find("44E1DB33-2455-4728-AEA2-ECBD724B5E7B");
assertEqual( task.name, "Finish book" );
```

If no record exists for the given ID, an exception will be raised. You can check whether a record exists without fear of an exception using the `exists()` function:

```
var taskExists = Task.exists("44E1DB33-2455-4728-AEA2-ECBD724B5E7B");
assert( taskExists );
```

You can remove a record from the local cache by using the `destroy()` function:

```
var task = Task.create({name: "Thanks for all the fish"});

assert( task.exists() );
task.destroy();
assertEqual( task.exists(), false );
```

Fetching Records

Retrieving records by ID is only one way of fetching them. Typically, it's useful to iterate through all the records or to return a filtered subset. Spine lets you do this using `all()`, `select()`, and `each()`:

```
// Return all tasks
Task.all(); //=> [Object]

// Return all tasks with a false done attribute
var pending = Task.select(function(task){ return !task.done });

// Invoke a callback for each task
Task.each(function(task){ /* ... */ });
```

In addition, Spine provides a few helpers for finding records by attribute:

```
// Finds first task with the specified attribute value
Task.findByAttribute(name, value);     //=> Object

// Finds all tasks with the specified attribute value
Task.findAllByAttribute(name, value); //=> [Object]
```

Model Events

You can bind to model events to get callbacks when records change:

```
Task.bind("save", function(record){
  console.log(record.name, "was saved!");
});
```

If a record is involved, it will be passed to the event callback. You can bind a listener to the model to receive global callbacks for every record, or you can bind a listener to a specific record:

```
Task.first().bind("save", function(){
  console.log(this.name, "was saved!")
});

Task.first().updateAttributes({name: "Tea with the Queen"});
```

Although you can obviously create custom events using `trigger()`, the following are available:

save
Record was saved (either created/updated)

update
Record was updated

create
Record was created

destroy
Record was destroyed

change
Any of the above; record was created/updated/destroyed

refresh
All records invalidated and replaced

error
Validation failed

You'll find that model events are crucial when creating your application, especially when it comes to binding models up to the view.

Validation

Validation is achieved in the simplest possible way, by overriding the model instance's `validate()` function. `validate()` is called whenever the record is saved. If `validate()` returns anything, the validation fails. Otherwise, the save continues unhindered, persisting the record to local memory:

```
Task.include({
  validate: function(){
    if ( !this.name ) return "Name required";
  }
});
```

If validation fails, you should return a string from `validate()` with an explanation. Use this message to notify the user of what went wrong and how to correct it:

```
Task.bind("error", function(record, msg){
  // Very basic error notification
  alert("Task didn't save: " + msg);
});
```

The model's *error* event will be invoked whenever validation fails. Callbacks will be passed the invalid record and error message.

Persistence

Spine's records are always persisted in memory, but you have a choice of storage backends, such as HTML5's Local Storage or Ajax.

Using Local Storage is trivial. Just include the *spine.model.local.js* JavaScript file, and extend your model with `Spine.Model.Local`:

```
// Save with local storage
Task.extend(Spine.Model.Local);
Task.fetch();
```

The records won't be retrieved automatically from the browser's local storage, so you'll need to call `fetch()` to populate your model with preexisting data. This is typically done after everything else in your application has been initialized. Once the model has been populated with new data, the *refresh* event will be triggered:

```
Task.bind("refresh", function(){
  // New tasks!
  renderTemplate(Task.all());
});
```

Using Ajax persistence is similar; just include the *spine.model.ajax.js* script and extend your model with `Spine.Model.Ajax`:

```
// Save to server
Task.extend(Spine.Model.Ajax);
```

By default, Spine detects the model name and uses some basic pluralization to generate a URL. So, for the example above, the `Task` model's URL would be `/tasks`. You can override this default behavior by providing your own URL property on the class:

```
// Add a custom URL
Task.extend({
  url: "/tasks"
});

// Fetch new tasks from the server
Task.fetch();
```

As soon as `Task.fetch()` is called, Spine will make an Ajax GET request to `/tasks`, expecting a JSON response containing an array of tasks. If the server returns a successful response, the records will be loaded and the *refresh* event triggered.

Spine will send Ajax requests to the server whenever you create, update, or destroy a record, keeping the two in sync. The library expects your server to be structured in a RESTful way so it works seamlessly, although you can obviously override this to suit a custom setup. Spine expects these endpoints to exist:

```
read    → GET    /collection
create  → POST   /collection
update  → PUT    /collection/id
destroy → DELETE /collection/id
```

After a record has been created client side, Spine will send off an HTTP POST to your server, including a JSON representation of the record. Let's create a Task with a name of "Buy eggs"; this is the request that would be sent to the server:

```
POST /tasks HTTP/1.0
Host: localhost:3000
Origin: http://localhost:3000
Content-Length: 66
Content-Type: application/json

{"id": "44E1DB33-2455-4728-AEA2-ECBD724B5E7B", "name": "Buy eggs"}
```

Likewise, destroying a record will trigger a DELETE request to the server, and updating a record will trigger a PUT request. For PUT and DELETE requests, the record's ID is referenced inside the URL:

```
PUT /tasks/44E1DB33-2455-4728-AEA2-ECBD724B5E7B HTTP/1.0
Host: localhost:3000
Origin: http://localhost:3000
Content-Length: 71
Content-Type: application/json

{"id": "44E1DB33-2455-4728-AEA2-ECBD724B5E7B", "name": "Buy more eggs"}
```

Spine has a different take on Ajax syncing than most other libraries. It sends a request to the server after the record has been saved client side, so the client is never waiting for a response. This means your client is totally decoupled from your server— i.e., it doesn't need a server to be present in order to function.

Having a decoupled server offers three major advantages. First, your interface is fast and nonblocking, so users are never waiting to interact with your application. The second is that it simplifies your code—you don't need to plan for a record that may be displayed in the user interface but isn't editable due to a pending server response. Third, it makes it much easier to add offline support, if that's ever required.

What about server-side validation? Spine assumes you'll do all necessary validation client side. The only time a server should respond with an error is if there's been an exception (a problem with your code), which should only happen in exceptional circumstances.

When the server returns an unsuccessful response, an *ajaxError* event will be fired on the model, including the record, an XMLHttpRequest object, Ajax settings, and the thrown error:

```
Task.bind("ajaxError", function(record, xhr, settings, error){
  // Invalid response
});
```

Controllers

Controllers are the last component to Spine, and they provide the glue that will tie the rest of your application together. Controllers generally add event handlers to DOM elements and models, render templates, and keep the view and models in sync. To create a Spine controller, you need to subclass `Spine.Controller` by calling `create()`:

```
jQuery(function(){
  window.Tasks = Spine.Controller.create({
    // Controller properties
  });
});
```

It's recommended to load controllers only after the rest of the page has loaded, so you don't have to deal with different page states. In all the Spine examples, you'll notice each controller is contained inside a call to `jQuery()`. This ensures that the controller will be created only when the document's ready.

In Spine, the convention is to give controllers camel-cased plural names—usually, the plural of the model with which they're associated. Most controllers just have instance properties, as they're used after instantiation only. Instantiating controllers is the same as instantiating any other class, by calling `init()`:

```
var tasks = Tasks.init();
```

Controllers always have a DOM element associated with them, which can be accessed through the `el` property. You can optionally pass this through on instantiation; otherwise, the controller will generate a default `div` element:

```
var tasks = Tasks.init({el: $("#tasks")});
assertEqual( tasks.el.attr("id"), "tasks" );
```

This element can be used internally to append templates and render views:

```
window.Tasks = Spine.Controller.create({
  init: function(){
    this.el.html("Some rendered text");
  }
});

var tasks = Tasks.init();
$("body").append(tasks.el);
```

In fact, any arguments you pass to `init()` will be set as properties on the controller. For example:

```
var tasks = Tasks.init({item: Task.first()});
assertEqual( Task.first(), tasks.item );
```

Proxying

You'll notice in the previous examples that we're wrapping all event callbacks with `this.proxy()` to ensure that they always run in the correct context. Because this is such a common pattern, Spine provides a shortcut, `proxied`. Onto your controller, simply add a `proxied` property containing an array of function names that should always be executed in the context of the controller:

```
// Equivalent to using proxyAll
var Tasks = Spine.Controller.create({
  proxied: ["render", "addAll"],

  render: function(){ /* ... */ },
  addAll: function(){ /* ... */ }
});
```

Now you can pass callbacks like `render()` to event listeners without being concerned about execution context. Those functions will always be invoked in the correct context.

Elements

It's often useful to access elements inside your controller as local properties. Spine provides a shortcut for this: `elements`. Just add the `elements` property on your controller, containing an object of selectors to names. In the example below, `this.input` refers to the element selected by `form input[type=text]`. All selections are done in the context of the controller's element (el), not the whole page:

```
// The `input` instance variable
var Tasks = Spine.Controller.create({
  elements: {
    "form input[type=text]": "input"
  },

  init: function(){
    // this.input refers to the form's input
    console.log( this.input.val() );
  }
});
```

Keep in mind, though, that if you replace the HTML of the controller's element (el), you'll need to call `refreshElements()` to refresh all the element's references.

Delegating Events

Spine's `events` property gives you an easy way to add event listeners in bulk. Behind the scenes, Spine takes advantage of event bubbling, so only one event listener is added onto the controller's element (el). Like the `events` property, all event delegation is scoped by el.

Events take the form of {"eventName selector": "callback"}. The selector is optional and, if it isn't provided, the event will be placed straight on el. Otherwise, the event will be delegated (*http://api.jquery.com/delegate*), and it will be triggered if the event type is fired on a child matching the selector. This happens dynamically, so it doesn't matter whether the contents of el change:

```
var Tasks = Spine.Controller.create({
  events: {
    "keydown form input[type=text]": "keydown"
  },

  keydown: function(e){ /* ... */ }
});
```

In the example above, whenever the input matching the selector receives a *keydown* event, the controller's keydown callback is executed. Spine makes sure that it's executed with the correct context, so you don't need to worry about proxying event callbacks in this case.

The event object is passed along to the callback, which is useful in this example because we can tell which key was pressed. Additionally, the element in question can be retrieved from the event's target property.

Controller Events

As well as event delegation, Spine's controllers support custom events. By default, controllers are extending with Spine.Events, meaning they have all the event functionality that entails, like bind() and trigger(). You can use this to ensure that your controllers are decoupled from each other, or as part of the controller's internal structure:

```
var Sidebar = Spine.Controller.create({
  events: {
    "click [data-name]": this.click
  },

  init: function(){
    this.bind("change", this.change);
  },

  change: function(name){ /* ... */ },

  click: function(e){
    this.trigger("change", $(e.target).attr("data-name"));
  }

  // ...
});

var sidebar = Sidebar.init({el: $("#sidebar")});
sidebar.bind("change", function(name){
  console.log("Sidebar changed:", name);
})
```

In the example above, other controllers can bind to Sidebar's *change* event or even trigger it. As we explored in Chapter 2, custom events can be a great way of structuring applications internally, even if they're never used externally.

Global Events

Spine lets you bind to and trigger events on a global basis. This is a form of PubSub, and it lets controllers communicate without even knowing about one another, ensuring they're properly decoupled. This is achieved by having a global object, Spine.App, which anything can bind to or trigger events on:

```
var Sidebar = Spine.Controller.create({
  proxied: ["change"],

  init: function(){
    this.App.bind("change", this.change);
  },

  change: function(name){ /* ... */ }
});
```

Spine's controllers aliased Spine.App to a shortened this.App, saving you a bit of typing. You can see in the example above that the Sidebar controller is binding to the global event *change*. Other controllers or scripts can then trigger this event, passing any required data:

```
Spine.App.trigger("change", "messages");
```

The Render Pattern

Now that we've covered all the main options available in controllers, let's look at some typical use cases.

The *render pattern* is a really useful way of binding models and views. When the controller is instantiated, it adds an event listener to the relevant model, invoking a callback when the model is refreshed or changed. The callback will update el, usually by replacing its contents with a rendered template:

```
var Tasks = Spine.Controller.create({
  init: function(){
    Task.bind("refresh change", this.proxy(this.render));
  },

  template: function(items){
    return($("#tasksTemplate").tmpl(items));
  },

  render: function(){
    this.el.html(this.template(Task.all()));
  }
});
```

This simple but blunt method for data binding updates every element whenever a single record is changed. This is fine for uncomplicated and small lists, but you may find you need more control over individual elements, such as adding event handlers to items. This is where the *element pattern* comes in.

The Element Pattern

The element pattern essentially gives you the same functionality as the render pattern, but with a lot more control. It consists of two controllers: one that controls a collection of items, and one that deals with each individual item. Let's dive right into the code to give you a good indication of how it works:

```
var TasksItem = Spine.Controller.create({
  // Delegate the click event to a local handler
  events: {
    "click": "click"
  },

  // Ensure functions have the correct context
  proxied: ["render", "remove"],

  // Bind events to the record
  init: function(){
    this.item.bind("update", this.render);
    this.item.bind("destroy", this.remove);
  },

  // Render an element
  render: function(item){
    if (item) this.item = item;

    this.el.html(this.template(this.item));
    return this;
  },

  // Use a template, in this case via jQuery.tmpl.js
  template: function(items){
    return($("#tasksTemplate").tmpl(items));
  },

  // Called after an element is destroyed
  remove: function(){
    this.el.remove();
  },

  // We have fine control over events, and
  // easy access to the record too
  click: function(){ /* ... */ }
});

var Tasks = Spine.Controller.create({
  proxied: ["addAll", "addOne"],
```

```
init: function(){
  Task.bind("refresh", this.addAll);
  Task.bind("create",  this.addOne);
},

addOne: function(item){
  var task = TasksItem.init({item: item});
  this.el.append(task.render().el);
},

addAll: function(){
  Task.each(this.addOne);
  }
});
```

In the example above, Tasks has responsibility for adding records when they're initially created, and TasksItem takes responsibility for the record's *update* and *destroy* events, rerendering the record when necessary. Although it's more complicated, this gives us some advantages over the previous render pattern.

For one thing, it's more efficient—the list doesn't need to be redrawn whenever a single element changes. Furthermore, we now have a lot more control over individual items. We can place event handlers, as demonstrated with the click callback, and manage rendering on an item-by-item basis.

Building a Contacts Manager

So, let's take our knowledge of Spine's API and apply it to something practical, like a contacts manager. We want to give users a way of reading, creating, updating, and deleting contacts, as well as searching them.

Figure 11-1 shows the finished result so you can have an idea of what we're creating.

The contact manager is one of a set of open source Spine examples. You can follow along with the tutorial below, or download the full code from the project's repository (*http://github.com/maccman/spine.contacts*).

As you can see in Figure 11-1, the contact manager has two main sections, the sidebar and the contacts view. These two will make up our respective controllers, Sidebar and Contacts. As for models, the manager only has one: the Contact model. Before we expand on each individual component, let's take a look at the initial page structure:

```
<div id="sidebar">
  <ul class="items">
  </ul>

  <footer>
    <button>New contact</button>
  </footer>
</div>

<div class="vdivide"></div>
```

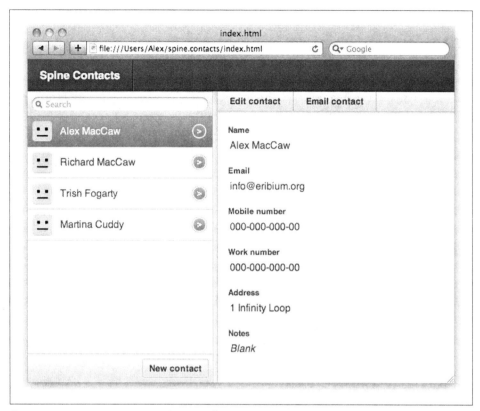

Figure 11-1. Listing contacts in a Spine application

```
<div id="contacts">
  <div class="show">
    <ul class="options">
      <li class="optEdit">Edit contact</li>
      <li class="optEmail">Email contact</li>
    </ul>
    <div class="content"></div>
  </div>

  <div class="edit">
    <ul class="options">
      <li class="optSave default">Save contact</li>
      <li class="optDestroy">Delete contact</li>
    </ul>
    <div class="content"></div>
  </div>
</div>
```

We have a #sidebar div and a #contacts div for our respective sections. Our application is going to fill the .items list with contact names and have a currently selected contact showing in #contacts. We'll listen to clicks on .optEmail and .optSave, toggling between the show and edit states as required. Finally, we'll listen for *click* events on .optDestroy, which destroys the current contact and selects another.

Contact Model

With just a half-dozen lines of code, the contact model is exceedingly straightforward. Contact has three attributes: first_name, last_name, and email. We'll also provide a helper function that will give a full name, which will be useful in templates:

```
// Create the model
var Contact = Spine.Model.setup("Contact", ["first_name", "last_name", "email"]);

// Persist model between page reloads
Contact.extend(Spine.Model.Local);

// Add some instance functions
Contact.include({
  fullName: function(){
    if ( !this.first_name && !this.last_name ) return;
    return(this.first_name + " " + this.last_name);
  }
});
```

Notice that Spine.Model.Local is extending the model. This will ensure that records are saved to the browser's local storage, making them available the next time the page loads.

Sidebar Controller

Now let's take a look at the Sidebar controller, which has the responsibility of listing contacts and keeping track of the currently selected one. Whenever contacts change, the Sidebar controller must update itself to reflect those changes. In addition, the sidebar has a "New contact" button that it will listen to, creating new blank contacts when it's clicked.

Here's the full controller in all its glory. This might be an overwhelming piece of code at first—especially if you're not familiar with Spine—but it's heavily commented, so it should be understandable under closer examination:

```
jQuery(function($){

  window.Sidebar = Spine.Controller.create({
    // Create instance variables:
    //   this.items //=> <ul></ul>
    elements: {
      ".items": "items"
    },

    // Attach event delegation
    events: {
      "click button": "create"
    },
```

```javascript
      // Ensure these functions are called with the current
      // scope as they're used in event callbacks
      proxied: ["render"],

      // Render template
      template: function(items){
        return($("#contactsTemplate").tmpl(items));
      },

      init: function(){
        this.list = Spine.List.init({
          el: this.items,
          template: this.template
        });

        // When the list's current item changes, show the contact
        this.list.bind("change", this.proxy(function(item){
          this.App.trigger("show:contact", item);
        }));

        // When the current contact changes, i.e., when a new contact is created,
        // change the list's currently selected item
        this.App.bind("show:contact edit:contact", this.list.change);

        // Rerender whenever contacts are populated or changed
        Contact.bind("refresh change", this.render);
      },

      render: function(){
        var items = Contact.all();
        this.list.render(items);
      },

      // Called when 'Create' button is clicked
      create: function(){
        var item = Contact.create();
        this.App.trigger("edit:contact", item);
      }
    });

  });
```

You'll notice that the controller's init() function is using a class called Spine.List, something we haven't yet covered. Spine.List is a utility controller that's great for generating lists of records. What's more, Spine.List will keep track of a currently selected item, and then notify listeners with a *change* event when the user selects a different item.

The list is completely rerendered whenever contacts are changed or refreshed. This keeps the example nice and simple, but it may be something we want to change in the future if performance issues arise.

The #contactsTemplate referenced in template() is a script element that contains our contact's template for individual list items:

```
<script type="text/x-jquery-tmpl" id="contactsTemplate">
  <li class="item">
    {{if fullName()}}
      <span>${fullName()}</span>
    {{else}}
      <span>No Name</span>
    {{/if}}
  </li>
</script>
```

We are using jQuery.tmpl (*http://api.jquery.com/jquery.tmpl*) for the templating, which should be familiar to you if you've read Chapter 5. Spine.List will use this template to render each item, and it will set a class of current on the <li> if it's associated with the currently selected item.

Contacts Controller

Our Sidebar controller is now displaying a list of contacts, allowing users to select individual ones. But how about showing the currently selected contact? This is where the Contacts controller comes in:

```
jQuery(function($){

  window.Contacts = Spine.Controller.create({
    // Populate internal element properties
    elements: {
      ".show": "showEl",
      ".show .content": "showContent",
      ".edit": "editEl"
    },

    proxied: ["render", "show"],

    init: function(){
      // Initial view shows contact
      this.show();

      // Rerender the view when the contact is changed
      Contact.bind("change", this.render);

      // Bind to global events
      this.App.bind("show:contact", this.show);
    },

    change: function(item){
      this.current = item;
      this.render();
    },

    render: function(){
      this.showContent.html($("#contactTemplate").tmpl(this.current));
    },

    show: function(item){
```

```
        if (item && item.model) this.change(item);

        this.showEl.show();
        this.editEl.hide();
      }
    });
```

Whenever a new contact is selected in the sidebar, the global *show:contact* event will be triggered. We're binding to this event in Contacts, executing the show() function, which gets passed the newly selected contact. We're then rerendering the showCon tent div, replacing it with the currently selected record.

You can see we've referenced a #contactTemplate template, which will display Con tacts' current contact to our users. Let's go ahead and add that template to the page:

```
<script type="text/x-jquery-tmpl" id="contactTemplate">
  <label>
    <span>Name</span>
    ${first_name} ${last_name}
  </label>

  <label>
    <span>Email</span>
    {{if email}}
      ${email}
    {{else}}
      <div class="empty">Blank</div>
    {{/if}}
  </label>
</script>
```

We've now got functionality to show contacts, but how about editing and destroying them? Let's rewrite the Contacts controller to do that. The main difference is that we're going to toggle between two application states, showing and editing when the .opt Edit and .optSave elements are clicked. We're also going to add a new template into the fray: #editContactTemplate. When saving records, we'll read the edit form's inputs and update the record's attributes:

```
jQuery(function($){

  window.Contacts = Spine.Controller.create({
    // Populate internal element properties
    elements: {
      ".show": "showEl",
      ".edit": "editEl",
      ".show .content": "showContent",
      ".edit .content": "editContent"
    },

    // Delegate events
    events: {
      "click .optEdit": "edit",
      "click .optDestroy": "destroy",
      "click .optSave": "save"
```

```
  },

  proxied: ["render", "show", "edit"],

  init: function(){
    this.show();
    Contact.bind("change", this.render);
    this.App.bind("show:contact", this.show);
    this.App.bind("edit:contact", this.edit);
  },

  change: function(item){
    this.current = item;
    this.render();
  },

  render: function(){
    this.showContent.html($("#contactTemplate").tmpl(this.current));
    this.editContent.html($("#editContactTemplate").tmpl(this.current));
  },

  show: function(item){
    if (item && item.model) this.change(item);

    this.showEl.show();
    this.editEl.hide();
  },

  // Called when the 'edit' button is clicked
  edit: function(item){
    if (item && item.model) this.change(item);

    this.showEl.hide();
    this.editEl.show();
  },

  // Called when the 'delete' button is clicked
  destroy: function(){
    this.current.destroy();
  },

  // Called when the 'save' button is clicked
  save: function(){
    var atts = this.editEl.serializeForm();
    this.current.updateAttributes(atts);
    this.show();
  }
});

});
```

As mentioned previously, we're using a new template called #editContactTemplate.
We need to add this to the page so it can be referenced successfully. Essentially,
#editContactTemplate is very similar to #contactTemplate, except that it's using input
elements to display the record's data:

```
<script type="text/x-jquery-tmpl" id="editContactTemplate">
  <label>
    <span>First name</span>
    <input type="text" name="first_name" value="${first_name}" autofocus>
  </label>

  <label>
    <span>Last name</span>
    <input type="text" name="last_name" value="${last_name}">
  </label>

  <label>
    <span>Email</span>
    <input type="text" name="email" value="${email}">
  </label>
</script>
```

App Controller

So, we've got two controllers—Sidebar and Contacts—that deal with selecting, displaying, and editing Contact records. Now all that's needed is an App controller that instantiates every other controller, passing them the page elements they require:

```
jQuery(function($){
  window.App = Spine.Controller.create({
    el: $("body"),

    elements: {
      "#sidebar": "sidebarEl",
      "#contacts": "contactsEl"
    },

    init: function(){
      this.sidebar = Sidebar.init({el: this.sidebarEl});
      this.contact = Contacts.init({el: this.contactsEl});

      // Fetch contacts from local storage
      Contact.fetch();
    }
  }).init();
});
```

Notice we're calling `.init()` immediately after creating the App controller. We're also calling `fetch()` on the Contact model, retrieving all the contacts from local storage.

So, that's all there is to it! Two main controllers (Sidebar and Contacts), one model (Contact), and a couple of views. To see the finished product, check out the source repository (*http://github.com/maccman/spine.contacts*) and see Figure 11-2.

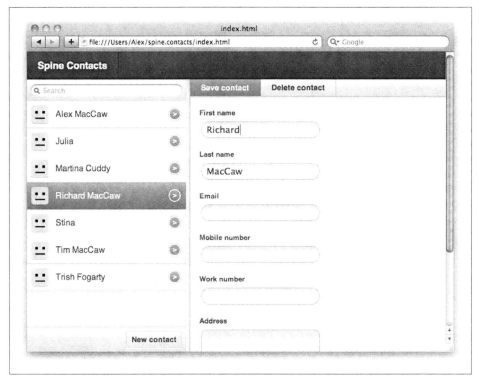

Figure 11-2. Editing contacts in the example Spine application

## CHAPTER 12

The Backbone Library

Backbone is an excellent library for building JavaScript applications. Its beauty is in its simplicity; the library is very lightweight, giving you a great deal of flexibility while covering all the basics. As with the rest of this book, MVC is the name of the game, and that pattern runs right through the core of Backbone. The library gives you models, controllers, and views—the building blocks for your application.

How is Backbone different from other frameworks, such as SproutCore or Cappuccino? Well, the main difference is Backbone's lightweight nature. SproutCore and Cappuccino provide rich UI widgets and vast core libraries, and they determine the structure of your HTML for you. Both frameworks measure in the hundreds of kilobytes when packed and gzipped, as well as many megabytes of JavaScript, CSS, and images when loaded in the browser. By comparison, Backbone measures just 4 KB, providing purely the core concepts of models, events, collections, views, controllers, and persistence.

Backbone's only hard dependency is underscore.js (*http://documentcloud.github.com/underscore*), a library full of useful utilities and general-purpose JavaScript functions. Underscore provides more than 60 functions that deal with—among other things—array manipulation, function binding, JavaScript templating, and deep-equality testing. It's definitely worth checking out Underscore's API, especially if you're doing a lot of work with arrays. Other than Underscore, you can safely use jQuery or Zepto.js to help Backbone with view functionality.

Although it's well documented, Backbone can be a little overwhelming when you first get into it. The aim of this chapter is to rectify that situation, giving you an in-depth and practical introduction to the library. The first few sections will be an overview of Backbone's components, and then we'll finish with a practical application. Feel free to skip straight to the end if you want to see Backbone in action.

Models

Let's start with probably the most key component to MVC: models. Models are where your application's data is kept. Think of models as a fancy abstraction upon the application's raw data, adding utility functions and events. You can create Backbone models by calling the extend() function on Backbone.Model:

```
var User = Backbone.Model.extend({
  initialize: function() {
    // ...
  }
});
```

The first argument to extend() takes an object that becomes the instance properties of the model. The second argument is an optional class property hash. You can call extend() multiple times to generate subclasses of models, which inherit all their parents' class and instance properties:

```
var User = Backbone.Model.extend({
  // Instance properties
  instanceProperty: "foo"
}, {
  // Class properties
  classProperty: "bar"
});

assertEqual( User.instanceProperty, "foo" );
assertEqual( User.prototype.classProperty, "bar" );
```

When a model is instantiated, the model's initialize() instance function is called with any instantiation arguments. Behind the scenes, Backbone models are constructor functions, so you can instantiate a new instance by using the new keyword:

```
var User = Backbone.Model.extend({
  initialize: function(name) {
    this.set({name: name});
  }
});

var user = new User("Leo McGarry");
assertEqual( user.get("name"), "Leo McGarry");
```

Models and Attributes

Use the set() and get() functions for setting and retrieving an instances' attributes:

```
var user = new User();
user.set({name: "Donna Moss"})

assertEqual( user.get("name"), "Donna Moss" );
assertEqual( user.attributes, {name: "Donna Moss"} );
```

set(attrs, [options]) takes a hash of attributes to apply to the instance, and get(attr) takes a single string argument—the name of the attribute—returning its value. The instance keeps track of its current attributes with a local hash called attributes. You shouldn't manipulate this directly; as with the get() and set() functions, make sure the appropriate validation and events are invoked.

You can validate an instance's attributes by using the `validate()` function. By default, this is left undefined, but you can override it to add any custom validation logic:

```
var User = Backbone.Model.extend({
  validate: function(atts){
    if (!atts.email || atts.email.length < 3) {
      return "email must be at least 3 chars";
    }
  }
});
```

If the model and attributes are valid, don't return anything from `validate()`; if the attributes are invalid, you can either return a string describing the error or an `Error` instance. If validation fails, the `set()` and `save()` functions will not continue and an *error* event will be triggered. You can bind to the *error* event, ensuring that you'll be notified when any validation fails:

```
var user = new User;

user.bind("error", function(model, error) {
  // Handle error
});

user.set({email: "ga"});

// Or add an error handler onto the specific set
user.set({"email": "ga"}, {error: function(model, error){
  // ...
}});
```

Specify default attributes with a `default` hash. When creating an instance of the model, any unspecified attributes will be set to their default value:

```
var Chat = Backbone.Model.extend({
  defaults: {
    from: "anonymous"
  }
});

assertEqual( (new Chat).get("from"), "anonymous" );
```

Collections

In Backbone, arrays of model instances are stored in collections. It might not be immediately obvious why it's useful to separate collections from models, but it's actually quite a common scenario. If you were recreating Twitter, for example, you'd have two collections, `Followers` and `Followees`, both populated by `User` instances. Although both collections are populated by the same model, each contains an array of different `User` instances; as a result, they are separate collections.

As with models, you can create a collection by extending `Backbone.Collection`:

```
var Users = Backbone.Collection.extend({
  model: User
});
```

In the example above, you can see we're overriding the model property to specify which model we want associated with the collection—in this case, the User model. Although it's not absolutely required, it's useful to set this to give the collection a default model to refer to if it's ever required. Normally, a collection will contain instances of only a single model type, rather than a multitude of different ones.

When creating a collection, you can optionally pass an initial array of models. Like with Backbone's models, if you define an initialize instance function, it will be invoked on instantiation:

```
var users = new Users([{name: "Toby Ziegler"}, {name: "Josh Lyman"}]);
```

Alternatively, you can add models to the collection using the add() function:

```
var users = new Users;

// Add an individual model
users.add({name: "Donna Moss"});

// Or add an array of models
users.add([{name: "Josiah Bartlet"}, {name: "Charlie Young"}]);
```

When you add a model to the collection, the *add* event is fired:

```
users.bind("add", function(user) {
  alert("Ahoy " + user.get("name") + "!");
});
```

Similarly, you can remove a model from the collection using remove(), which triggers a *remove* event:

```
users.bind("remove", function(user) {
  alert("Adios " + user.get("name") + "!");
});

users.remove( users.models[0] );
```

Fetching a specific model is simple; if the model's ID is present, you can use the controller's get() function:

```
var user = users.get("some-guid");
```

If you don't have a model's ID, you can fetch a model by *cid*—the client ID created automatically by Backbone whenever a new model is created:

```
var user = users.getByCid("c-some-cid");
```

In addition to the *add* and *remove* events, whenever the model in a collection has been modified, a *change* event will be fired:

```
var user = new User({name: "Adam Buxton"});

var users = new Backbone.Collection;
```

```
users.bind("change", function(rec){
  // A record was changed!
});
users.add(user);

user.set({name: "Joe Cornish"});
```

Controlling a Collection's Order

You can control a collection's order by providing a `comparator()` function, returning a value against which you want the collection sorted:

```
var Users = Backbone.Collection.extend({
  comparator: function(user){
    return user.get("name");
  }
});
```

You can return either a string or numeric value to sort against (unlike JavaScript's regular sort). In the example above, we're making sure the `Users` collection is sorted alphabetically by name. Ordering will happen automatically behind the scenes, but if you ever need to force a collection to re-sort itself, you can call the `sort()` function.

Views

Backbone views are not templates themselves, but are control classes that handle a model's presentation. This can be confusing, because many MVC implementations refer to views as chunks of HTML or templates that deal with events and rendering in controllers. Regardless, in Backbone, it is a view "because it represents a logical chunk of UI, responsible for the contents of a single DOM."

Like models and collections, views are created by extending one of Backbone's existing classes—in this case, `Backbone.View`:

```
var UserView = Backbone.View.extend({
  initialize: function(){ /* ... */ },
  render: function(){ /* ... */ }
});
```

Every view instance has the idea of a current DOM element, or `this.el`, regardless of whether the view has been inserted into the page. `el` is created using the attributes from the view's `tagName`, `className`, or `id` properties. If none of these is specified, `el` is an empty div:

```
var UserView = Backbone.View.extend({
  tagName: "span",
  className: "users"
});

assertEqual( (new UserView).el.className, "users" );
```

If you want to bind the view onto an existing element in the page, simply set el directly. Clearly, you need to make sure this view is set up after the page has loaded; otherwise, the element won't yet exist:

```
var UserView = Backbone.View.extend({
  el: $(".users")
});
```

You can also pass el as an option when instantiating a view, as with the tagName, className, and id properties:

```
new UserView({id: "followers"});
```

Rendering Views

Every view also has a render() function, which by default is a no-op (an empty function). Your view should call this function whenever the view needs to be redrawn. You should override this function with functionality specific to your view, dealing with rendering templates and updating el with any new HTML:

```
var TodoView = Backbone.View.extend({
  template: _.template($("#todo-template").html()),

  render: function() {
    $(this.el).html(this.template(this.model.toJSON()));
    return this;
  }
});
```

Backbone is pretty agnostic about how you render views. You can generate the elements yourself or using a templating library. The latter approach is advocated, though, because it's generally the cleanest method—keeping HTML out of your JavaScript programs. Since Underscore.js, being a dependency of Backbone, is on the page, you can use _.template() (*http://documentcloud.github.com/underscore/#template*)—a handy utility for generating templates.

Above, you'll notice that we're using a local property called this.model. This actually points to a model's instance and is passed through to the view upon instantiation. The model's toJSON() function essentially returns the model's raw attributes, ready for the template to use:

```
new TodoView({model: new Todo});
```

Delegating Events

Through delegation, Backbone's views provide an easy shortcut for adding event handlers onto el. Here's how you can set a hash of events and their corresponding callbacks on the view:

```
var TodoView = Backbone.View.extend({
  events: {
```

```
      "change input[type=checkbox]" : "toggleDone",
      "click .destroy"              : "clear",
    },

    toggleDone: function(e){ /* ... */},
    clear: function(e){ /* ... */}
});
```

The event hash is in the format {"eventType selector": "callback"}. The selector is optional, and if it isn't provided, the event is bound straight to el. If the selector is provided, the event is delegated (*http://api.jquery.com/delegate*), which basically means it's bound dynamically to any of el's children that match the selector. Delegation uses event bubbling, meaning that events will still fire regardless of whether el's contents have changed.

The callback is a string, and it refers to the name of an instance function on the current view. When the view's event callbacks are triggered, they're invoked in the current view's context, rather than the current target or window's context. This is rather useful because you have direct access to this.el and this.model from any callbacks, such as in the example toggleDone() and clear() functions above.

Binding and Context

So, how is the view's render() function actually invoked? Well, typically this is called by the view's model when it changes, using the *change* event. This means your application's views and HTML are kept in sync (bound) with your model's data:

```
var TodoView = Backbone.View.extend({
  initialize: function() {
    _.bindAll(this, 'render', 'close');
    this.model.bind('change', this.render);
  },

  close: function(){ /* ... */ }
});
```

One thing to watch out for is context changes in event callbacks. Underscore provides a useful function to get around this: _.bindAll(context, *functionNames) (*http://docu mentcloud.github.com/underscore/#bindAll*). This function binds a context and function names (as strings). _.bindAll() ensures that all the functions you indicate are always invoked in the specified context. This is especially useful for event callbacks, as their context is always changing. In the example above, the render() and close() functions will always execute in the TodoView's instance context.

Catering to model destruction works similarly. Your views just need to bind to the model's *delete* event, removing el when it's triggered:

```
var TodoView = Backbone.View.extend({
  initialize: function() {
    _.bindAll(this, 'render', 'remove');
    this.model.bind('change',  this.render);
```

```
      this.model.bind('delete', this.remove);
    },

    remove: function(){
      $(this.el).remove();
    }
});
```

Note that you can render Backbone's views without using models or event callbacks. You could easily call the `render()` function from `initialize()`, rendering the view when it's first instantiated. However, I've been covering model and view integration because it's the typical use case for views—the binding capabilities are one of Backbone's most useful and powerful features.

Controllers

Backbone controllers connect the application's state to the URL's hash fragment, providing shareable, bookmarkable URLs. Essentially, controllers consist of a bunch of routes and the functions that will be invoked when those routes are navigated to.

Routes are a hash—the key consisting of paths, parameters, and splats—and the value is set to the function associated with the route:

```
routes: {                                // Matches:
  "help":                 "help",   // #help
  "search/:query":        "search", // #search/kiwis
  "search/:query/p:page": "search"  // #search/kiwis/p7
  "file/*path":           "file"    // #file/any/path.txt
}
```

You can see in the example above that parameters start with a : and then the name of the parameter. Any parameters in a route will be passed to its action when the route is invoked. Splats, specified by a *, are basically a wildcard, matching anything. As with parameters, splats will be passed matched values onto their route's action.

Routes are parsed in the reverse order they're specified in the hash. In other words, your most general "catch all" routes should be located at the end of the `routes` hash.

Per usual, controllers are created by extending `Backbone.Controllers`, passing in an object containing instance properties:

```
var PageController = Backbone.Controller.extend({
  routes: {
    "":                     "index",
    "help":                 "help",   // #help
    "search/:query":        "search", // #search/kiwis
    "search/:query/p:page": "search"  // #search/kiwis/p7
  },

  index: function(){ /* ... */ },

  help: function() {
```

```
    // ...
  },

  search: function(query, page) {
    // ...
  }
});
```

In the example above, when the user navigates to *http://example.com#search/coconut*, whether manually or by pushing the back button, the `search()` function will be invoked with the `query` variable pointing to `"coconut"`.

If you want to make your application compliant with the Ajax Crawling specification (*http://code.google.com/web/ajaxcrawling/index.html*) and indexable by search engines (as discussed in Chapter 4), you need to prefix all your routes with !/, as in the following example:

```
var PageController = Backbone.Controller.extend({
  routes: {
    "!/page/:title": "page", // #!/page/foo-title
  }
  // ...
}):
```

You'll also need to make changes server side, as described by the specification.

If you need more route functionality, such as making sure certain parameters are integers, you can pass a regex directly to `route()`:

```
var PageController = Backbone.Controller.extend({
  initialize: function(){
    this.route(/pages\/(\d+)/, 'id', function(pageId){
      // ...
    });
  }
}):
```

So, routes tie up changes to the URL's fragment with controllers, but how about setting the fragment in the first place? Rather than setting `window.location.hash` manually, Backbone provides a shortcut—`saveLocation(fragment)`:

```
Backbone.history.saveLocation("/page/" + this.model.id);
```

When `saveLocation()` is called and the URL's fragment is updated, none of the controller's routes will be invoked. This means you can safely call `saveLocation()` in a view's `initialize()` function, for example, without any controller intervention.

Internally, Backbone will listen to the *onhashchange* event in browsers that support it, or implement a workaround using iframes and timers. However, you'll need to initiate Backbone's history support by calling the following:

```
Backbone.history.start();
```

You should only start Backbone's history once the page has loaded and all of your views, models, and collections are available. As it stands, Backbone doesn't support the new HTML5 `pushState()` and `replaceState()` history API. This is because `push State()` and `replaceState()` currently need special handling on the server side and aren't yet supported by Internet Explorer. Backbone may add support once those issues have been addressed. For now, all routing is done by the URL's hash fragment.

Syncing with the Server

By default, whenever you save a model, Backbone will notify your server with an Ajax request, using either the jQuery or Zepto.js library. Backbone achieves this by calling `Backbone.sync()` before a model is created, updated, or deleted. Backbone will then send off a RESTful JSON request to your server which, if successful, will update the model client side.

To take advantage of this, you need to define a `url` instance property on your model and have a RESTfully compliant server. Backbone will take care of the rest:

```
var User = Backbone.Model.extend({
  url: '/users'
});
```

The `url` property can either be a string or a function that returns a string. The path can be relative or absolute, but it must return the model's endpoint.

Backbone maps create, read, update, and delete (CRUD) actions into the following methods:

```
create → POST   /collection
read   → GET    /collection[/id]
update → PUT    /collection/id
delete → DELETE /collection/id
```

For example, if you were creating a `User` instance, Backbone would send off a POST request to `/users`. Similarly, updating a `User` instance would send off a PUT request to the endpoint `/users/id`, where `id` is the model's identifier. Backbone expects you to return a JSON hash of the instance's attributes in response to POST, PUT, and GET requests, which will be used to update the instance.

To save a model to the server, call the model's `save([attrs], [options])` function, optionally passing in a hash of attributes and request options. If the model has an `id`, it is assumed to exist on the server side, and `save()` sends will be a PUT (update) request. Otherwise, `save()` will send a POST (create) request:

```
var user = new User();
user.set({name: "Bernard"});

user.save(null, {success: function(){
  // user saved successfully
}});
```

All calls to `save()` are asynchronous, but you can listen to the Ajax request callbacks by passing the `success` and `failure` options. In fact, if Backbone is using jQuery, any options passed to `save()` will also be passed to `$.ajax()`. In other words, you can use any of jQuery's Ajax options (*http://api.jquery.com/jQuery.ajax*), such as `timeout`, when saving models.

If the server returns an error and the save fails, an *error* event will be triggered on the model. If it succeeds, the model will be updated with the server's response:

```
var user = new User();

user.bind("error", function(e){
  // The server returns an error!
});

user.save({email: "Invalid email"});
```

You can refresh a model by using the `fetch()` function, which will request the model's attributes from the server (via a GET request). A *change* event will trigger if the remote representation of the model differs from its current attributes:

```
var user = Users.get(1);
user.fetch();
```

Populating Collections

So, we've covered creating and updating models, but what about fetching them from the server in the first place? This is where Backbone collections come in, requesting remote models and storing them locally. Like models, you should add a `url` property to the collection to specify its endpoint. If a `url` isn't provided, Backbone will fall back to the associated model's `url`:

```
var Followers = Backbone.Collection.extend({
  model: User,
  url: "/followers"
});

Followers.fetch();
```

The collection's `fetch()` function will send off a GET request to the server—in this case, to `/followers`—retrieving the remote models. When the model data returns from the server, the collection will refresh, triggering a *refresh* event.

You can refresh collections manually with the `refresh()` function, passing in an array of model objects. This comes in really handy when you're first setting up the page. Rather than firing off another GET request on page load, you can prepopulate collection data by passing in a JSON object inline via `refresh()`. For example, here's how it would look using Rails:

```
<script type="text/javascript">
  Followers.refresh(<%= @users.to_json %>);
</script>
```

On the Server Side

As mentioned previously, your server needs to implement a number of RESTful endpoints in order to integrate seamlessly with Backbone:

```
create → POST    /collection
read   → GET     /collection
read   → GET     /collection/id
update → PUT     /collection/id
delete → DELETE  /collection/id
```

Backbone will serialize models into JSON before sending them. Our `User` model would look like this:

```
{"name": "Yasmine"}
```

Notice that the data isn't prefixed by the current model, something that can especially trip up Rails developers. I'm going to go through some of the specifics of integrating Rails with Backbone, so if you're not using the framework, feel free to skip to the next section.

Inside your CRUD methods, you should be using the plain, unprefixed parameters. For example, here's how our Rails controller's `update` method could work:

```
def update
  user = User.find(params[:id])
  user.update_attributes!(params)
  render :json => user
end
```

Obviously, you should be securing your model from malicious input by whitelisting attributes (*http://guides.rubyonrails.org/security.html#mass-assignment*) using the `attr_accessible` method, but that's beyond the scope of this book. Every controller method, except for `destroy`, should return a JSON representation of the record.

Serializing attributes to JSON is also an issue because, by default, Rails prefixes any record data with the model, like this:

```
{"user": {"name": "Daniela"}}
```

Unfortunately, Backbone won't be able to parse that object correctly. You need to ensure Rails doesn't include the model name inside JSON serializations of records by creating an initializer file:

```
# config/initializers/json.rb
ActiveRecord::Base.include_root_in_json = false
```

Custom Behavior

`Backbone.sync()` is the function Backbone calls every time it attempts to read or save a model to the server. You can override its default behavior (sending an Ajax request) in order to use a different persistence strategy, such as WebSockets, XML transport, or

Local Storage. For example, let's replace `Backbone.sync()` with a no-op function that just logs the arguments with which its called:

```
Backbone.sync = function(method, model, options) {
  console.log(method, model, options);
  options.success(model);
};
```

As you can see, `Backbone.sync()` gets passed a `method`, `model`, and `options`, which have the following properties:

method
:   The CRUD method (`create`, `read`, `update`, or `delete`)

model
:   The model to be saved (or collection to be read)

options
:   The request options, including success and failure callbacks

The only thing Backbone expects you to do is invoke either the `options.success()` or `options.error()` callback.

It's also possible to override the sync function per model or collection, rather than globally:

```
Todo.prototype.sync = function(method, model, options){ /* ... */ };
```

A good example of a custom `Backbone.sync()` function is in the local storage adapter (*https://github.com/jeromegn/Backbone.localStorage*). Including the adapter and setting the `localStorage` option on the relevant models or collections enables Backbone to use HTML5 `localStorage`, rather than a backend server. As you can see in the example below, `Backbone.sync()` CRUDs the `store` object, depending on the method, and finally calls `options.success()` with the appropriate model:

```
// Save all of the todo items under the "todos" localStorage namespace.
Todos.prototype.localStorage = new Store("todos");

// Override Backbone.sync() to use a delegate to the model or collection's
// localStorage property, which should be an instance of Store.
Backbone.sync = function(method, model, options) {

  var resp;
  var store = model.localStorage || model.collection.localStorage;

  switch (method) {
    case "read":    resp = model.id ? store.find(model) : store.findAll(); break;
    case "create":  resp = store.create(model);                    break;
    case "update":  resp = store.update(model);                    break;
    case "delete":  resp = store.destroy(model);                   break;
  }

  if (resp) {
    options.success(resp);
  } else {
```

```
      options.error("Record not found");
    }
  }
};
```

Building a To-Do List

Let's put what we've learned about Backbone into practice with a simple to-do list application. We want the user to be able to CRUD to-dos, and we want items to be persisted between page refreshes. You can build the application using the examples below, or see the finished application in *assets/ch12/todos*.

The initial page structure looks like the following; we're loading in CSS, JavaScript libraries, and our Backbone application contained in *todos.js*:

```
<html>
<head>
  <link href="todos.css" media="all" rel="stylesheet" type="text/css"/>
  <script src="lib/json2.js"></script>
  <script src="lib/jquery.js"></script>
  <script src="lib/jquery.tmpl.js"></script>
  <script src="lib/underscore.js"></script>
  <script src="lib/backbone.js"></script>
  <script src="lib/backbone.localstorage.js"></script>
  <script src="todos.js"></script>
</head>

<body>
  <div id="todoapp">
    <div class="title">
      <h1>Todos</h1>
    </div>

    <div class="content">
      <div id="create-todo">
        <input id="new-todo" placeholder="What needs to be done?" type="text" />
      </div>

      <div id="todos">
        <ul id="todo-list"></ul>
      </div>
    </div>
  </div>
</body>
</html>
```

The page structure is very straightforward; it just contains a text input for creating new to-dos (#new-todo) and a list showing existing to-dos (#todo-list).

Now let's move on to the todos.js script, where the core of our Backbone application is located. We're going to wrap everything we put in this class with jQuery(), ensuring that it will be run only after the page has loaded:

```
// todos.js
jQuery(function($){
  // Application goes here...
})
```

Let's create a basic Todo model that has content and done attributes. We're providing a toggle() helper for easily inverting the model's done attribute:

```
window.Todo = Backbone.Model.extend({
  defaults: {
    done: false
  },

  toggle: function() {
    this.save({done: !this.get("done")});
  }
});
```

We're setting the Todo model on the window object to ensure that it's accessible globally. Also, by using this pattern, it's easy to see which global variables a script is declaring—just look through the script for window references.

The next step is to set up a TodoList collection, where the array of Todo models will be stored:

```
window.TodoList = Backbone.Collection.extend({
  model: Todo,

  // Save all of the to-do items under the "todos" namespace.
  localStorage: new Store("todos"),

  // Filter down the list of all to-do items that are finished.
  done: function() {
    return this.filter(function(todo){ return todo.get('done'); });
  },

  remaining: function() {
    return this.without.apply(this, this.done());
  }
});

// Create our global collection of Todos.
window.Todos = new TodoList;
```

We're using the Backbone local storage provider (*backbone.localstorage.js*), which requires us to set a localStorage attribute on any collections or models wanting to store data. The other two functions in TodoList, done(), and remaining() deal with filtering the collection, returning to-do models that have or have not been completed. Because there will only ever be one TodoList, we're instantiating a globally available instance of it: window.Todos.

And now for the view that will show individual to-dos, TodoView. This will bind to the *change* event on Todo models, rerendering the view when it's triggered:

```
window.TodoView = Backbone.View.extend({

  // View is a list tag.
  tagName:  "li",

  // Cache the template function for a single item.
  template: $("#item-template").template(),

  // Delegate events to view functions
  events: {
    "change    .check"         : "toggleDone",
    "dblclick .todo-content" : "edit",
    "click     .todo-destroy" : "destroy",
    "keypress .todo-input"    : "updateOnEnter",
    "blur      .todo-input"    : "close"
  },

  initialize: function() {
    // Make sure functions are called in the right scope
    _.bindAll(this, 'render', 'close', 'remove');

    // Listen to model changes
    this.model.bind('change', this.render);
    this.model.bind('destroy', this.remove);
  },

  render: function() {
    // Update el with stored template
    var element = jQuery.tmpl(this.template, this.model.toJSON());
    $(this.el).html(element);
    return this;
  },

  // Toggle model's done status when the checkbox is checked
  toggleDone: function() {
    this.model.toggle();
  },

  // Switch this view into `"editing"` mode, displaying the input field.
  edit: function() {
    $(this.el).addClass("editing");
    this.input.focus();
  },

  // Close the `"editing"` mode, saving changes to the to-do.
  close: function(e) {
    this.model.save({content: this.input.val()});
    $(this.el).removeClass("editing");
  },

  // If you hit `enter`, we're through editing the item.
  // Fire the blur event on the input, triggering close()
  updateOnEnter: function(e) {
    if (e.keyCode == 13) e.target.blur();
  },
```

```
// Remove element when model is destroyed
remove: function() {
  $(this.el).remove();
},

// Destroy model when '.todo-destroy' is clicked
destroy: function() {
  this.model.destroy();
}
});
```

You can see we're delegating a bunch of events to the view that manage updating, completing, and deleting the to-do. For example, whenever the checkbox is changed, toggleDone() gets called, toggling the model's done attribute. That in turn triggers the model's *change* event, which causes the view to rerender.

We're using jQuery.tmpl (*http://api.jquery.com/category/plugins/templates*) for the HTML templating, replacing the contents of el with a regenerated template whenever the view renders. The template refers to an element with an ID of #item-template, which we haven't yet defined. Let's do that now, placing the template inside our *index.html* body tags:

```
<script type="text/template" id="item-template">
  <div class="todo {{if done}}done{{/if}}">
    <div class="display" title="Double click to edit...">
      <input class="check" type="checkbox" {{if done}}checked="checked"{{/if}} />
      <div class="todo-content">${content}</div>
      <span class="todo-destroy"></span>
    </div>
    <div class="edit">
      <input class="todo-input" type="text" value="${content}" />
    </div>
  </div>
</script>
```

That templating syntax should look fairly familiar to you if you've read Chapter 5, where jQuery.tmpl is covered in some depth. Essentially, we're interoperating the to-do's contents inside the #todo-content and #todo-input elements. Additionally, we're making sure the checkbox has the correct "checked" state.

TodoView is pretty self-contained—we just need to give it a model on instantiation and append its el attribute to the to-do list. This is basically the job of AppView, which ensures that our initial to-do list is populated by instantiating TodoView instances. The other role AppView performs is creating new Todo records when a user hits Return on the #new-todo text input:

```
// Our overall AppView is the top-level piece of UI.
window.AppView = Backbone.View.extend({

  // Instead of generating a new element, bind to the existing skeleton of
  // the App already present in the HTML.
  el: $("#todoapp"),
```

```
      events: {
        "keypress #new-todo":  "createOnEnter",
        "click .todo-clear a": "clearCompleted"
      },

      // At initialization, we bind to the relevant events on the `Todos`
      // collection, when items are added or changed. Kick things off by
      // loading any preexisting to-dos that might be saved in *localStorage*.
      initialize: function() {
        _.bindAll(this, 'addOne', 'addAll', 'render');

        this.input = this.$("#new-todo");

        Todos.bind('add',     this.addOne);
        Todos.bind('refresh', this.addAll);

        Todos.fetch();
      },

      // Add a single to-do item to the list by creating a view for it and
      // appending its element to the `<ul>`.
      addOne: function(todo) {
        var view = new TodoView({model: todo});
        this.$("#todo-list").append(view.render().el);
      },

      // Add all items in the Todos collection at once.
      addAll: function() {
        Todos.each(this.addOne);
      },

      // If you hit return in the main input field, create new Todo model
      createOnEnter: function(e) {
        if (e.keyCode != 13) return;

        var value = this.input.val();
        if ( !value ) return;

        Todos.create({content: value});
        this.input.val('');
      },

      clearCompleted: function() {
        _.each(Todos.done(), function(todo){ todo.destroy(); });
        return false;
      }
    });

    // Finally, we kick things off by creating the App.
    window.App = new AppView;
```

When the page initially loads, the Todos collection will be populated and the *refresh* event called. This invokes addAll(), which fetches all the Todo models, generates Todo View views, and appends them to #todo-list. Additionally, when new Todo models are added to `Todos`, the `Todos` *add* event is triggered, invoking `addOne()` and appending a new `TodoView` to the list. In other words, the initial population and `Todo` creation is being handled by `AppView`, while the individual `TodoView` views handle updating and destroying themselves.

Now let's refresh the page and see the result of our handiwork. Notwithstanding any bugs and typos, you should see something like Figure 12-1.

Figure 12-1. The finished Backbone Todo application

We have functionality for adding, checking, updating, and removing to-dos, all with a relatively small amount of code. Because we're using the local storage Backbone adapter, to-dos are persisted between page reloads. This example should give you a good idea of how useful Backbone is, as well as how to go about creating your own applications.

You can find the full application inside this book's accompanying files, in *assets/ch12/todos*.

## CHAPTER 13

The JavascriptMVC Library

Justin Meyer (http://jupiterjs.com/pages/justin-meyer), the author of JavaScriptMVC, kindly contributed this chapter

JavaScriptMVC (JMVC) is an open source jQuery-based JavaScript framework. It is nearly a comprehensive (holistic) frontend development framework, packaging utilities for testing, dependency management, documentation, and a host of useful jQuery plug-ins.

Yet every part of JavaScriptMVC can be used without every other part, making the library lightweight. Its class, model, view, and controller combined are only 7k minified and compressed, yet even they can be used independently. JavaScriptMVC's independence lets you start small and scale to meet the challenges of the most complex applications on the Web.

This chapter covers JavaScriptMVC's `$.Class`, `$.Model`, `$.View`, and `$.Controller`. The following describes each component:

`$.Class`
> The JavaScript-based class system

`$.Model`
> The traditional model layer

`$.View`
> The client-side template system

`$.Controller`
> The jQuery widget factory

JavaScriptMVC's naming conventions deviate slightly from the traditional Model-View-Controller (*http://en.wikipedia.org/wiki/Model–view–controller#Concepts*) design pattern. For example, `$.Controller` is used to create traditional view controls, like pagination buttons and lists, as well as traditional controllers that coordinate between the traditional views and models.

Setup

JavaScriptMVC can be used as a single download that includes the entire framework. But since this chapter covers only the MVC parts, go to the download builder (*http://javascriptmvc.com/builder.html*); check Controller, Model, and View's EJS templates; and click Download.

The download will come with minified and unminified versions of jQuery and your selected plug-ins. Load these with script tags in your page:

```
<script type='text/javascript' src='jquery-1.6.1.js'></script>
<script type='text/javascript' src='jquerymx-1.0.custom.js'></script>
```

Classes

JMVC's controller and model inherit from its class helper: `$.Class`. To create a class, call `$.Class(NAME, [classProperties, ] instanceProperties])`:

```
$.Class("Animal",{
  breathe : function(){
    console.log('breathe');
  }
});
```

In the example above, instances of `Animal` have a `breathe()` method. We can create a new `Animal` instance and call `breathe()` on it:

```
var man = new Animal();
man.breathe();
```

If you want to create a subclass, simply call the base class with the subclass's name and properties:

```
Animal("Dog",{
  wag : function(){
    console.log('wag');
  }
})

var dog = new Dog;
dog.wag();
dog.breathe();
```

Instantiation

When a new class instance is created, it calls the class's `init` method with the arguments passed to the constructor function:

```
$.Class('Person',{
  init : function(name){
    this.name = name;
  },
```

```
  speak : function(){
    return "I am " + this.name + ".";
  }
});

var payal = new Person("Payal");
assertEqual( payal.speak() , 'I am Payal.' );
```

Calling Base Methods

Call base methods with this._super. The following overwrites person to provide a more "classy" greeting:

```
Person("ClassyPerson", {
  speak : function(){
    return "Salutations, " + this._super();
  }
});

var fancypants = new ClassyPerson("Mr. Fancy");
assertEquals( fancypants.speak() , 'Salutations, I am Mr. Fancy.')
```

Proxies

Class' callback method returns a function that has "this" set appropriately, similar to $.proxy (*http://api.jquery.com/jQuery.proxy/*). The following creates a Clicky class that counts how many times it was clicked:

```
$.Class("Clicky",{
  init : function(){
    this.clickCount = 0;
  },

  clicked: function(){
    this.clickCount++;
  },

  listen: function(el){
    el.click( this.callback('clicked') );
  }
})
var clicky = new Clicky();
clicky.listen( $('#foo') );
clicky.listen( $('#bar') ) ;
```

Static Inheritance

Class lets you define inheritable static properties and methods. The following allows you to retrieve a person instance from the server by calling Person.findOne(ID, success(person)). Success is called back with an instance of `Person`, which has the speak method:

```
$.Class("Person",{
  findOne : function(id, success){
    $.get('/person/'+id, function(attrs){
      success( new Person( attrs ) );
    },'json')
  }
},{
  init : function(attrs){
    $.extend(this, attrs)
  },
  speak : function(){
    return "I am "+this.name+".";
  }
})

Person.findOne(5, function(person){
  assertEqual( person.speak(), "I am Payal." );
})
```

Introspection

Class provides namespacing and access to the name of the class and namespace object:

```
$.Class("Jupiter.Person");

Jupiter.Person.shortName; //-> 'Person'
Jupiter.Person.fullName;  //-> 'Jupiter.Person'
Jupiter.Person.namespace; //-> Jupiter

var person = new Jupiter.Person();

person.Class.shortName; //-> 'Person'
```

A Model Example

Putting it all together, we can make a basic ORM-style model layer. Just by inheriting from `Model`, we can request data from REST services and get it back wrapped in instances of the inheriting `Model`:

```
$.Class("Model",{
  findOne : function(id, success){
    $.get('/' + this.fullName.toLowerCase() + '/' + id,
      this.callback(function(attrs){
        success( new this( attrs ) );
      })
    },'json')
  }
},{
  init : function(attrs){
    $.extend(this, attrs)
  }
```

```
})

Model("Person",{
  speak : function(){
    return "I am "+this.name+".";
  }
});

Person.findOne(5, function(person){
  alert( person.speak() );
});

Model("Task");

Task.findOne(7,function(task){
  alert(task.name);
});
```

This is similar to how JavaScriptMVC's model layer works.

Model

JavaScriptMVC's model and its associated plug-ins provide lots of tools around organizing model data, such as validations, associations, lists, and more. But the core functionality is centered around service encapsulation, type conversion, and events.

Attributes and Observables

Of absolute importance to a model layer is the ability to get and set properties on the modeled data, and to listen for changes on a model instance. This is the Observer pattern, and it lies at the heart of the MVC approach—views listen to changes in the model.

Fortunately, with JavaScriptMVC, it is easy to make any data observable. A great example is pagination. It's very common for multiple pagination controls to exist on the page. For example, one control might provide Next and Previous page buttons; another control might detail the items the current page is viewing (e.g., "Showing items 1-20"). All pagination controls need the exact same data:

offset
    The index of the first item to display

limit
    The number of items to display

count
    The total number of items

We can model this data with JavaScriptMVC's $.Model:

```
var paginate = new $.Model({
  offset: 0,
  limit: 20,
  count: 200
});
```

The paginate variable is now observable. We can pass it to pagination controls that can read from, write to, and listen for property changes. You can read properties like normal or by using the model.attr(NAME) method:

```
assertEqual( paginate.offset, 0 );
assertEqual( paginate.attr('limit') , 20 );
```

If we click the next button, we need to increment the offset. Change property values with model.attr(NAME, VALUE). The following moves the offset to the next page:

```
paginate.attr('offset', 20);
```

When paginate's state is changed by one control, the other controls need to be notified. You can bind to a specific attribute change with model.bind(ATTR, success(ev, new Val)) and update the control:

```
paginate.bind('offset', function(ev, newVal){
  $('#details').text( 'Showing items ' + (newVal + 1 ) + '-' + this.count )
})
```

You can also listen to any attribute change by binding to the 'updated.attr' event:

```
paginate.bind('updated.attr', function(ev, newVal){
  $('#details').text( 'Showing items ' + (newVal+1 )+ '-' + this.count )
})
```

The following is a next-previous jQuery plug-in that accepts paginate data:

```
$.fn.nextPrev = function(paginate){
  this.delegate('.next','click', function(){
    var nextOffset = paginate.offset + paginate.limit;
    if( nextOffset < paginate.count){
      paginate.attr('offset', nextOffset );
    }
  });

  this.delegate('.prev','click', function(){
    var nextOffset = paginate.offset-paginate.limit;
    if( 0 < paginate.offset ){
      paginate.attr('offset', Math.max(0, nextOffset) );
    }
  });

  var self = this;
  paginate.bind('updated.attr', function(){
    var next = self.find('.next'),
        prev = self.find('.prev');
    if( this.offset == 0 ){
      prev.removeClass('enabled');
    } else {
      prev.removeClass('disabled');
```

```
        }
      if( this.offset > this.count - this.limit ){
        next.removeClass('enabled');
      } else {
        next.removeClass('disabled');
      }
    });
  };
```

There are a few problems with this plug-in. First, if the control is removed from the page, it is not unbinding itself from paginate. We'll address this when we discuss controllers.

Second, the logic protecting a negative offset or offset above the total count is done in the plug-in. This logic should be done in the model. To fix this problem, we'll need to create a pagination class, where we can add additional constraints to limit what values limit, offset, and count can be.

Extending Models

JavaScriptMVC's model inherits from $.Class. Thus, you create a model class by inheriting from $.Model(NAME, [STATIC,] PROTOTYPE):

```
$.Model('Paginate',{
  staticProperty: 'foo'
},{
  prototypeProperty: 'bar'
})
```

There are a few ways to make the Paginate model more useful. By adding setter methods, discussed next, we can limit what values count and offsets can be set to.

Setters

Setter methods are model prototype methods that are named setNAME. They get called with the val passed to model.attr(NAME, val), as well as a success and error callback. Typically, the method should return the value that should be set on the model instance, or call an error with an error message. Success is used for asynchronous setters.

The Paginate model uses setters to prevent invalid counts and offsets values from being set. For example, we make sure the value isn't negative:

```
$.Model('Paginate',{
  setCount : function(newCount, success, error){
    return newCount < 0 ? 0 : newCount;
  },

  setOffset : function(newOffset, success, error){
    return newOffset < 0 ? 0 :
Math.min(newOffset, !isNaN(this.count - 1) ? this.count : Infinity )
  }
});
```

Now, the `nextPrev` plug-in can set offsets with reckless abandon:

```
this.delegate('.next','click', function(){
  paginate.attr('offset', paginate.offset+paginate.limit);
});

this.delegate('.prev','click', function(){
    paginate.attr('offset', paginate.offset-paginate.limit );
});
```

Defaults

We can add default values to `Paginate` instances by setting the static `defaults` property. When a new `paginate` instance is created, if no value is provided, it initializes with the default value:

```
$.Model('Paginate',{
  defaults : {
    count: Infinity,
    offset: 0,
    limit: 100
  }
},{
  setCount : function(newCount, success, error){ ... },
  setOffset : function(newOffset, success, error){ ... }
});

var paginate = new Paginate({count: 500});
assertEqual(paginate.limit, 100);
assertEqual(paginate.count, 500);
```

The `Paginate` model can make it even easier to move to the next or previous page and know whether it's possible by adding helper methods.

Helper Methods

These are prototype methods that help set or get useful data on model instances. The following, completed `Paginate` model includes `next` and `prev` methods that will move to the next and previous pages, if possible. It also provides a `canNext` and `canPrev` method that returns whether or not the instance can move to the next page:

```
$.Model('Paginate',{
  defaults : {
    count: Infinity,
    offset: 0,
    limit: 100
  }
},{
  setCount : function( newCount ){
    return Math.max(0, newCount );
  },
  setOffset : function( newOffset ){
    return Math.max( 0 , Math.min(newOffset, this.count ) )
```

```
    },
    next : function(){
      this.attr('offset', this.offset+this.limit);
    },
    prev : function(){
      this.attr('offset', this.offset - this.limit )
    },
    canNext : function(){
      return this.offset > this.count - this.limit
    },
    canPrev : function(){
      return this.offset > 0
    }
  })
```

Thus, our jQuery widget becomes much more refined:

```
$.fn.nextPrev = function(paginate){
    this.delegate('.next','click', function(){
      paginate.attr('offset', paginate.offset+paginate.limit);
    })
    this.delegate('.prev','click', function(){
      paginate.attr('offset', paginate.offset-paginate.limit );
    });
    var self = this;
    paginate.bind('updated.attr', function(){
      self.find('.prev')[paginate.canPrev() ? 'addClass' : 'removeClass']('enabled')
      self.find('.next')[paginate.canNext() ? 'addClass' : 'removeClass']('enabled');
    })
};
```

Service Encapsulation

We've just seen how $.Model is useful for modeling client-side state. However, for most applications, the critical data is on the server, not on the client. The client needs to create, retrieve, update, and delete (CRUD) data on the server. Maintaining the duality of data on the client and server is tricky business; $.Model simplifies this problem.

$.Model is extremely flexible. It can be made to work with all sorts of service and data types. This book covers only how $.Model works with the most common and popular service and data types: Representational State Transfer (REST) and JSON.

A REST service uses URLs and the HTTP verbs POST, GET, PUT, and DELETE to create, retrieve, update, and delete data, respectively. For example, a task service that allows you to create, retrieve, update, and delete tasks might look like:

```
create    → POST    /tasks
read all  → GET     /tasks
read      → GET     /tasks/2
update    → PUT     /tasks/2
delete    → DELETE  /tasks/2
```

The following connects to task services, letting us create, retrieve, update, and delete tasks from the server:

```
$.Model("Task",{
  create  : "POST /tasks.json",
  findOne : "GET /tasks/{id}.json",
  findAll : "GET /tasks.json",
  update  : "PUT /tasks/{id}.json",
  destroy : "DELETE /tasks/{id}.json"
},{ });
```

Let's go through every step needed to use the Task model to CRUD tasks.

Create a task

```
new Task({ name: 'do the dishes'}).save(
  success( task, data ),
  error( jqXHR)
) //=> taskDeferred
```

To create an instance of a model on the server, first create an instance with new Model(attributes). Then call save(). save() checks as to whether the task has an ID. In this case it does not, so save() makes a create request with the task's attributes. It takes two parameters:

success
> A function that gets called if the save is successful. Success gets called with the task instance and the data returned by the server.

error
> A function that gets called if there is an error with the request. It gets called with jQuery's wrapped XHR object.

save() returns a deferred that resolves to the created task.

Get a task

```
Task.findOne(params,
  success( task ),
  error( jqXHR)
) //=> taskDeferred
```

Retrieves a single task from the server. It takes three parameters:

params
> The data to pass to the server; typically, an ID like {id: 2}.

success
> A function that gets called if the request is successful. Success gets called with the task instance.

error
> A function that gets called if there is an error with the request.

findOne() returns a deferred that resolves to the task.

Get tasks

```
Task.findAll(params,
  success( tasks ),
  error( jqXHR)
) //=> tasksDeferred
```

Retrieves an array of tasks from the server. It takes three parameters:

params
> The data to pass to the server. Typically, it's an empty object ({}) or filters {limit: 20, offset: 100}.

success
> A function that gets called if the request is successful. Success gets called with an array of task instances.

error
> A function that gets called if there is an error with the request.

findAll() returns a deferred that resolves to an array of tasks.

Update a task

```
task.attr('name','take out recycling');
task.save(
  success( task, data ),
  error( jqXHR)
) //=> taskDeferred
```

To update the server, first change the attributes of a model instance with attr. Then call save(). save() takes the same arguments and returns the same deferred as the create task case.

Destroy a task

```
task.destroy(
  success( task, data ),
  error( jqXHR)
) //=> taskDeferred
```

destroy() deletes a task on the server. destroy() takes two parameters:

success
> A function that gets called if the save is successful. Success gets called with the task instance and the data returned by the server.

error
> A function that gets called if there is an error with the request.

Like with save(), destroy() returns a deferred that resolves to the destroyed task. The Task model has essentially become a contract to our services!

Type Conversion

Did you notice how the server responded with createdAt values as numbers like 1303173531164? This number is actually April 18th, 2011. Instead of getting a number back from task.createdAt, it would be much more useful if it returned a JavaScript date created with new Date(1303173531164). We could do this with a setCreatedAt setter, but if we have lots of date types, this will get repetitive quickly.

To make this easy, $.Model lets you define the type of an attribute as well as a converter function for those types. Set the type of attributes on the static attributes object, and set the converter methods on the static convert object:

```
$.Model('Task',{
  attributes : {
    createdAt : 'date'
  },

  convert : {
    date : function(date){
      return typeof date == 'number' ? new Date(date) : date;
    }
  }
},{});
```

Task now converts createdAt to a Date type. To list the year of each task, write:

```
Task.findAll({}, function(tasks){
  $.each(tasks, function(){
    console.log( "Year = "+this.createdAt.fullYear() )
  })
});
```

CRUD Events

The model publishes events when an instance has been created, updated, or destroyed. You can listen to these events globally on the model or on an individual model instance. Use MODEL.bind(EVENT, callback(ev, instance)) to listen for created, updated, or destroyed events.

Let's say we want to know when a task is created, so we can then add it to the page. After it's been added, we'll listen for updates on that task to make sure we are showing its name correctly. Here's how we can do this:

```
Task.bind('created', function(ev, task){
  var el = $('<li>').html(todo.name);
  el.appendTo($('#todos'));

  task.bind('updated', function(){
    el.html(this.name);
  }).bind('destroyed', function(){
    el.remove();
  })
});
```

Using Client-Side Templates in the View

JavaScriptMVC's views are really just client-side templates, which take data and return a string. Typically, the strings are HTML intended to be inserted into the DOM.

`$.View` is a templating interface that uses templates to take care of complexities. It offers:

- Convenient and uniform syntax
- Template loading from HTML elements or external files
- Synchronous or asynchronous template loading
- Template preloading
- Caching of processed templates
- Bundling of processed templates in production builds
- `$.Deferred` support

JavaScriptMVC comes prepackaged with four different template engines:

- EJS
- JAML
- Micro
- Tmpl

This tutorial uses EJS templates, but the following techniques will work with any template engine (with minor syntax differences).

Basic Use

When using views, you almost always want to insert the results of a rendered template into the page. `jQuery.View` overwrites the jQuery modifiers, so using a view is as easy as:

```
$("#foo").html('mytemplate.ejs',{message: 'hello world'})
```

This code:

1. Loads the template in the file *mytemplate.ejs*. It might look like:

    ```
    <h2><%= message %></h2>
    ```

2. Renders it with {`message: 'hello world'`}, resulting in:

    ```
    <h2>hello world</h2>
    ```

3. Inserts the result into the `foo` element, which might look like:

    ```
    <div id='foo'><h2>hello world</h2></div>
    ```

jQuery Modifiers

You can use a template with the following jQuery modifier methods:

```
$('#bar').after('temp.ejs',{});
$('#bar').append('temp.ejs',{});
$('#bar').before('temp.ejs',{});
$('#bar').html('temp.ejs',{});
$('#bar').prepend('temp.ejs',{});
$('#bar').replaceWith('temp.ejs',{});
$('#bar').text('temp.ejs',{});
```

Loading from a Script Tag

View can load from script tags or from files. To load from a script tag, create a script tag with a `type` attribute set to the template type (`text/ejs`), and an `id` to label the template:

```
<script type='text/ejs' id='recipesEJS'>
<% for(var i=0; i < recipes.length; i++){ %>
  <li><%=recipes[i].name %></li>
<%} %>
</script>
```

Render with this template, like so:

```
$("#foo").html('recipesEJS', recipeData)
```

Notice that we passed the `id` of the element we want to render.

$.View and Subtemplates

Sometimes you simply want the rendered string. In this case, you can use `$.View(TEM PLATE , data )` directly. Pass `$.View` the path to the template, as well as the data you want to render:

```
var html = $.View("template/items.ejs", items );
```

The most common use case is subtemplates. It's common practice to separate out an individual item's template from the list template (*items.ejs*). We'll make `template/items.ejs` render a `<>` for each item, but use the template in `template/item.ejs` for the content of each item:

```
<% for( var i = 0; i < this.length; i++){ %>
  <li>
    <%= $.View("template/item.ejs", this[i]);
  </li>
< % } %>
```

`this` refers to the data passed to the template. In the case of `template/items.ejs`, `this` is the array of items. In `template/item.ejs`, it will be the individual item.

Deferreds

It's extremely common behavior to make an Ajax request and use a template to render the result. Using the `Task` model from the previous `$.Model` section, we could render tasks like:

```
Task.findAll({}, function(tasks){
  $('#tasks').html("views/tasks.ejs" , tasks )
})
```

`$.View` supports deferred (*http://api.jquery.com/category/deferred-object/*) allows very powerful, terse, and high-performance syntax. If a deferred is found in the render data passed to `$.View` or the jQuery modifiers, `$.View` will load the template asynchronously and wait until all deferreds and the template are loaded before rendering the template.

The model methods `findAll`, `findOne`, `save`, and `destroy` return deferreds. This allows us to rewrite the rendering of tasks into one line:

```
$('#tasks').html("views/tasks.ejs" , Task.findAll() )
```

This also works with multiple deferreds:

```
$('#app').html("views/app.ejs" , {
  tasks: Task.findAll(),
  users: User.findAll()
})
```

Packaging, Preloading, and Performance

By default, `$.View` loads templates synchronously because it expects that you are:

- Putting templates in script tags
- Packaging templates with your JavaScript build
- Preloading templates

JavaScriptMVC does not recommend putting templates in script tags. Script tag templates make it hard to reuse templates across different JavaScript applications. They can also reduce load performance if your app doesn't need the templates immediately.

JavaScriptMVC recommends initially packaging used templates with your application's JavaScript, and then preloading templates that will be used later.

StealJS, JavaScriptMVC's build system, can process and package templates, adding them to a minified production build. Simply point `steal.views(PATH, ...)` to your template:

```
steal.views('tasks.ejs','task.ejs');
```

Later, when `$.View` looks for that template, it will use a cached copy, saving an extra Ajax request.

For templates that are not used immediately, preload and cache them with jQuery.get. Simply give the URL to the template and provide a dataType of 'view' (it's best to do this a short time after the initial page has loaded):

```
$(window).load(function(){
  setTimeout(function(){
    $.get('users.ejs',function(){},'view');
    $.get('user.ejs',function(){},'view');
  },500)
})
```

$.Controller: The jQuery Plug-in Factory

JavaScriptMVC's controllers are many things. They are a jQuery plug-in factory. They can be used as a traditional view, making pagination widgets and grid controls. They can also be used as a traditional controller, initializing controllers and hooking them up to models. Mostly, controllers are a really great way of organizing your application's code.

Controllers provide a number of handy features, such as:

- jQuery plug-in creation
- Automatic binding
- Default options
- Automatic determinism

But the controller's most important feature is not obvious to anyone but the most hardcore JS ninjas. The following code creates a tooltip-like widget that displays itself until the document is clicked:

```
$.fn.tooltip = function(){
  var el = this[0];

  $(document).click(function(ev){
    if (ev.target !== el)
      $(el).remove();
  });

  $(el).show();
  return this;
});
```

To use it, add the element to be displayed to the page, and then call tooltip on it:

```
$("<div class='tooltip'>Some Info</div>")
  .appendTo(document.body)
  .tooltip()
```

But this code has a problem. Can you spot it? Here's a hint: what if your application is long-lived and lots of these tooltip elements are created?

The problem is that this code leaks memory! Every tooltip element, and any tooltip child elements, are kept in memory forever. This is because the click handler is not removed from the document, and it has a closure reference to the element.

This is a very easy mistake to make. jQuery removes all event handlers from elements that are removed from the page, so developers often don't have to worry about unbinding event handlers. But in this case, we bound to something outside the widget's element—the document—and did not unbind the event handler.

But within a Model-View-Controller architecture, controllers listen to the view, and views listen to the model. You are constantly listening to events outside the widget's element. For example, the nextPrev widget from the $.Model section listens to updates in the paginate model:

```
paginate.bind('updated.attr', function(){
  self.find('.prev')[this.canPrev() ? 'addClass' : 'removeClass']('enabled')
  self.find('.next')[this.canNext() ? 'addClass' : 'removeClass']('enabled');
})
```

But it doesn't unbind from paginate! Forgetting to remove event handlers is potentially a source of errors. However, both the tooltip and nextPrev will not error. Instead, both will silently kill an application's performance. Fortunately, $.Controller makes this easy and organized. Here's how we can write tooltip:

```
$.Controller('Tooltip',{
  init: function(){
    this.element.show()
  },
  "{document} click": function(el, ev){
    if(ev.target !== this.element[0]){
      this.element.remove()
    }
  }
})
```

When the document is clicked and the element is removed from the DOM, $.Controller will unbind the document click handler automatically.

$.Controller can do the same thing for the nextPrev widget, binding to the Paginate model:

```
$.Controller('Nextprev',{
  ".next click" : function(){
    var paginate = this.options.paginate;
    paginate.attr('offset', paginate.offset+paginate.limit);
  },
  ".prev click" : function(){
    var paginate = this.options.paginate;
    paginate.attr('offset', paginate.offset-paginate.limit );
  },
  "{paginate} updated.attr" : function(ev, paginate){
    this.find('.prev')[paginate.canPrev() ? 'addClass' : 'removeClass']('enabled')
    this.find('.next')[paginate.canNext() ? 'addClass' : 'removeClass']('enabled');
  }
```

```
})
// create a nextprev control
$('#pagebuttons').nextprev({ paginate: new Paginate() })
```

If the element #pagebuttons is removed from the page, the NextPrev controller instance will automatically unbind from the Paginate model.

Now that your appetite for error-free code is properly whetted, the following details how $.Controller works.

Overview

$.Controller inherits from $.Class. To create a controller class, call $.Controller (NAME, classProperties, instanceProperties) with the name of your controller, static methods, and instance methods. The following is the start of a reusable list widget:

```
$.Controller("List", {
  defaults : {}
},{
  init : function(){  },
  "li click" : function(){  }
})
```

When a controller class is created, it creates a jQuery helper method of a similar name. The helper method is primarily used to create new instances of controllers on elements in the page. The helper method name is the controller's name underscored, with any periods replaced with underscores. For example, the helper for $.Controller('App.Foo Bar') is $(el).app_foo_bar().

Controller Instantiation

To create a controller instance, you can call new Controller(element, options) with an HTML element or jQuery-wrapped element, as well as an optional options object to configure the controller. For example:

```
new List($('ul#tasks'), {model : Task});
```

You can also use the jQuery helper method to create a List controller instance on the #tasks element:

```
$('ul#tasks').list({model : Task})
```

When a controller is created, it calls the controller's prototype init method with:

this.element
    Set to the jQuery-wrapped HTML element

this.options
    Set to the options passed to the controller merged with the class' defaults object

The following code updates the List controller to request tasks from the model and then render them with an optional template passed to the list:

```
$.Controller("List", {
  defaults : {
    template: "items.ejs"
  }
}, {
  init : function(){
    this.element.html( this.options.template, this.options.model.findAll() );
  },
  "li click" : function(){  }
});
```

We can now configure Lists to render tasks with a the provided template. How flexible!

```
$('#tasks').list({model: Task, template: "tasks.ejs"});
$('#users').list({model: User, template: "users.ejs"})
```

If we don't provide a template, List will default to using *items.ejs*.

Event Binding

As mentioned in `$.Controller`'s introduction, its most powerful feature is its ability to bind and unbind event handlers.

When a controller is created, it looks for action methods. Action methods are methods that look like event handlers—for example, `"li click"`. These actions are bound using `jQuery.bind` or `jQuery.delegate`. When the controller is destroyed by removing the controller's element from the page or calling destroy on the controller, these events are unbound, preventing memory leaks.

The following are examples of actions with descriptions of what they listen for:

`"li click"`
Clicks on or within `li` elements within the controller element

`"mousemove"`
Moves the mouse within the controller element

`"{window} click"`
Clicks on or within the window

Action functions get called back with the jQuery-wrapped element or object that the event happened on, as well as the event. For example:

```
"li click": function( el, ev ) {
  assertEqual(el[0].nodeName, "li" )
  assertEqual(ev.type, "click")
}
```

Templated Actions

`$.Controller` supports templated actions. Templated actions can be used to bind to other objects, customize the event type, or customize the selector.

Controller replaces the parts of your actions that look like `{OPTION}` with a value in the controller's options or the window.

The following is a skeleton of a menu that lets you customize it to show submenus on different events:

```
$.Controller("Menu",{
  "li {openEvent}" : function(){
    // show subchildren
  }
});

//create a menu that shows children on click
$("#clickMenu").menu({openEvent: 'click'});

//create a menu that shows children on mouseenter
$("#hoverMenu").menu({openEvent: 'mouseenter'});
```

We could enhance the menu further to allow customization of the menu element tag:

```
$.Controller("Menu",{
  defaults : {menuTag : "li"}
},{
  "{menuTag} {openEvent}" : function(){
    // show subchildren
  }
});

$("#divMenu").menu({menuTag : "div"})
```

Templated actions let you bind to elements or objects outside the controller's element. For example, the `Task` model from the `$.Model` section produces a "created" event when a new `Task` is created. We can make our list widget listen to tasks being created, and then add these tasks to the list automatically:

```
$.Controller("List", {
  defaults : {
    template: "items.ejs"
  }
},{
  init : function(){
    this.element.html( this.options.template, this.options.model.findAll() );
  },
  "{Task} created" : function(Task, ev, newTask){
    this.element.append(this.options.template, [newTask])
  }
})
```

The "{Task} create" gets called with the Task model, the created event, and the newly created Task. The function uses the template to render a list of tasks (in this case there is only one) and add the resulting HTML to the element.

But it's much better to make List work with any model. Instead of hardcoding tasks, we'll make the controller take a model as an option:

```
$.Controller("List", {
  defaults : {
    template: "items.ejs",
    model: null
  }
},{
  init : function(){
    this.element.html( this.options.template, this.options.model.findAll() );
  },
  "{model} created" : function(Model, ev, newItem){
    this.element.append(this.options.template, [newItem])
  }
});

// create a list of tasks
$('#tasks').list({model: Task, template: "tasks.ejs"});
```

Putting It All Together: An Abstract CRUD List

Now we will enhance the list to not only add items when they are created, but to update and remove them when they are destroyed. To do this, we start by listening to updated and destroyed:

```
"{model} updated" : function(Model, ev, updatedItem){
  // find and update the LI for updatedItem
},
"{model} destroyed" : function(Model, ev, destroyedItem){
  // find and remove the LI for destroyedItem
}
```

You'll notice that we have a problem. Somehow, we need to find the element that represents the particular model instance. To do this, we need to label the element as belonging to the model instance. Fortunately, $.Model and $.View make it very easy to label an element with an instance and find that element.

To label the element with a model instance within an EJS view, simply write the model instance to the element. The following might be tasks.ejs:

```
<% for(var i =0 ; i < this.length; i++){ %>
  <% var task = this[i]; %>
  <li <%= task %> > <%= task.name %> </li>
<% } %>
```

tasks.ejs iterates through a list of tasks. For each task, it creates an li element with the task's name. But it also adds the task to the element's jQuery data with <li><%= task %></li>.

To later get that element given a model instance, call `modelInstance.elements([CON TEXT])`. This returns the jQuery-wrapped elements that represent the model instance.

Putting it together, the list becomes:

```
$.Controller("List", {
  defaults : {
    template: "items.ejs",
    model: null
  }
},{
  init : function(){
    this.element.html( this.options.template, this.options.model.findAll() );
  },
  "{model} created" : function(Model, ev, newItem){
    this.element.append(this.options.template, [newItem])
  },
  "{model} updated" : function(Model, ev, updatedItem){
    updatedItem.elements(this.element)
      .replaceWith(this.options.template, [updatedItem])
  },
  "{model} destroyed" : function(Model, ev, destroyedItem){
    destroyedItem.elements(this.element)
      .remove()
  }
});

// create a list of tasks
$('#tasks').list({model: Task, template: "tasks.ejs"});
```

It's almost frighteningly easy to create abstract, reusable, memory-safe widgets with JavaScriptMVC.

jQuery Primer

A lot of libraries have been developed to make the DOM easier to work with, but few have the popularity and praise of jQuery. And for good reason: jQuery's API is excellent and the library is lightweight and namespaced, so it shouldn't conflict with anything else you're using. What's more, jQuery is easily extendable; a whole host of plug-ins (*http://plugins.jquery.com*) have been developed, from JavaScript validation to progress bars.

jQuery is namespaced behind the `jQuery` variable, which is aliased with a dollar sign (`$`). Unlike libraries such as Prototype (*http://prototypejs.org*), jQuery doesn't extend any native JavaScript objects, largely to avoid conflicts with other libraries.

The other important thing to understand about jQuery is selectors. If you're familiar with CSS, selectors will be second nature to you. All of jQuery's instance methods are performed on selectors, so rather than iterating over elements, you can just use a selector to collect them. Any functions called on the jQuery selector will be executed on every element selected.

To demonstrate this, let me show you an example of adding a class name `selected` to all the elements with the class `foo`. The first example will be in pure JavaScript, and the second will use jQuery:

```javascript
// Pure JavaScript example
var elements = document.getElementsByClassName("foo");
for (var i=0; i < elements.length; i++) {
  elements[i].className += " selected";
}

// jQuery example
$(".foo").addClass("selected");
```

So, you can see how jQuery's selectors API greatly reduces the code required. Let's take a closer look at those selectors. Just as you'd use a hash (#) in CSS to select elements by ID, you can do the same with jQuery:

```javascript
// Select an element by ID (wem)
var element = document.getElementById("wem");
```

```
var element = $("#wem");
```

```
// Select all elements by class (bar)
var elements = document.getElementsByClassName("bar");
var elements = $(".bar");
```

```
// Select all elements by tag (p)
var elements = document.getElementsByTagName("p");
var elements = $("p");
```

As with CSS, you can combine selectors to make them more specific:

```
// Select the children of 'bar' with a class of 'foo'
var foo = $(".bar .foo");
```

You can even select by an elements attribute:

```
var username = $("input[name='username']");
```

Or, you can select the first matched element:

```
var example = $(".wem:first");
```

Whenever we call a function on the selector, all elements selected are affected:

```
// Add a class to all elements with class 'foo'
$(".foo").addClass("bar");
```

As I mentioned, all of jQuery's functions are namespaced, so if you call a function directly on a DOM element, it will fail:

```
// This will fail!
var element = document.getElementById("wem");
element.addClass("bar");
```

Instead, if you want to use jQuery's API, you'll have to wrap up the element into a jQuery instance:

```
var element = document.getElementById("wem");
$(element).addClass("bar");
```

DOM Traversal

Once you've selected some elements, jQuery gives you a number of ways (*http://api .jquery.com/category/traversing*) of finding other elements relative to elements in the selector:

```
var wem = $("#wem");
```

```
// Find scoped children
wem.find(".test");
```

```
// Select the direct parent
wem.parent();
```

```
// Or get an array of parents, scoped by an optional selector
wem.parents(".optionalSelector");
```

```
// Select the direct descendants (of the first element)
wem.children();
```

Or, you can traverse elements inside the selector:

```
var wem = $("#wem");

// Returns the element at the specified index (0)
wem.eq( 0 );

// Returns the first element (equivalent to $.fn.eq(0))
wem.first();

// Reduce elements to those that match a selector (".foo")
wem.filter(".foo");

// Reduce elements to those that pass the test function
wem.filter(function(){
  // this, is the current element
  return $(this).hasClass(".foo");
});

// Reduce elements to those that have descendants that match a selector (".selected")
wem.has(".selected");
```

jQuery has some iterators, map() and each(), that accept a callback:

```
var wem = $("#wem");

// Pass each element selected into a function,
// constructing a new array based on the return values
wem.map(function(element, index){
  assertEqual(this, element);

  return this.id;
});

// Iterate a callback over selected elements, equivalent to a `for` loop.
wem.each(function(index, element){
  assertEqual(this, element);

  /* ... */
});
```

It's also possible to add elements to a selector manually:

```
// Add all p elements to the selector
var wem = $("#wem");
wem.add( $("p") );
```

DOM Manipulation

jQuery isn't all about selectors, though; it has a powerful API for manipulating and interfacing with the DOM. In addition to selectors, jQuery's constructor takes HTML tags, which you can use to generate new elements:

```
var element = $("p");
element.addClass("bar")
element.text("Some content");
```

Appending the new element to the DOM is easy—just use jQuery's append() or pre pend() functions. For performance reasons, you ideally want to do any manipulation on generated elements before you attach them to the DOM:

```
// Append an element
var newDiv = $("<div />");
$("body").append(newDiv);

// Add an element as the first child
$(".container").prepend($("<hr />"));
```

Or, you can insert an element before/after another:

```
// Insert an element after another
$(".container").after( $("<p />") );

// Insert an element before another
$(".container").before( $("<p />") );
```

Removing elements is also simple:

```
// Removing elements
$("wem").remove();
```

What about changing an element's attributes? jQuery has support for that, too. For example, you can add class names using the addClass() function:

```
$("#foo").addClass("bar");

// Remove a class
$("#foo").removeClass("bar");

// Does an element have this class?
var hasBar = $("#foo").hasClass("bar");
```

Setting and fetching CSS styles is simple enough, too. The css() function acts as both a getter and setter, depending on the type of arguments passed to it:

```
var getColor = $(".foo").css("color");

// Set the color style
$(".foo").css("color", "#000");

// Or, pass a hash to set multiple styles
$(".foo").css({color: "#000", backgroundColor: "#FFF"});
```

jQuery has a number of shortcuts for the most common style changes:

```
// Set display to none, hiding elements
$(".bar").hide();

// Set display to block, showing elements
$(".bar").show();
```

Or, if you want the opacity to change slowly:

```
$(".foo").fadeOut();
$(".foo").fadeIn();
```

jQuery's getter and setter functions aren't limited to CSS. For example, you can set the contents of elements using the html() function:

```
// Retrieving the HTML of the first element in the selector
var getHTML = $("#bar").html();

// Setting the HTML of selected elements
$("#bar").html("<p>Hi</p>");
```

The same goes for the text() function, although the arguments are escaped:

```
var getText = $("#bar").text();

$("#bar").text("Plain text contents");
```

And, finally, to remove all of an element's children, use the empty() function:

```
$("#bar").empty();
```

Events

Event handling in browsers has had a turbulent history, which has resulted in inconsistent APIs. jQuery resolves that problem for you, ironing out all the differences among browsers and providing a great API. Here's a brief overview of jQuery's event handling, but for more information, see Chapter 2, as well as the official docs (*http://api.jquery.com/category/events*).

To add an event handler, use the bind() function, passing the event type and callback:

```
$(".clicky").bind("click", function(event){
  // Executed on click
});
```

jQuery provides shortcuts for the more common events, so rather than calling bind, you can do something like this:

```
$(".clicky").click(function(){ /* ... */ });
```

One event you're very likely to use is *document.ready*. This is fired during the page load, when the DOM is ready but before elements such as images are loaded. jQuery provides a neat shortcut for the event—just pass a function straight to the jQuery object:

```
jQuery(function($){
  // Executed on document.ready
});
```

What often confuses jQuery newcomers is the context change inside callbacks. For instance, in the example above, the context of the callback is changed to reference the element, in this case $(".clicky"):

```
$(".clicky").click(function(){
  // 'this' equals the event target
  assert( $(this).hasClass(".clicky") );
});
```

The context change becomes a problem if you're using this in the callback. A common idiom is to store the context in a local variable, often called self:

```
var self = this;
$(".clicky").click(function(){
  self.clickedClick();
});
```

An alternative is to wrap the callback in a proxy function using jQuery.proxy(), like so:

```
$(".clicky").click($.proxy(function(){
  // Context isn't changed
}, this));
```

For a further explanation of event delegation and context, see Chapter 2.

Ajax

Ajax, or XMLHttpRequest, is another feature that has wildly different implementations across browsers. Again, jQuery abstracts them, ironing out any differences, giving you a nice API (*http://api.jquery.com/category/ajax*). We covered jQuery's Ajax API in greater detail in Chapter 3, but here's a brief overview.

jQuery has one low-level function, ajax(), and several higher-level abstractions of it. The ajax() function takes a hash of options, such as the endpoint url, the type of request, and success callbacks:

```
$.ajax({
  url: "http://example.com",
  type: "GET",
  success: function(){ /* ... */ }
});
```

However, jQuery's shortcuts make the API even more succinct:

```
$.get("http://example.com", function(){ /* on success */ })
$.post("http://example.com", {some: "data"});
```

jQuery's dataType option tells jQuery how to deal with Ajax responses. If you don't provide it, jQuery will make an intelligent guess based on the response's header data type. If you know what the response is, it's better to set it explicitly:

```
// Request JSON
$.ajax({
  url: "http://example.com/endpoint.jso",
  type: "GET",
  dataType: "json",
  success: function(json){ /* ... */ }
});
```

jQuery also provides shortcuts for common datatypes, like `getJSON()`, which is equivalent to the `ajax()` function above:

```
$.getJSON("http://example.com/endpoint.json", function(json){ /* .. */ });
```

For a more in-depth analysis of the options in jQuery's Ajax API, check out Chapter 3, as well as the official documentation.

Being a Good Citizen

jQuery prides itself on being a good web citizen; as such, it is completely namespaced and doesn't pollute global scope. However, the object `jQuery` is aliased to the `$`, which is often used by other libraries, such as Prototype (*http://www.prototypejs.org/*). Therefore, to stop the libraries from conflicting, you need to use jQuery's `noConflict` mode to change the alias and free up `$`:

```
var $J = jQuery.noConflict();

assertEqual( $, undefined );
```

When you're writing jQuery extensions, you need to assume that jQuery's no conflict mode has been switched on and that `$` doesn't reference jQuery. In practice, though, `$` is a useful shortcut, so just make sure it's a local variable:

```
(function($){

  // $ is a local variable
  $(".foo").addClass("wem");

})(jQuery);
```

To simplify things, jQuery will also pass a reference to itself with the *document.ready* event:

```
jQuery(function($){
  // Runs when the page loads
  assertEqual( $, jQuery );
});
```

Extensions

Extending jQuery couldn't be easier. If you want to add class functions, just create the function straight on the `jQuery` object:

```
jQuery.myExt = function(arg1){ /*...*/ };

// Then, to use
$.myExt("anyArgs");
```

If you want to add instance functions that will be available on the element selector, just set the function on the jQuery.fn object, which is an alias for jQuery.prototype. It's good practice to return the context (i.e., this) at the end of the extension, which enables chaining:

```
jQuery.fn.wemExt = function(arg1){
  $(this).html("Bar");
  return this;
};


$("#element").wemExt(1).addClass("foo");
```

It's also good practice to encapsulate your extension in the module pattern (*http://yuiblog.com/blog/2007/06/12/module-pattern/*),which prevents any scope leaks and variable conflicts. Wrap your extension in an anonymous function, keeping all the variables local:

```
(function($){
  // Local context in here
  var replaceLinks = function(){
    var re = /((http|https|ftp):\/\/[\w?=&.\/-;#~%-]+(?![\w\s?&.\/;#~%"=-]*>))/g;
    $(this).html(
      $(this).html().replace(re, '<a target="_blank" href="$1">$1</a> ')
    );
  };

  $.fn.autolink = function() {
    return this.each(replaceLinks);
  };
})(jQuery);
```

Creating a Growl jQuery Plug-in

Let's put our knowledge of jQuery into practice and create a Growl library. For those of you unfamiliar with Growl, it's a notification library (*http://growl.info*) for Mac OS X that applications can use to show messages unobtrusively on the desktop. We're going to emulate the OS X library somewhat and display messages from JavaScript in the page, as demonstrated in Figure A-1.

The first step is to create a #container div from which all our message elements will descend. As you can see, we're including both jQuery and jQuery UI libraries—we'll use the latter later to add a few effects. When the page loads, we'll append the container div:

```
//= require <jquery>
//= require <jquery.ui>
```

Figure A-1. Example Growl messages

```
(function($){
  var container = $("<div />");
  container.attr({id: "growl"});

  $(function(){
    // On page load, append the div
    $("body").append(container);
  });

  /* ... */
})(jQuery);
```

Now for the plug-in's logic. Whenever we have a new message, we append a div to the container element. We're adding a **drop** effect to the message and then, after a period of time, fading and removing it—just like Growl's behavior on OS X:

```
$.growl = function(body){
  // Create the Growl div
  var msg = $("<div />").addClass("msg");
  msg.html(body);

  // Append it to the list
  container.append(msg);

  // Add a drop effect, and then remove
  msg.show("drop", {
    direction: "down",
    distance: 50
  }, 300).
    delay(2000).
    fadeOut(300, function(){
      $(this).remove();
    });

  return msg;
};
```

That's all the JavaScript required. It's looking rather ugly at the moment, so we can spice it up with a bit of CSS3. We want the #container div to be positioned absolutely, at the bottom right of the page:

```css
#growl {
  position: absolute;
  bottom: 10px;
  right: 20px;
  overflow: hidden;
}
```

Now let's style the message elements. I quite like the HUD Growl theme, so let's try to emulate that. We'll make the background slightly transparent using rgba and then add an inset box-shadow, giving the element the appearance of a light source:

```css
#growl .msg {
  width: 200px;
  min-height: 30px;
  padding: 10px;
  margin-bottom: 10px;

  border: 1px solid #171717;
  color: #E4E4E4;
  text-shadow: 0 -1px 1px #0A131A;
  font-weight: bold;
  font-size: 15px;

  background: #141517;
  background: -webkit-gradient(
    linear, left top, left bottom,
    from(rgba(255, 255, 255, 0.3)),
    color-stop(0.8, rgba(255, 255, 255, 0))),
    rgba(0, 0, 0, 0.8);

  -webkit-box-shadow: inset 0 1px 1px #8E8E8E;
  -moz-box-shadow: inset 0 1px 1px #8E8E8E;
  box-shadow: inset 0 1px 1px #8E8E8E;

  -webkit-border-radius: 7px;
  -moz-border-radius: 7px;
  border-radius: 7px;
}
```

That's all there is to it. You see how trivially easy it is to create jQuery plug-ins. As with the other examples, you can see the full source in *assets/appA/growl.html*.

CSS Extensions

In the words of its author, Alexis Sellier, Less (*http://lesscss.org*) is a "dynamic stylesheet language, which builds upon CSS's syntax." Less is a superset of CSS that extends it with variables, mixins, operations, and nested rules.

It's great because it can really reduce the amount of CSS you need to write—especially when it comes to CSS3 vendor-specific rules. You can then compile your Less files down to pure CSS.

In other words, instead of writing this:

```
.panel {
  background: #CCC;
  background: -webkit-gradient(linear, left top, left bottom, from(#FFF), to(#CCC));
  background: -moz-linear-gradient(top, #FFF, #CCC);
}
```

You can write this:

```
.panel {
  .vbg-gradient(#FFF, #CCC);
}
```

Variables

If you're reusing colors and rule attributes, using Less variables allows you to amalgamate them in one place, letting you make global changes without a find and replace!

Specifying a variable is easy:

```
@panel-color: #CCC;
```

Then, you can use it inside your style rules:

```
header {
  color: @panel-color;
}
```

Mixins

Less mixins behave a lot like C macros. Basically, you define a mixin, which can take optional arguments, like so:

```
.vbg-gradient(@fc: #FFF, @tc: #CCC) {
  background: @fc;
  background: -webkit-gradient(linear, left top, left bottom, from(@fc), to(@tc));
  background: -moz-linear-gradient(top, @fc, @tc);
  background: linear-gradient(top, @fc, @tc);
}
```

The example above takes two arguments, `fc` and `tc`, with default values of `#FFF` and `#CCC`, respectively. These are then interpolated in the class contents. Think of it as defining a variable, but for whole classes.

Since CSS3 hasn't yet finished the standardization process, the browser vendors generally specify their own prefixes, such as `-webkit` and `-moz`. This is great, in a way, because we can start using the features immediately; but often it's a really verbose syntax, as you need to define styles two or three times for the different browsers.

As you've probably guessed, Less can really cut down on the amount of typing you need to do—you just need to turn vendor-specific styles into a mixin.

Here are some other mixins that might be useful:

```
/* Rounded borders */
.border-radius(@r: 3px) {
  -moz-border-radius: @r;
  -webkit-border-radius: @r;
  border-radius: @r;
}

/* Shadow */
.box-shadow (@h: 0px, @v: 0px, @b: 4px, @c: #333) {
  -moz-box-shadow: @h @v @b @c;
  -webkit-box-shadow: @h @v @b @c;
  box-shadow: @h @v @b @c;
}
```

Nested Rules

Instead of specifying long selector names to get elements, you can nest selectors. The full selector is generated behind the scenes, but nested rules make your stylesheets clearer and more readable:

```
button {
  .border-radius(3px);
  .box-shadow(0, 1px, 1px, #FFF);
  .vbg-gradient(#F9F9F9, #E3E3E3);

  :active {
    .vbg-gradient(#E3E3E3, #F9F9F9);
```

```
        }
    }
```

One word of warning, though: I wouldn't go beyond two levels of nesting because you can seriously abuse this feature if you're not careful, and your stylesheets will look the worse for it.

Including Other Stylesheets

If you're planning on splitting up your stylesheet, which I highly recommend, you can use @import to include other stylesheets within the current one. Less will actually fetch that stylesheet and include it inline, which improves performance because clients won't have another HTTP request to make.

This use case is often used with mixins. Say you have a CSS3 mixin file; you can import it like so:

```
@import "utils";
```

Colors

This feature is so new to Less that it hasn't yet been documented, but it's so useful that it deserves mentioning. Less lets you manipulate colors with various functions:

```
background: saturate(#319, 10%);
background: desaturate(#319, 10%);
background: darken(#319, 10%);
background: lighten(#319, 10%)
```

A lot of designs are based on the same colors, but they use different shades. Indeed, combined with variables, you can make branded themes very quickly.

How Do I Use Less?

There are various methods for compiling Less code into CSS.

Via the Command Line

Install the Less gem, and then call the lessc command:

```
gem install less
lessc style.less
```

Via Rack

If you're using a Rack-based framework like Rails 3, there's an even simpler solution: the rack-less gem. Just include the relevant gem in your *Gemfile*:

```
gem "rack-less"
```

And inject the middleware in *application.rb*:

```
require "rack/less"
config.middleware.use "Rack::Less"
```

Any Less stylesheets under */app/stylesheets* will be compiled automatically. You can even cache and compress the result by configuring rack-less in your *production.rb* config file:

```
Rack::Less.configure do |config|
  config.cache    = true
  config.compress = :yui
end
```

Via JavaScript

Development seems to have slowed on the Ruby libraries, but luckily there's a more up-to-date option: Less.js (*http://github.com/cloudhead/less.js*) is Less written in JavaScript. You can specify Less stylesheets in the page and include the *less.js* JavaScript file, which compiles them automatically:

```
<link rel="stylesheet/less" href="main.less" type="text/css">
<script src="less.js" type="text/javascript"></script>
```

Less.js is 40 times faster than the Ruby version of the library. However, you may want to precompile the Less stylesheets so clients don't take the performance hit. If you have Node.js installed, you can compile it via the command line:

```
node bin/lessc style.less
```

Less.app

This Mac OS X application (*http://incident57.com/less*) makes it even easier to use Less. It uses Less.js behind the scenes, and you can specify certain folders to be "watched"—i.e., the Less stylesheets will be automatically compiled into CSS when you save them. See Figure B-1.

Figure B-1. Compiling Less files automatically with Less.app

CSS3 Reference

Producing beautiful interfaces in CSS2.1 was pretty tricky because it usually involved a lot of extra markup, images, and JavaScript. CSS3 attempts to solve these problems, providing a variety of really useful attributes and selectors to help you create amazing user interfaces.

Often, when designing web applications, I skip Photoshop and jump straight into CSS3 and HTML5. Now that there are these powerful technologies, designing static PSD mockups seems a bit redundant. Clients also tend to appreciate this because they can interact with an HTML prototype of the product, getting a much better feel for the user experience.

"But what about older browsers?" I hear you cry! Surely CSS3 isn't ready for prime time yet? Well, the answer to that is *graceful degradation*. Older browsers will ignore your CSS3 styles, falling back to the standard ones. For example, in Chrome, your users will see the application in its full glory, gradients and all, whereas in IE7, the application will be just as functional, only a lot less pretty.

As for Internet Explorer 6, I advocate you to drop support altogether. Facebook, Amazon, and Google are all starting to drop support, and the small percentage of IE6 users just doesn't make the effort to support it viable. The Web is moving on, and older technologies need to be dropped.

The major browsers are IE, Firefox, Chrome, and Safari. Chrome and Safari have a different JavaScript engine, but they share the same rendering engine, WebKit. Although there are subtle differences between the two browsers—they use different graphics libraries—fixes to Chrome are pushed upstream to WebKit, and vice versa.

Microsoft released IE9 as this book was being written. Hopefully it will be widely adopted before too long, because it's quite an improvement on its previous browsers, and it includes a lot of CSS3 support.

It's an incredibly exciting time to be a frontend developer, and you should consider using these new technologies immediately.

Prefixes

The browser vendors were implementing CSS3 before it had been completely standardized. For that reason, while the syntax is still in flux, some CSS3 styles have a browser-specific prefix. For example, the CSS3 gradient style is different in Firefox and Safari. Firefox uses `-moz-linear-gradient`, and Safari (WebKit) uses `-webkit-gradient`; both syntaxes are prefixed with the vendor type.

The different prefixes used are:

- Chrome: `-webkit-`
- Safari: `-webkit-`
- Firefox: `-moz-`
- IE: `-ms-`
- Opera: `-o-`

For the moment, you should specify styles with the vendor prefix and then without. This is to ensure that when the browsers remove the prefix and switch over to the standardized CSS3 specification, your styles will still work:

```
#prefix-example {
  -moz-box-shadow: 0 3px 5px #FFF;
  -webkit-box-shadow: 0 3px 5px #FFF;
  box-shadow: 0 3px 5px #FFF;
}
```

Colors

CSS3 gives you some new ways of specifying colors, including alpha transparency.

The old way of creating transparent colors was using 1px × 1px background images, but you can put that behind you now.

The `rgb` style lets you specify colors with red, green, and blue fills—the primary colors—rather than the traditional hex values. You can convert between the two easily by using Safari's Web Inspector—just click on a color in the Styles section.

The example below is equivalent to the #FFF hex value—i.e., white:

```
#rgb-example {
  //    rgb(red, green, blue);
  color: rgb(255, 255, 255);
}
```

You can also use the `hsl` style, which stands for hue, saturation, and lightness.

HSL takes three values:

Hue
> A degree on the color wheel; 0 (or 360) is red, 120 is green, 240 is blue. Numbers in between create different shades.

Saturation
> A percentage value; 100% shows the full color.

Lightness
> Also a percentage; 0% is dark (black), 100% is light (white), and 50% is the average.

Adding alpha transparency to `rgb` or `hsl` is simple—just use `rgba` and `hsla`, respectively. Alpha transparency is specified as a number between 0 (transparent) and 1 (opaque).

```
#alpha-example {
  background: hsla(324, 100%, 50%, .5);
  border: 1em solid rgba(0, 0, 0, .3);
  color: rgba(255, 255, 255, .8);
}
```

Browser support:

- Firefox: full support
- Chrome: full support
- Opera: full support
- Safari: full support
- IE: full support
- Opera: full support

Rounded Corners

Rounding corners in CSS 2.1 was quite a slog, often involving a lot of extra markup, multiple images, and even JavaScript.

Now it's much easier—just use the `border-radius` style. As with the padding and margin styles, you can specify multiple radii to target different corners, two to target the horizontal and vertical radii, or one radius to target all of them. By providing a large-enough radius, you can even create a circle:

```
border-radius: 20px;

// horizonal, vertical
border-radius: 20px 20px;

// top left, top right, bottom right, bottom left
border-radius: 20px 20px 20px 20px;
```

Browser support:

- Firefox: full support

- Chrome: full support
- Safari: with `-webkit-`
- IE >= 9.0: full support
- Opera: full support

Drop Shadows

Prior to CSS3, a lot of people didn't bother with drop shadows because it was such a hassle. However, CSS3 gives you `box-shadow` style, which makes implementing them a breeze. Just don't go overboard in addition to creating a potential eyesore; drop shadows can be quite performance-intensive.

`box-shadow` takes a few options: the horizontal offset, vertical offset, blur radius, optional spread distance, and color. By providing the `inset` option, the shadow will be drawn inside the element; otherwise, the default is outside. You can also include multiple shadows by comma-separating them, as in the examples below:

```
// horizonal offset, vertical offset, blur radius, color
box-shadow: 10px 5px 15px #000;

// inset shadows
box-shadow: 10px 5px 15px #000 inset;

// horizonal offset, vertical offset, blur radius, spread distance, color
box-shadow: 10px 5px 15px 15px #000;

// multiple shadows
box-shadow: 0 1px 1px #FFF inset, 5px 5px 10px #000;
```

Designers often specify a light source in their designs, which makes the interface seem a bit more tangible and interactive. You can do that easily with `box-shadow`—just specify a 1px, white inset shadow. In this case, the light source is from the top of the page; we'll need to keep that consistent across all our styles:

```
#shadow-example {
  -moz-box-shadow: 0 1px 1px #FFF inset;
  -webkit-box-shadow: 0 1px 1px #FFF inset;
  box-shadow: 0 1px 1px #FFF inset;
}
```

Browser support:

- Firefox: full support
- Chrome: with `-webkit-`
- Safari: with `-webkit-`
- IE >= 9.0: full support
- Opera: full support

Text Shadow

Before CSS3, the only way to do text shadows was to replace the text with images—a nasty workaround. CSS3 lets you add shadows to text with the `text-shadow` style. Just pass it the horizontal offset, vertical offset, optional blur radius, and color:

```
// horizonal offset, vertical offset, color
text-shadow: 1px 1px #FFF;

// horizonal offset, vertical offset, blur radius, color
text-shadow: 1px 1px .3em rgba(255, 255, 255, .8);
```

Text shadows are different from `box-shadows` because as there is no support for spread distances or inset shadows. However, you can trick the eye to believe that a text shadow is inset or outset with the shadow position. If the shadow has a negative vertical offset and is above the text, it appears inset. Accordingly, if the shadow is below the text, it looks outset.

Browser support:

- Firefox: full support
- Chrome: full support
- Safari: full support
- IE: no support
- Opera: full support

Gradients

Previously, gradients were implemented by using repeating background images. This meant they had a fixed width or height, and you needed to open up an image editor to alter them.

CSS3 adds support for linear and radial gradients, which is one of its most useful features. There are a few CSS functions you call to generate the gradients, and you can use them wherever you would normally use a color.

For linear gradients, just pass the `linear-gradient` function a list of colors you want to transition through:

```
linear-gradient(#CCC, #DDD, white)
```

By default, the gradients are vertical; however, you can change that by passing in a position:

```
// horizontal gradient
linear-gradient(left, #CCC, #DDD, #FFF);

// or with a specific angle
linear-gradient(-45deg , #CCC , #FFF)
```

If you want more control over where a gradient transition begins, you can use color stops. Just specify a percentage or pixel value along with the color:

```
linear-gradient(white , #DDD 20% , black)
```

You can also transition to and from a transparency:

```
radial-gradient( rgba(255, 255, 255, .8) , transparent )
```

Safari currently has a markedly different syntax. It will soon align with the standard, but, for now, here's how to use it:

```
// -webkit-gradient(<type>, <point> [, <radius>]?, <point> [, <radius>]?
//[, <stop>]*);
-webkit-gradient(linear, left top, left bottom,
from(#FFF), color-stop(10%, #DDD), to(#CCC));
```

Although most major browsers support the CSS gradient standard, each prefixes the syntax with its own vendor name:

- Firefox: with -moz-
- Chrome: with -webkit-
- Safari: alternative implementation
- IE >= 10: with -ms-
- Opera >= 11.1: with -o-

So, a gradient that works cross-browser looks like this:

```
#gradient-example {
  /* Fallback */
  background: #FFF;
  /* Chrome < 10, Safari < 5.1 */
  background: -webkit-gradient(linear, left top, left bottom, from(#FFF), to(#CCC));
  /* Chrome >= 10, Safari >= 5.1 */
  background: -webkit-linear-gradient(#FFF, #CCC);
  /* Firefox >= 3.6 */
  background: -moz-linear-gradient(#FFF, #CCC);
  /* Opera >= 11.1 */
  background: -o-linear-gradient(#FFF, #CCC);
  /* IE >= 10 */
  background: -ms-linear-gradient(#FFF, #CCC);
  /* The standard */
  background: linear-gradient(#FFF, #CCC);
}
```

Phew, that's quite a mouthful! Luckily, projects like Less and Sass take the pain out of it, which I'll elaborate on later in this chapter.

Multiple Backgrounds

Just as you can specify multiple shadows in CSS3, you can specify multiple backgrounds. Previously, to have many background images, you'd have to create a lot of nested elements—i.e., too much extraneous markup. CSS3 lets you give a comma-separated list to the background style, greatly reducing the amount of markup required:

```
background: url(snowflakes.png) top repeat-x,
  url(chimney.png) bottom no-repeat,
  -moz-linear-gradient(white, #CCC),
  #CCC;
```

Browser support:

- Firefox: full support
- Chrome: full support
- Safari: full support
- IE >= 9.0: full support
- Opera: full support

Selectors

CSS3 gives you a bunch of new selectors for targeting elements:

:first-child
:   Selects the first item in the selector

:last-child
:   Selects the last item in the selector

:only-child
:   Selects elements with only one child

:target
:   Selects elements targeted in the current URL's hash

:checked
:   Selects checked checkboxes

Selectors I want to cover in greater detail are listed below.

Nth Child

:nth-child lets you alternate styling for every *n* children. For example, this selects every third child:

```
#example:nth-child( 3n ) { /* ... */ }
```

You can use this to select even or odd children:

```
/* Even children */
#example:nth-child( 2n )   { /* ... */ }
#example:nth-child( even ) { /* ... */ }

/* Odd children */
```

```
#example:nth-child( 2n+1 ) { /* ... */ }
#example:nth-child( odd )  { /* ... */ }
```

You can also reverse the selector:

```
/* Last child */
#example:nth-last-child( 1 )
```

In fact, :first-child is equivalent to :nth-child(1), and :last-child is equivalent to :nth-last-child(1).

Direct Descendants

You can limit the selector to only directly descendant children by using the greater-than symbol, >:

```
/* Only directly descendant divs */
#example > div { }
```

Selector Negation

You can negate selectors by using :not, which you can pass a simple selector. At the moment, negation doesn't support the more complex selectors, like p:not(h1 + p):

```
/* Only directly descendant children, except ones with the "current" class */
#example > *:not(.current) {
  display: none
}
```

Browser support:

- Firefox: full support
- Chrome: full support
- Safari: full support
- IE >= 9.0: full support
- Opera: full support

Transitions

CSS3 adds transition support, letting you create simple animations when a style changes. You need to pass a duration, property, and optional animation type to the transition property. You can specify the duration in seconds (s) or milliseconds (ms):

```
/* duration, property, animation type (optional) */
transition: 1.5s opacity ease-out

/* Multiple transitions */
transition: 2s opacity , .5s height ease-in
transition: .5s height , .5s .5s width
```

In the first example, when the opacity changes (say, a style gets applied inline), the original and new values will be animated between.

There are various types of timing functions:

- `linear`
- `ease-in`
- `ease-out`
- `ease-in-out`

Or, you can specify a custom timing sequence using a cubic bezier curve, which describes the animation speed, such as this bouncing animation:

```
#transition-example {
  position: absolute;
  /* cubic-bezier(x1, y1, x2, y2) */
  transition: 5s left cubic-bezier(0.0, 0.35, .5, 1.3);
}
```

In Safari and Chrome, once the transition is complete, a *WebKitTransitionEvent* will be fired on the element. In Firefox, the event is called *transitionend*. Unfortunately, there are several caveats to using CSS3 transitions: you get little control over playback and not all values are transitionable. That said, transitions are very useful for simple animations, and some browsers (such as Safari) even hardware-accelerate them:

```
#transition-example {
  width: 50px;
  height: 50px;
  background: red;
  -webkit-transition: 2s background ease-in-out;
  -moz-transition: 2s background ease-in-out;
  -o-transition: 2s background ease-in-out;
  transition: 2s background ease-in-out;
}

#transition-example:hover {
  background: blue;
}
```

For one reason or another, you can only transition between gradients if at least one gradient has a touch of alpha transparency. You also can't transition between some values, like `height:0` to `height:auto`.

Browser support:

- Firefox: with `-moz-`
- Chrome: with `-webkit-`
- Safari: with `-webkit-`
- IE >= 10.0: with `-ms-`
- Opera: with `-o-`

Border Images

With `border-image`, you can use an image for the border of an element. The first argument specifies the image's URL; the subsequent ones describe how the image is sliced. The last part is the stretch value, which describes how the slices for the sides and the middle are scaled and tiled. Available stretch values are `round`, `repeat`, and `stretch`:

```
border-image: url(border.png) 14 14 14 14 round round;
```

```
border-image: url(border.png) 14 14 14 14 stretch stretch;
```

Browser support:

- Firefox: with `-moz-`
- Chrome: with `-webkit-`
- Safari: with `-webkit-`
- IE: no support
- Opera: with `-o-`

Box Sizing

Have you ever wanted to make an element with 100% width but still have padding or margins? Using the traditional box model, CSS calculates percentage widths using the parent element's width, and then adds on margins and padding. In other words, a 100% width element with padding, margins, or a border will always overflow.

However, by setting `box-sizing` to `border-box`—instead of its default value `content-box`—you can change the way the size is measured, taking into account borders, margins, padding, and content:

```
.border-box {
  -webkit-box-sizing: border-box;
  -moz-box-sizing: border-box;
  box-sizing: border-box;
}
```

This has great support among the major browsers, and it can be used safely unless you plan to support any browsers prior to Internet Explorer 8.

Transformations

With CSS3, we get basic 2D transformations, which lets elements be translated, rotated, scaled, and skewed. For example, we can rotate an element 30 degrees counterclockwise:

```
transform: rotate( -30deg );
```

You can also skew the element around the x and y axes by the specified angles:

```
transform: skew( 30deg , -10deg );
```

An element's position can be transformed in the x or y axis using `translateX` or `translateY`:

```
translateX(30px);
translateY(500px);
```

You can increase or decrease an element's size using the `scale` transform. By default, an element's scale is set to 1:

```
transform: scale(1.2);
```

You can specify multiple transformations by concatenating them:

```
transform: rotate(30deg) skewX(30deg);
```

Browser support:

- Firefox: with `-moz-`
- Chrome: with `-webkit-`
- Safari: with `-webkit-`
- IE >= 9: with `-ms-`
- Opera: with `-o-`

Flexible Box Model

CSS3 introduces the flexible box model, a new way of displaying content. It's really useful, as it brings some features to CSS that GUI frameworks, such as Adobe Flex, have had for a while. Traditionally, if you wanted a list aligned horizontally, you used floats. The flexible box model lets you do that and more. Let's take a look at the code:

```
.hbox {
  display: -webkit-box;
  -webkit-box-orient: horizontal;
  -webkit-box-align: stretch;
  -webkit-box-pack: left;

  display: -moz-box;
  -moz-box-orient: horizontal;
  -moz-box-align: stretch;
  -moz-box-pack: left;
}

.vbox {
  display: -webkit-box;
  -webkit-box-orient: vertical;
  -webkit-box-align: stretch;

  display: -moz-box;
  -moz-box-orient: vertical;
```

```
    -moz-box-align: stretch;
}
```

We're setting the display to `-webkit-box` or `-moz-box`, and then setting the direction in which the children will be laid out. By default, all the children will expand equally to fit their parent. However, you can alter this behavior by setting the `box-flex` attribute.

By setting `box-flex` to 0, you're specifying that an element shouldn't expand, whereas if you set the flex to 1 or higher, the element will expand to fit the available content. For example, a sidebar may have a flex attribute of 0, and the main content may have a flex attribute of 1:

```
#sidebar {
  -webkit-box-flex: 0;
  -moz-box-flex: 0;
  box-flex: 0;

  width: 200px;
}

#content {
  -webkit-box-flex: 1;
  -moz-box-flex: 1;
  box-flex: 1;
}
```

Browser support:

- Firefox: with `-moz-`
- Chrome: with `-webkit-`
- Safari: with `-webkit-`
- IE >= 10: with `-ms-`
- Opera: no support

Fonts

`@font-face` allows you to use custom fonts to display text on your web pages. So, you no longer need to depend on a limited number of system fonts users have installed.

Supported font formats are TrueType and OpenType. Fonts are subject to the same domain policy restriction—the files must be on the same domain as the page using them.

You can specify a `@font-face` like this, giving it a `font-family` and the URL location where the font is located:

```
@font-face {
  font-family: "Bitstream Vera Serif Bold";
  src: url("/fonts/VeraSeBd.ttf");
}
```

Then, you can use it as you would any other font:

```
#font-example {
  font-family: "Bitstream Vera Serif Bold";
}
```

Fonts will be downloaded asynchronously and applied when they've finished downloading. This means a user will see one of her system's default fonts until the custom font has downloaded. Therefore, it's a good idea to specify a fallback font that's available locally.

Browser support:

- Firefox: full support
- Chrome: full support
- Safari: full support
- IE >= 9: full support
- Opera: full support

Graceful Degradation

If you write your CSS correctly, your application will degrade gracefully. It will be functional in browsers that don't support CSS3—it just won't be very pretty.

The key to graceful degradation is that browsers ignore things they don't understand, such as unknown CSS properties, values, and selectors. CSS properties override one another, so if one is defined twice in the same rule, the first property will be overridden. You should put the property that's CSS 2.1-compliant first, so it will be overridden if rgba is supported:

```
#example-gd {
  background: white;
  background: rgba(255, 255, 255, .75);
}
```

What about vendor prefixes? Well, the same rule applies. Just include prefixes for each browser—it will use the one it understands. You should put the prefixless version last, as it will be used when the browser's CSS3 support is standardized and prefixes are removed:

```
#example-gd {
  background: #FFF;
  background: -webkit-gradient(linear, left top, left bottom, from(#FFF), to(#CCC));
  background: -webkit-linear-gradient(#FFF, #CCC);
  background: -moz-linear-gradient(#FFF, #CCC);
  background: linear-gradient(#FFF, #CCC);
}
```

Modernizr

Modernizr (*http://www.modernizr.com*) detects support for various CSS3 properties, letting you target specific browser behavior in your stylesheet:

```
.multiplebgs div p {
  /* properties for browsers that
     support multiple backgrounds */
}
.no-multiplebgs div p {
  /* optional fallback properties
     for browsers that don't */
}
```

Some of the features Modernizr detects support for are:

- `@font-face`
- `rgba()`
- `hsla()`
- `border-image:`
- `border-radius:`
- `box-shadow:`
- `text-shadow:`
- Multiple backgrounds
- Flexible box model
- CSS animations
- CSS gradients
- CSS 2D transforms
- CSS transitions

To see a full list or to download Modernizr, visit the project page (*http://www.modernizr.com*).

Using Modernizr is very simple—just include the JavaScript file and add a class of *no-js* to the `<html>` tag:

```
<script src="/javascripts/modernizr.js"></script>
<html class="no-js">
```

Modernizr then adds some classes to the `<html>` tag, which you can use in your selectors to target specific browser behaviors:

```
/* Alternate layout when the Flexible Box Model is not available */
.no-flexbox #content {
  float: left;
}
```

Google Chrome Frame

Google Chrome Frame (GCF) is an Internet Explorer extension that lets you switch IE's renderer to Google Chrome's renderer, Chromium (*http://www.chromium.org*).

Once the extension is installed, you can enable GCF with a `meta` tag in the page's head:

```
<meta http-equiv="X-UA-Compatible" content="chrome=1">
```

Or, an alternative is to add the setting to the response's header:

```
X-UA-Compatible: chrome=1
```

That's all that's required to enable GCF rendering for your web page. However, GCF has some more features, like prompting users to install it if they're running IE (and it's not already installed). The prompt can just overlay on top of the page and will refresh automatically when GCF is installed—no browser restart is necessary.

The first step is to include the GCF JavaScript:

```
<script src="http://ajax.googleapis.com/ajax/libs/chrome-frame/1/CFInstall.min.js"
```

Then, in a page load handler or at the bottom of the page, we need to invoke CFInstall:

```
<script>
  jQuery(function(){
    CFInstall.check({
      mode: "overlay",
    });
  });
</script>
```

CFInstall takes several options:

mode
> Inline, overlay, or popup

destination
> The address to navigate to on installation, usually the current page

node
> The ID of an element that will contain the installation prompt

Once GCF is installed, the browser's `User-Agent` header will be extended with the string `chromeframe`. GCF cleverly uses Internet Explorer's network stack to perform URL requests. This ensures that requests have the same cookies, history, and SSL state when using GCF, which basically preserves the user's existing sessions.

For further information, see the getting started guide (*http://www.chromium.org/devel opers/how-tos/chrome-frame-getting-started*).

Creating a Layout

Let's take what we've learned and apply it to creating a simple layout, inspired by Holla.

First, let's create the basic page markup. We're going to have a header and two columns—a sidebar with fixed width and a main content container:

```
<body>
  <header id="title">
    <h1>Holla</h1>
  </header>

  <div id="content">
    <div class="sidebar"></div>
    <div class="main"></div>
  </div>
</body>
```

Next, let's add the basic reset and body styles:

```
body, html {
  margin: 0;
  padding: 0;
}

body {
  font-family: Helvetica, Arial, "MS Trebuchet", sans-serif;
  font-size: 16px;
  color: #363636;
  background: #D2D2D2;
  line-height: 1.2em;
}
```

And now the h tags:

```
h1, h2 {
  font-weight: bold;
  text-shadow: 0 1px 1px #ffffff;
}

h1 {
  font-size: 21pt;
  color: #404040;
}

h2 {
  font-size: 24pt;
  color: #404040;
  margin: 1em 0 0.7em 0;
}

h3 {
  font-size: 15px;
  color: #404040;
  text-shadow: 0 1px 1px #ffffff;
}
```

Now let's define a header for our layout. We're using the CSS3 background gradients, but we're defaulting back to a plain hex code color if they're not supported:

```css
#title {
  border-bottom: 1px solid #535353;
  overflow: hidden;
  height: 50px;
  line-height: 50px;

  background: #575859;
  background: -webkit-gradient(linear, left top, left bottom,
  from(#575859), to(#272425));
  background: -webkit-linear-gradient(top, #575859, #272425);
  background: -moz-linear-gradient(top, #575859, #272425);
  background: linear-gradient(top, #575859, #272425);
}

#title h1 {
  color: #ffffff;
  text-shadow: 0 1px 1px #000000;
  margin: 0 10px;
}
```

Now, if we look in the browser, there's a dark header with our application's name, as shown in Figure C-1.

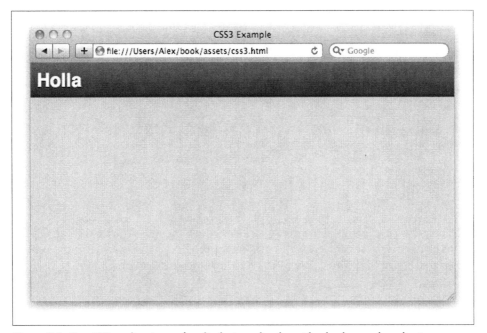

Figure C-1. Our CSS application so far, displaying a header with a background gradient

Let's create a #content div that will contain the main part of the application. We want it stretched across the page in both the x and y directions, so we'll make its position absolute. Its immediate children are aligned horizontally, so we'll set its display to the flexible box type:

```
#content {
  overflow: hidden;

  /*
    The content div will cover the whole page,
    but leave enough room for the header.
  */
  position: absolute;
  left: 0;
  right: 0;
  top: 50px;
  bottom: 0;

  /* The children are horizontally aligned */
  display: -webkit-box;
  -webkit-box-orient: horizontal;
  -webkit-box-align: stretch;
  -webkit-box-pack: left;

  display: -moz-box;
  -moz-box-orient: horizontal;
  -moz-box-align: stretch;
  -moz-box-pack: left;
}
```

Now let's create a lefthand column called .sidebar. It's got a fixed width, so we're setting box-flex to 0:

```
#content .sidebar {
  background: #EDEDED;
  width: 200px;

  /* It's got a fixed width, we don't want it to expand */
  -webkit-box-flex: 0;
  -moz-box-flex: 0;
  box-flex: 0;
}
```

Let's create a list of menu items inside .sidebar. Each menu is separated by an *h3*, the menu header. As you can see, we're using a lot of CSS3, which—due to the vendor prefixes—is rather repetitive. We can clean it up using Less mixins:

```
#content .sidebar ul {
  margin: 0;
  padding: 0;
  list-style: none;
}

#content .sidebar ul li {
  display: block;
```

```
    padding: 10px 10px 7px 20px;
    border-bottom: 1px solid #cdcdcc;
    cursor: pointer;

    -moz-box-shadow: 0 1px 1px #fcfcfc;
    -webkit-box-shadow: 0 1px 1px #fcfcfc;
    box-shadow: 0 1px 1px #fcfcfc;
}

#content .sidebar ul li.active {
    color: #ffffff;
    text-shadow: 0 1px 1px #46677f;

    -webkit-box-shadow: none;
    -moz-box-shadow: none;

    background: #7bb5db;
    background: -webkit-gradient(linear, left top, left bottom,
    from(#7bb5db), to(#4775b8));
    background: -webkit-linear-gradient(top, #7bb5db, #4775b8);
    background: -moz-linear-gradient(top, #7bb5db, #4775b8);
    background: linear-gradient(top, #7bb5db, #4775b8);
}
```

Let's add some example menus to the HTML markup:

```
<div class="sidebar">
  <h3>Channels</h3>
  <ul>
    <li class="active">Developers</li>
    <li>Sales</li>
    <li>Marketing</li>
    <li>Ops</li>
  </ul>
</div>
```

All the CSS that's left is the `.main` div, which stretches right across the page:

```
#content .main {
    -moz-box-shadow: inset 0 1px 3px #7f7f7f;
    -webkit-box-shadow: inset 0 1px 3px #7f7f7f;
    box-shadow: inset 0 1px 3px #7f7f7f;

    /* We want .main to expand as far as possible */
    -webkit-box-flex: 1;
    -moz-box-flex: 1;
    box-flex: 1;
}
```

Let's take another look; as Figure C-2 shows, we've now got a basic application layout upon which we can expand.

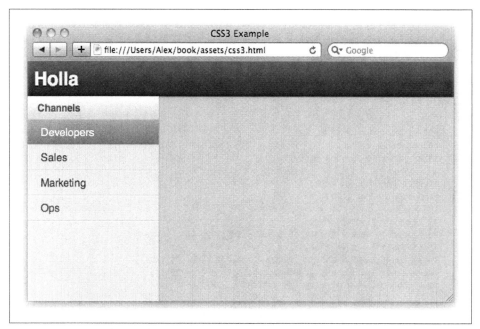

Figure C-2. Basic application layout

As I mentioned before, the CSS3 syntax is rather verbose and repetitive due to the vendor prefixes we have to use. We can clean it up using Less mixins. For example:

```
#content .sidebar h3 {
  .vbg-gradient(#FFF, #DEDFE0);
  .box-shadow(0, -5px, 10px, #E4E4E4);
}
```

See Appendix B for more information, and view the Holla stylesheets for some good examples.

Index

Symbols

$ shortcut, jQuery, 50
$$() function, 127
$() function, 126
$x() function, 127
() braces, anonymous functions, 50
_ (underscore), prefixing private properties, 16
_.bindAll(), 171

A

Access-Control-Allow-Origin header, 42
Access-Control-Request-Headers header, 42
addEventListener(), 19, 24
addressing references, 37
Adobe Flash, 44
afterEach() function, 114
Ajax
    crawling, 62
    jQuery, 212
    loading data with, 39–43
    progress, 93
    syncing and Spine, 150
ajax() function, 212
ajaxError event, 150
alpha transparency, 225
AMD format, 77
Apache web server, relative expiration date, 134
APIs
    History API, 63
    HTML5 file APIs, 81
    jQuery.tmpl templating API, 68
    jQuery's selectors API, 207
    pushState() and replaceState() history API, 174
    Underscore's AP, 165
    WebSocket API, 99
    XMLHttpRequest API, 92
App.log() function, 126
append() function, 210
apply(), 12
arguments variable, 14
assert libraries, 110
assert() function, 109
assertEqual() function, 110
assertion types, 112
assertions, 109
async attribute, 134
attributes
    async attribute, 134
    Backbone library models, 166
    defer attribute, 134
    files in HTML5, 82
    JavaScriptMVC library models, 189–191
    multiple attribute, 82
    originalEvent attribute, 84
    returning, 46
    validating an instance's attributes, 167
    whitelisting, 176
auditors, deployment, 139
autoLink() function, 69

B

Backbone library, 165–183
    collections, 167
    controllers, 172
    models, 165
    syncing with the server, 174–177

We'd like to hear your suggestions for improving our indexes. Send email to *index@oreilly.com*.

cubic bezier curve, 231

D

data
    loading, 38–44
        including data inline, 39
        JSONP, 43
        security with cross-domain requests, 43
        with Ajax, 39–43
    models, 3
    storing locally, 44
dataTransfer object, 84, 86
dataTransfer.getData() function, 86
dataType option, 212
deactivate() function, 59
debugging, 123–131
    (see also testing)
    console, 125
    inspectors, 123
    network requests, 129
    profile and timing, 130–131
    using the debugger, 127
declaring CommonJS modules, 74
defaults
    browsers and default actions to events, 21
    caching, 134
    constructor function return context, 7
    controllers extending, 153
    JavaScriptMVC library models, 192
defer attribute, 134
deferreds, JavaScriptMVC library client-side
        templates, 199
define() function, 78
degradation, graceful degradation: CSS3, 235
delegate() function, 24, 57
delegating
    Backbone library events, 170
    events, 24, 56
dependency management, 73–80
    CommonJS, 74
    FUBCs, 80
    module alternative, 79
    module loaders, 76
    wrapping up modules, 78
deployment, 133–139
    auditors, 139
    caching, 134
    CDNs, 138
    Gzip compression, 137

minification, 136
performance, 133
resources, 139
descendants, CSS3, 230
describe() function, 114
destroy() function, 4, 144, 147
dir() function, 127
direct descendants, CSS3, 230
distributed testing, 121
document.createElement(), 65
document.ready event, 211, 213
DOM elements
    controllers, 151
    creating, 65
DOM, jQuery, 208–211
domains
    same origin policy, 41
    whitelist of, 44
DOMContentLoaded event, 23, 129
DownloadURL type, 85
drag and drop
    files, 83–86
    jQuery drag-and-drop uploader, 95–96
dragenter event, 85
dragover event, 85
dragstart event, 84
drivers, testing, 116
drop areas, 95
drop event, 95
drop shadows, CSS3, 226
dropping files, 85
dynamically rendering views, 65

E

el property, 151
element pattern, 155
elements
    associated with events, 22
    DOM elements, 65
    mapping, 55
    Spine libraries' controllers, 152
    tooltip element, 201
empty() function, 211
Envjs, 119
equals() function, 112
error event, 148, 167
ETags, 136
event bubbling, 20
event callbacks

About the Author

Alex MacCaw is a Ruby/JavaScript developer and entrepreneur. He has written a JavaScript framework, Spine; has developed major applications, including Taskforce and Socialmod; and has done a host of open source work. He speaks at Ruby/Rails conferences in New York City, San Francisco, and Berlin. In addition to programming, he is currently traveling around the world with a Nikon D90 and a surfboard.

Colophon

The animal on the cover of *JavaScript Web Applications* is a Long-eared owl.

The Long-eared owl (*Asio otus*) is a slender, grayish-brown woodland owl that's characterized by long, upright ear tufts positioned in the middle of its head. At one time, its distinctive ears earned it the nickname "cat owl."

Long-eared owls can be found in the open woodlands, thickets, and forest edges of North America, Europe, Asia, and northern Africa. Their diets consist almost entirely of small mammals, primarily voles and mice, which they're able to locate in complete darkness due to the asymmetrical positioning of their ear openings. They fly back and forth over low-cover areas to locate their food; their flight is light and buoyant and is often compared to that of a large moth.

Long-eared owls do not build their own nests; instead, they settle in abandoned stick nests of magpies, crows, hawks, and squirrels. They tend to become dispersed and territorial during their breeding season (which typically occurs between mid-March and early June), whereas during the winter months, they roost communally to keep warm, often in clusters of 7–50 birds.

The cover image is from Wood's *Animate Creations*. The cover font is Adobe ITC Garamond. The text font is Linotype Birka; the heading font is Adobe Myriad Condensed; and the code font is LucasFont's TheSansMonoCondensed.

Get even more for your money.

Join the O'Reilly Community, and register the O'Reilly books you own. It's free, and you'll get:

* $4.99 ebook upgrade offer
* 40% upgrade offer on O'Reilly print books
* Membership discounts on books and events
* Free lifetime updates to ebooks and videos
* Multiple ebook formats, DRM FREE
* Participation in the O'Reilly community
* Newsletters
* Account management
* 100% Satisfaction Guarantee

Signing up is easy:

1. Go to: oreilly.com/go/register
2. Create an O'Reilly login.
3. Provide your address.
4. Register your books.

Note: English-language books only

To order books online:
oreilly.com/store

For questions about products or an order:
orders@oreilly.com

To sign up to get topic-specific email announcements and/or news about upcoming books, conferences, special offers, and new technologies:
elists@oreilly.com

For technical questions about book content:
booktech@oreilly.com

To submit new book proposals to our editors:
proposals@oreilly.com

O'Reilly books are available in multiple DRM-free ebook formats. For more information:
oreilly.com/ebooks

O'REILLY®

Spreading the knowledge of innovators   oreilly.com

CPSIA information can be obtained at www.ICGtesting.com
Printed in the USA
LVOW052028221112

308391LV00005B/193/P